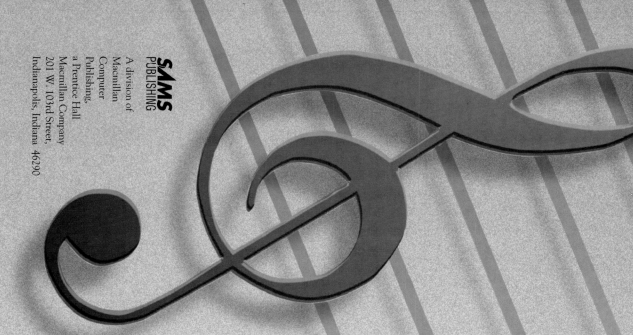

Becoming a Computer Musician

Jeff Bowen

SAMS PUBLISHING

A division of
Macmillan
Computer
Publishing,
a Prentice Hall
Macmillan Company
201 W. 103rd Street,
Indianapolis, Indiana 46290

Trademarks

OVERVIEW

CONTENTS

ACKNOWLEDGMENTS

Becoming a Computer Musician would not exist without the assistance and support of the following special friends:

Diana N. Bowen

Mark Evans

Steve Cooper

Larry Fast

Dr. Martin L. Norris

James Irsay

Debra Stohl—IBM

Kyle McCartney and Steve Meek—CompUSA

Paul DeBenedictus, Tim Self, Mac McCormick and all at Opcode Systems

Chuck Surack—Sweetwater Sound

Jack Falk and Hal Jordy—Electronic Arts

Theresa Fagan—Midisoft Corporation

Dave Kilkenny and Chris Rice—Twelve Tone Systems

Jeff Boone—Alaska Software

Gary Dauphin—Apple Computers

Dave Wymer—Softronics

Mike Lawson and Tony Margolese—Gibson Guitar Corporation

And I *would* be remiss if I did not also acknowledge the following people and companies who furnished special information and/or hardware, which contributed greatly to the information pool in this book:

Daniel Rose—Mark of The Unicorn

Lisa Marcus—Kurzweil Music Systems

Akai Professional

Alesis Studio Electronics

Apple Computer

Audio Technica, US

Berklee College of Music

Blue Ribbon Soundworks

Creative Labs, Incorporated

Digidesign

E-mu Systems

Fostex, USA

MacSystems—Jim Neely

MiBAC Music Software

Morning Star Solutions

Passport Designs

Music Quest, Incorporated

Musicware

Orchid Technology

OSC

Roland, USA

Samson Technologies

Software Toolworks

Spectral Innovations

Tascam, USA

Turtle Beach Systems

Also, special thanks to the entire Sams Publishing editorial, development, and production staff; to Grace Buechlein and David Bradford, for seemingly tireless assistance; to Wayne Blankenbeckler, who originated the concept for this book; and to Richard Swadley, for giving us the green light to proceed with making it a reality.

About the Author

Jeff Bowen owns and operates Bowen Music Productions of Indianapolis, where he and his staff provide many services for the film, video, and broadcast industry. Jeff combines formal science and music education with years of studio and stage experience to provide a fresh resource for creative educational productions.

Since 1985, Jeff has pioneered concepts of SMPTE time code synchronized audio engineering and music composition for video and film. He authors a regular column titled "Sound Advice," which is featured in the International Planetarium Society journal *The Planetarian*.

Prior to forming Bowen Music Productions, Jeff taught over 20,000 private music lessons. He maintains close involvement with education, speaking often to student groups and conducting sound and music workshops at numerous professional conferences. He has produced or scored over 300 film and video productions, including many nationally and internationally known works. His awards include: 1993 CINDY Gold Award, 1992 CINE Golden Eagle, NYC Bronze Apple, multiple Addys, and multiple Silver Screens (including the 1994 Silver Screen for Educational Video, Grades 9-12).

Introduction

Becoming a Computer Musician explores the many ways we can use computers for musical applications, including the following:

- ♪ Music education
- ♪ Music composition
- ♪ Hobby applications
- ♪ Careers in music
- ♪ Integrating computer music with live instrument recording
- ♪ The MIDI studio
- ♪ Multimedia presentations for school, business, or fun
- ♪ Music for film and broadcast

What Is a Computer Musician?

Computer musician is such a vague term. Let's define it:

Computer musician: One who uses computers and associated hardware and software to assist with the education, creation, and performance of musical applications for pleasure or profession.

This book is not intended to discourage or eliminate the use of natural or live instruments, or to eliminate traditional methods for teaching those instruments. I myself am accomplished on a number of live instruments and find that computers provide me with tools that enhance the technical *and* creative aspects of music production. I remember clearly how my early music instructors emphasized that good instrument technique (the ability to actually play your instrument well) would lead to better music performances. True. So it comes as no great shock that the introduction of a new technical development—integrating computers with music applications—should also enhance the entire process of music development and performance. This book is designed to assist in these respects.

What Computers Can You Use with this Book?

This book gives you training in how to integrate music creation with the PC and Macintosh computer platforms, but it does so in such a way that it remains useful for Amiga, Atari, Apple II and IIGS, and other computer systems as well. The fact is, the PC and Mac have achieved dominance in most of the marketplace, so this book will concentrate on their users. Visit your local software shop or music store to find specific manuals, software, and hardware for other computer platforms you may own or have access to. The information in this book is still invaluable to your development as a computer musician.

Who Will Find this Book Interesting?

I am told by others in the publishing and music fields that this book is unique in its approach. To date, it is the broadest and most comprehensive approach to the possibilities of using computers with music. Other books may present certain facets of this field very, very well, but this book has something for everyone interested in the subject. It will be useful not only to persons who are savvy in PC and Mac use and to keyboard players, but also to guitarists, wind instrument players, choral musicians, drummers, and percussionists.

Becoming a Computer Musician is different in yet another way. The academic word that describes this

book is *tutorial*. From day one, my vision of the book was that it would feature a lot of hands-on examples for you to work with. This is not a tell-me-all-about-it book, but rather one that encourages you to actually learn how to become a computer musician. It is a *do* book! I want you to get your hands on the tools of the computer musician and learn how to use them.

What the Book Includes

You will find that I have worked very hard to provide you with the following:

Ideas for using computers with music, even if you own very basic hardware

Easy-to-understand descriptions of the concepts behind computer music systems

Well-illustrated explanations of the hardware and software, including installation

Step-by-step tutorial examples that show you how to use the included hardware and software

Lots of application samples in the appendices at the end of the book

A good glossary of terms

A list of manufacturers' addresses and phone numbers

An enclosed CD-ROM full of sample software, exercises, and video demos by recording artists Kenny Aronoff and Peter Gabriel

How Is this Book Organized?

A brief study of the table of contents will show you that the book can be divided into the following parts:

Part 1   An Introduction to Basic Computer Music Applications

Part 2   Start-Up MIDI...The Music Instrument Digital Interface

Part 3   The Complete MIDI Musician

Part 4   The Computer Musician of Tomorrow

Part 5   Appendices

Part 6   Glossary

Part 7   Index

Listed below each part are the headings and contents for each chapter. Please read these to get an overview of how your skills will be developed. You will see some really exciting subjects, developed in such a way that you can get involved with computer music to any degree you wish. And don't be in a hurry; spend a good while on each area before moving on to the next—even months if you want. It's okay with me! Remember that the field of computer music has developed over years and years, and it may take a while to really learn how to manipulate your new music tools. But, hey, I'm a patient teacher. In fact, you will notice that I repeat information several times throughout his book to give you many opportunities to remind yourself of important ideas. I have a reason for doing everything I do here, and teaching you is the reason. If you do the things I suggest, you *will* learn. Trust me and you'll do fine.

As you continue to examine the table of contents, you'll notice that certain chapters introduce a new general concept as being applicable to both the PC *and* Mac platforms. At the end of each chapter you'll be instructed as to which chapter is next in line for the specific computer platform you're using. In many cases, Mac users will skip the immediately following chapter (which would be dedicated to the PC). This structure provides demonstrations and examples specific to *each* computer and its own dedicated software and hardware. Pretty neat, huh?

The Appendices Are Great!

Throughout the book, you will encounter many references to the Appendices, which contain very detailed information about specific areas of interest. Using an Appendix for this detailed information keeps the chapter text free-flowing and easy to use. You definitely will find yourself working in the Appendices often.

You may start using the Glossary immediately. The sooner you grasp the specialized language of the computer musician, the sooner you can begin to understand the subject. Refer to the Glossary often; it serves as a great clarifier.

Wow! A CD-ROM Full of Software!

Becoming a Computer Musician supplies you with *MusicPower*, a CD-ROM full of software. The software features demo versions of many popular computer music programs, such as MIDI sequencer programs, music notation programs, software that teaches music principles, and so on. You'll also find sample music compositions, special video clips, and much more. Read Appendix F for the full scoop on this cool CD-ROM.

Conventions Used in this Book

You will find some special icons and information guides throughout this book.

> **Note:** You can find special or unusual topic-related information here.

> **Tip:** Look here for shortcuts, innovations, and references to other sections in the book.

> **Warning:** Reading this can head off trouble before it finds you.

This book contains interviews and quotes from experts and musicians in the industry. Look here to find out how things are done in the industry.

In addition to these boxes, the following special icons can be found:

 Indicates a MIDI note or reference

 Indicates an example from the CD-ROM included with this book

 Indicates PC-specific information

 Indicates Macintosh-specific information

I have made every effort to avoid reviewing or recommending any specific hardware or software, although the products featured in this book have proven track records and are some of my personal favorites. That is why you will find a manufacturer's index in the Appendices, but not an actual buyer's guide. This book is dedicated to creating music as quickly as possible, and there is little room for reviewing products. An excellent source of such reviews (for PC computers) is Sams

Publishing's book *Multimedia Madness*[1], by Ron Wodaski. It is an especially good source for reviews of educational and consumer/hobby-level audio and music products. Thanks to Ron for a great job!

What You Will Need

Okay, now to get down to the nuts and bolts. Here are the general requirements for the use of this book.

For the PC user:

- 386SX, 25 MHz or higher, running DOS 5.0 and Windows 3.1 or higher[2]
- A hard drive with 80MB or more of total disk storage
- 4MB of RAM (8MB is faster)
- A mouse or trackball
- A MIDI-capable sound card
- A CD-ROM drive (recommended)

For the Macintosh user:

- Almost any Mac[3] will work for the Mac chapters
- Operating system 6.01 or higher (7.01 is *highly* recommended; see the documentation of each demo for specific requirements)
- 4MB of RAM or more

- A hard drive with 40MB or more of total disk storage
- Computer keyboard *and* a mouse or trackball
- A CD-ROM drive (recommended)

A list at the beginning of each chapter gives you additional requirements for the subjects featured in that chapter.

For users of either platform, the book assumes the following:

- The reader has already developed the necessary basic computer operating skills.
- The reader has already developed some basic music skills, including a fundamental understanding of music principles, notation, and reading.

On Your Mark…

All set? Great! Remember, Appendix F has the instructions you need to install the individual programs from the *MusicPower* CD-ROM.

Oh, yeah…one more thing. You're going to like this stuff so much that you might not be able to stop. Be careful not to let working with this book become a threat to the time you spend with friends and family! On the other hand, that's why the hours between 10:00 p.m. and 2:00 a.m. exist, right?

[1]Wodaski, Ron. Multimedia Madness. *Indianapolis: Sams Publishing, 1994.*

[2]*Bear in mind that you can do a lot with this book even if you have less or more than what's recommended here. This is just a good "get started" recommendation.*

[3]*The Macintosh has traditionally been the domain of the serious computer musician. Most (nearly all) of the early hardware and software dedicated to music applications was designed by third-party Mac developers, at a time when 1MB of RAM was standard and a 20MB hard drive was considered to be a luxury item. These early computer-music pioneers became proficient at coaxing incredible features out of these low-powered machines. Thus, some of the most flexible, most efficient, and easiest to use music software has been developed by Mac software designers. My experience indicates that you can do much more on a low-end, low-powered Mac than on a similarly equipped PC.*

1

Why Become a Computer Musician?

? You may be a music student.

? You might be a home music hobbyist.

? Do you teach music or fine arts at any academic level?

? Is your plan for the future to become a major recording artist?

? Perhaps you're on the creative staff at an ad agency, and you want to compose simple demos for client presentations.

? Maybe you author multimedia presentations for a business, a museum, or just for fun.

? Some readers are planning to own and operate their very own recording studio business.

? Some will want to establish careers as composers for film and video.

? A church choir director might enjoy creating and printing a new score for a cantata.

The list goes on and on.

If you're reading this list, you almost undoubtedly fall into one of the categories mentioned. This book is about a creative process, about inventing new ways to compose and produce music, about cutting your own path in the world of music. You shouldn't feel that the preceding list is totally complete. Hopefully, you will break the existing molds.

How We Used to Become Musicians

When I was young, the launch into serious music study could be accomplished through a couple of popularly followed paths. One path was to become involved with the school choral program, often because it provided an escape from study time.

Another path began with a visit to the school music room or auditorium, where all students interested in band or orchestra were given a series of test questions, including such examples as "Which of these sounds is higher in pitch—number one or number two?", or "Which of these songs is playing faster…" Well, you get the idea. If you attained a certain point score you were deemed to be potentially musical. That qualified you and your parents to attend a meeting with the school band director, at which time you would be given the opportunity to select the instrument of your future. My parents did not share my vision of me as a drummer. (When I mentioned this idea to them, I could almost hear that ugly sound a modern computer game makes when you fail the password to the next level.) So I first tried the trumpet, but I couldn't "buzz" the mouthpiece (it tickled too much to deal with!). So I tried the trombone (I could "buzz" this mouthpiece), but my arm was too short for fifth position. As I longingly stared at the snare drum my friend was plunking on, I heard a distant dreamy voice… Huh? What's that? A clarinet!?! Hmmm… Never thought of that one before! Well, as it turned out, I was on

my way, destined to become a perennial first chair clarinetist and career composer/performer/ recording artist/sound engineer/studio owner/ author. Whodathunkit!

Meanwhile, my wife was progressing on a third path commonly taken by people interested in music: piano lessons. The classic vision of child-as-pianist was often pictured clearly in the mind of the parent and teacher. Often this vision was not shared by the student, who thought primarily of playing four-square or guitar while pounding out a B-flat major scale in octaves.

Fortunately for all, teachers and parents with unbelievable patience and will were able to instill a passion for the musical experience in a great number of us who really dug in and made the genre our own. However, there were times when the entertainment value of these training methods was minimal and the rewards difficult to achieve. Many students fell by the wayside, interested but disappointed. In some cases, the original interest in music survived but remained dormant for years, only to surface in adult life, when one perhaps felt compelled to stop by the local music store and just "see what's going on these days" or maybe happened to walk by a piece of music software at the computer store while purchasing a box of floppies and found the contents fascinating.

It doesn't have to be that way anymore.

Preparing String Players for the 21st Century

An interview with Drew Tretick, Zeta Music Artistic Clinician

True story: I was strolling through the aisles of the 1994 Music Educators National Conference in Cincinnati when I found one of the most interesting music education subjects discussed in this book. Drew Tretick is the staff clinician for Zeta Music, manufacturer of a full line of high-quality MIDI string instruments. Drew sports a Masters of Music Degree from the Juilliard School and performed that school's *first ever* MIDI Master's recital, using his Zeta electronic violin (pictured with him). Drew has also served as an Assistant Professor at Berklee College of Music, and the author provides the following excerpts from a April 1994 interview with him.

"Well, all around us we hear sounds. We hear music in everything. So many of our environmental sounds have ended up in our music, our pop music—whether it is industrial music, you name it. It is rather interesting how the reality and music…are intertwined. …Young children, they hear pop music or whatever it is that excites them, and it is something that is with us and we just can't turn it off. Now, if they can begin working with instruments and making sounds on their own and start being creative, they are, for themselves, having a vital role in doing something. It is no longer, 'Here are some notes on the page. Now, you've got to play a tune…you've got to do this, you've got to do that.' It gives them a chance to really be more involved with the very nature of expression, which, as you and I know, you take a saxophone solo, and you play it on, you know, a flute, it is going to have a totally different feeling. You know, so often, we'll hear

certain instruments in orchestras, in orchestration, and that instrument is used to convey a certain type of feeling by a composer and that composer will always use it that way because of the tone colors. Well, here, for instance, for a violinist, now, you can not only experience playing rhythm and harmony but all of it. These are just the basic musical elements, and it's being able to take expression to a higher level. It will excite the students and, for the professionals, it actually lets them go a little bit higher in their own expression."

"There is incredible enthusiasm from young children who are just beginning to desire to pick an instrument. When they see [the Zeta MIDI violin] for the first time, suddenly, a violin is incredibly exciting. That is incentive for them to want to grow as a musician. If the excitement is there, they will naturally move in the direction toward working and studying on the instrument. There's a terrific amount of training available through the use of a MIDI instrument. For instance, it can be set up so that you would 'quantize' pitch for every note you play on the instrument. Now, on a keyboard, you can just play a scale and there is nothing between the cracks. On the [MIDI] violin, you can set it up the same way so, as you play up your scale or, in fact, slide up a string

continues

with one bow stroke. It will actually go da, da, da, da, da or da, da, da, up half steps. You can turn that on or off so it will slide with you. The advantage of that is you no longer have to have your teacher standing next to you playing the line that you are practicing on the piano, and say, 'No, you are starting to go off tune.' You stay right in tune. The MIDI instrument tracks right on and will play the corresponding pitch that you are playing.'"

"Certainly, the obvious thing is that a student can practice with headphones on, or hear themselves in a group ensemble, because the instruments produce no sound, no real audible sound except for a little scraping sound of the bow on the string, which isn't very audible I don't know if you are aware, but I was teaching at Berklee [College of Music] with Matt Glazer, and the students loved working with the violin as well as some ancillary technology, such as a MIDI event processor playing cannons. The students at that school are improvisers. They enjoy being creative."

"When I was doing the presentation for Technology for String Teachers and Performers at the Music Educators National Convention, before I even began, a retired dean from the School of Music in Illinois, a rather well-known university there, immediately remarked, 'Why do this?' And I said, 'What a great question!' He hadn't heard a note yet. He almost felt threatened to hear that we're going to be replacing acoustic instruments. I let him answer his own questions. I played for about five minutes and then spoke a little bit about what I was doing. What he heard was unlike anything you could ever imagine hearing before from a string instrument, from a violin MIDI controller. And, he just sat back, smiled and said, 'You answered my question.'"

"The discussion went on. We talked about all the applications; as a violinist, as a cellist, as a bass player or a violist, all of these instrumentalists have, for so long, wanted to be able to take their ideas, their imaginative ideas, capture them somehow and, if they are a composer, they'll sit down at the piano and record or they'll get out a pen and paper and put their ideas into music. With the MIDI string controller, of course, that can be done, directly, very intuitively, from the instrument, recording right into a computer."

"For instance, one of the head people from Roland came over to hear what I was doing with some of their electronics—which are generally...just plugged into either a computer or a keyboard—and he hadn't heard what I did before. He heard how I could control a synthesizer from a violin—just playing a traditional piece of violin music with a lead melody—and I had a prerecorded background sequence, the piece I was playing. And he said, 'Okay, that is fine. But what can you do that has never been heard before?' So I played a piece of mine entitled 'Montana Meadow,' which sounds like a virtual movie soundtrack. Real-time, harmonic processing...I can improvise, go anywhere I want and take with me actual moving lines, intelligent musical moving lines. Through MIDI, you can actually do true harmonizing, whereas most harmonizers around now are rather fixed and static in nature. So that was very exciting. And he came back to the booth the next day with a lot of other people, a camera, and he was just so amazed that so much was coming out of their synthesizer. You know, he had never heard anything like it before. There are powerful performances that can be unleashed from a string controller that you can't get from a keyboard—your vibrato, your crescendo. Imagine just putting under each string, you know, the richness of...a sample, let's say, of the whole string section and rolling across all the strings of an instrument and then processing that data in various ways through electronics to do so much more."

Author's note: Drew's educational video, "Presenting the Electric Violin," is available through string instrument retail stores, or by contacting Zeta Music (1-800-622-MIDI).

Computers Musicians Are Here to Stay

The personal-computer revolution has provided an opportunity that dramatically affects nearly every aspect of the music medium. Even the private music instructor working with the lone violin student uses sheet music typeset by a computer scoring program. Every rock album now produced uses computers extensively from start to finish. Composers of music for films, videos, and TV/radio commercials rely heavily on computers. Visionary music education teachers are incorporating music teaching labs into their school music programs—not to eliminate the interest in "live" instrumental and vocal performance, but rather to stimulate interest in music in general.

The musical computer enables us to experience the creation of new music ideas and assist with the teaching of traditional music concepts. For centuries, only a few fortunate humans were able to compose their works and hear them performed. For others, being musically interested meant performing the works of earlier composers or turning on a cassette or CD player. Now, the whole concept of music for the masses has been moved from the "playback" or "reproduction only" mode to the "create it" or "interactive" mode. It's a fact that most people with an interest in music find that it's much more rewarding to hear their own ideas come to life than to simply replay what has been done before.

I clearly remember the first time I witnessed the integration of computers and music. It was during

Figure 1.1. *A violin student using Claire pitch-training software for the Mac computer to improve the accuracy of intonation.*

an early '80s demonstration of the Fairlight music system, a terrifically expensive system dedicated to high-end commercial productions. It made my heart pound to envision how this gadget could turn the creative ideas inside my head into finished productions that I could share with others. That moment launched my new career as a composer/producer of soundtracks for motion pictures. I feel moments like that one every day. So can you. That's the greatest reward of becoming a computer musician.

I speak often about computer-based music production methods at secondary school classes, university and college groups, and conferences of professional trade and educational associations.

Questions People Ask about Computers and Music

What are some of the things musicians can do with computers?

Musicians of all sorts use computers daily, in all sorts of ways.

A student learning his or her first notes of music and the names of the lines and spaces can benefit from the fun and effective ways computers can teach music (Figure 1.1).

Composers for symphony orchestras use score notation software to print scores for the orchestral musicians who'll perform the compositions (Figure 1.2).

Every recording session for albums, film, radio, and TV uses computers to assist with the recording and mixing of the project. The entire film and video industry uses an industry-standard digital data stripe called SMPTE time code[1] to synchronize the music and sound with the moving pictures. Computers "read" this time-code and ensure that the sounds properly match the action in the finished project.

Many musicians "record" their performances onto MIDI[2] sequencing software, which then "plays" their synthesizer sounds for them (Figure 1.3). This is big-time important, as explained in Chapters 4 and 5.

Some people use computers and music as their main hobby, composing simple songs and printing sheet music for use with their friends, church

choirs, youth groups, and service organizations (Figure 1.4).

Progressive live performers incorporate computer-generated or computer-controlled music into their concert performances, sometimes integrated with multimedia presentations. For example, Peter Gabriel is pushing the music technology envelope by introducing the interactive CD-ROM XPlora,

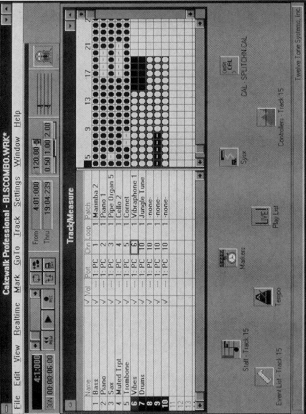

Figure 1.3. Cakewalk Professional "records" up to 256 tracks of MIDI event data.

Figure 1.2. The librarian for the Indianapolis Symphony Orchestra uses music notation software to arrange and archive scores to be performed by the Orchestra. Photo courtesy of The Indianapolis Symphony Orchestra.

[1] The computer, sound recording, and video industries all seem to share a great love for turning long chains of words into little short groups of letters, or acronyms. SMPTE actually stands for Society of Motion Picture and Television Engineers. This is an organization that determines all the standard protocols for data communications in the television and motion picture industry.

Time-code was actually invented by NASA (another acronym!) as a tool for analyzing launch and flight data, and it was adopted by SMPTE in the early '70s as a standard tool for film, video, and sound synchronizing and editing. See Chapter 14, "Adding Live Instrument and Voice Sounds to MIDI," for advanced SMPTE time code applications.

[2] MIDI is an acronym for Musical Instrument Digital Interface. This system, invented by a consortium of music instrument manufacturers in the early 1980s, uses computer data to communicate between electronic music instruments. MIDI is discussed in more detail beginning with Chapter 5.

Music for Disney's Kids, Incorporated

An Interview with Craig Sharmat, Music Director for the Disney Channel Show *Kids, Incorporated*

Since 1991, Craig Sharmat has provided music composition and production for the hit TV show *Kids, Incorporated*, which is a regular feature of the Disney Channel. Craig has also produced music scores for NBC Sports volleyball, ice skating, and gymnastics programs, and for the TV shows *Xuxa* and *Chartbusters*. Feature film credits include *Stone Cold* and *This is My Life*, and he has scored numerous pieces on made for TV movies. Craig and I talked one morning at 8:00 a.m. about produc-

ing music for TV shows. Here are a few of his comments.

"When I originally was asked to do *Kids, Incorporated* the question was whether it was going to be financially feasible for me to do it. The only way the job could get done is in a home studio environment [using] the computer. If I used live players, the situation was that I would take a 2-track mix of all of my basic music, put that on tape, and then just go and use the big studio to [record] live players, minimizing the cost of the production. At that point I can go back to my house and re-lay the [studio] tracks [to tracks] which are cinched on the computer. That allows me the flexibility of being able to add things and take away things from the mix that I normally wouldn't be able to in the old way of recording. I am able to...for example, I hear the vocals, and say, 'Okay, this other sound, a synth sound for example...no longer works here.' I could add another kind of sound. Producing in the back end is something which, in the old days of recording, wasn't really that accessible because you kind of had your tracks, and then you were done. Here [at home], I have unlimited free time in which to play with the track and to mix, so I can have just very basic tracks when going in to record, and then do most of the work on the back end at home after tracking. That allows me to keep my cost down and keep my creative freedom high—and that, to me,

was one of the biggest breakthroughs that I have had. It was enlightening. I can take on this project and make some money.'"

"I can't imagine right now not having [computer-assisted music technology], because it is just so powerful and the flexibility is just so great. One of the other things to consider here is that I *am* an accomplished guitar player by trade, but I can't cut a keyboard gig live. And, again, you know, on gigs, where it was an arranging gig, I could sit there maybe with a piece of music and write it out, but this [technology] gives me the whole thing, where I can hear everything right away. That doesn't sound like it is anything new or breath-taking, but, as a guitar player doing a lot of television, there aren't that many of us. There are mostly keyboard players."

"One really cool thing [about using the Pro Tools digital workstation] is that if I play a little bit of a phrase late on the guitar...let's say that I came from a jazz gig and I am playing a little bit behind the beat and now I am doing a rock gig and the rock gig doesn't want to be behind the beat. It wants to be a little bit pushed. They can take that whole Pro Tools track and just move it forward. And now your track is no longer being behind the beat, behind the track, but it is right on wherever they want to stick it. And you can't do that with tape. That in itself is great. And that, to me, is fascinating."

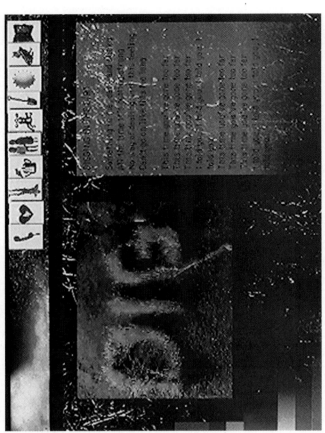

Figure 1.4. *Computers can assist with the composing, scoring, and printing of songs.*

Figure 1.5. *A scene from the interactive music CD-ROM XPlora, by British musician Peter Gabriel.*

which gives the "listener" the opportunity to help create the listening and viewing experience (Figure 1.5).

Music producers use computers to re-create and simulate the sounds of dozens of instruments, a technique that gives them a very accurate picture of what the finished work will sound like (Figure 1.6).

Computer-controlled sound editing and sound design help musicians create fresh, original, futuristic sounds, which they can then use to create their own new artistic sound. In Figure 1.7, ARY recording artist Andrew Young digitally records percussion, sound effect, and voice sounds, which he then edits and manipulates in creative

ways so as to help him sculpt a unique sound for his R&B recordings.

Of course, all musicians must find fast, reliable ways to handle their word processing, accounting, scheduling, and promotional ads. A great benefit of being a computer musician is that one of your musical tools (the computer) can double as your primary business office tool, too (Figure 1.8). It wasn't always that way…I never could get my 1983-issue Yamaha CS-80 synth to print out invoices!

Why do people use computers with music?

Computers have gained prominence in nearly every area of daily life by making daily tasks easier

and more enjoyable. The electronic ignition and fuel injection on your car are computer-controlled, as are the various settings on your food processor and the tuner on your TV set.

The TV commercial about IBM's participation in the design of the sites for the 1994 Winter Olympics touches a nerve in everyone, because we can relate to how tough it would have been to do all that work by hand. CAD (Computer-Assisted Design) architectural and accounting software makes accomplishing the tasks easier and faster.

A really fun example, the CD player, is basically a computer system that reads computer data from a compact disc and converts the 1s and 0s into

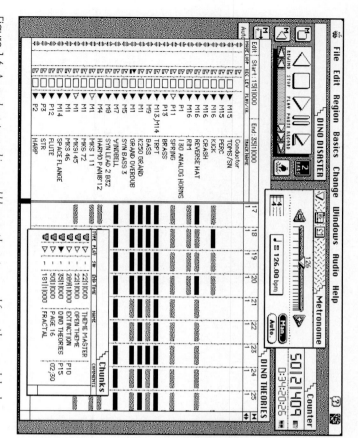

Figure 1.6. *An analog tape machine would have to play tape several feet wide to equal the sheer number of tracks available in software such as Performer, by Mark of the Unicorn.*

Figure 1.7. *ARY recording artist Andrew Young.*

analog electronic signals,[3] which your stereo speakers in turn converts into sound waves. These sound waves are heard by the listener as the exciting sounds of AC/DC, Paul McCartney, Bach, Mozart, Barbara Streisand, U2, Todd Rundgren, Peter Gabriel, and other recording artists. CD computers...oops, I mean players, not only sound better than older LP phonograph records, but they also allow more flexibility in the order in which tracks are played, require less

storage space and less maintenance, are more durable, and are easier to use.

Computers are used in musical applications for the same reasons. They help make some of the more difficult and tedious aspects of working with music easier, faster, and more enjoyable. One example, Digidesign's Pro Tools digital workstation, enables you to record verses and choruses and then cut, copy, and paste the musical passages much like you would edit sentences using a word processor

(Figure 1.9). Another benefit of using computers is that you can create musical passages that sound marvelous but would be impossible to perform manually.

Is it fun to use computers with music?

Using computers with music is a blast! I was a musician for 20 years before the technology to use a computer with music was realistically attainable. Using a computer enabled me to hear complete

[3]This is known as D to A (Digital to Analog) conversion. During today's recording sessions, sound waves are converted into digital data. This process is known as A to D (Analog to Digital) conversion. The converted data is then recorded or stored on disk or tape, or in RAM just like any other computer data. This sound data can then be manipulated (processed) in the digital domain so as to enhance the sonic quality of the recorded information. After this processing has taken place, the digitally recorded information is mastered and prepared for mass duplication, usually on compact disc (CD). The CD player in your home or car has a D to A converter that converts the digital data back to an easily usable analog form, which is reproduced by your stereo system's amplifiers and speakers.

Figure 1.8. *Computer music wizard Todd Rundgren keeps an impressive list of files and folders on his Powerbook. Wonder when they will design a computer with a fast enough clock speed to keep up with his busy music itinerary? Photo courtesy of Apple Computer, Incorporated.*

Figure 1.9. *Digidesign's Pro Tools digital workstation.*

compositions in a finished (or nearly finished) form, right in the comfort of my home. It sure is easier than renting a rehearsal hall and a sound system and calling a group of musicians with lots of equipment together so I could hear the songs I had composed. Using a computer to assist with music composition made me want to compose more, improving my composing skills in a really painless, fun way.

What changes have there been in the field of computer music?

Wow. That's a book of its own. I think the biggest changes have come in the areas of computer music

philosophy and computer music hardware. Computer musicians were first regarded by many music traditionalists as monsters who were allowing the computer to take over the creative process of music composition. Other live-instrument musicians feared being replaced by electronic versions of themselves. Both fears came true, to some degree.

Very progressive electronic music schools have experimented with artificial intelligence and random computer-generated compositions. While these compositions make for interesting lab experiments and may actually advance the cutting

edge of compositional theorems and logic, they aren't applicable to the mass commercial markets.

Some live musicians did feel the effect that computer/music integration had on their careers. As the '80s progressed, drum machines using digital recordings of actual drums (called samples) began to do a significant amount of the work once done by live drummers. Music producers and manufacturers pushed technology to its limit in the attempt to create the sounds of live instruments electronically.

Electronic instruments such as the Synclavier, the Fairlight, and the Kurzweil 250 specialized in providing high-quality digital sound samples of live instruments (Figure 1.10). These sampled sounds could then be triggered by on-board or computer-based MIDI sequencers to produce soundtracks that did an acceptable job of simulating performances of live instruments. The soundtracks for the enormously popular '80s TV series *Miami Vice* were created by composer Jan Hammer, with nearly every sound generated by the Fairlight digital music system.

Figure 1.10. *The Kurzweil 250 became an industry standard for playing back terrific-sounding digital samples of live instruments. Photo by Sweetwater Sound.*

[4] *This is exhibited in part by the wildly popular MTV Unplugged series, which features acoustic-only performances by well-known recording artists.*

[5] *Spot is an advertising industry nickname for thirty- and sixty-second ads that run on TV or radio.*

As the '90s began, it seemed that the public was reaching a saturation point with totally electronic music production[4] (a composer friend of mine called it being "box weary"), and musicians began to return to the idea of using computers to assist with composition and to enhance productions that use live musicians. As manufacturers turned more to the consumer market for revenue, the result was that the student or home musician could purchase hardware and software similar to that used by "the big guys" at a far lower cost than once was possible. In 1986, I would have spent a couple of thousand dollars for the computer music capabilities that now exist on some of the sound cards that home computer musicians can purchase for a couple of hundred dollars.

How have computers affected music career opportunities?

As the cost of hardware has plummeted, the market for original music has actually increased. To produce music for a 30-second TV spot,[5] you once would have taken the following steps:

1. Meet with the client.
2. Prepare a demo of the music for the spot.
3. Write out charts by hand for musicians.
4. Book the musicians for the demo.
5. Book the studio for the demo.
6. Go to the studio to record the demo.
7. Mix the demo.
8. Send the demo to the client for approval.
9. Revise the demo.
10. Prepare charts for musicians by hand for the "final" version of the music.
11. Book the musicians for the "final."
12. Book the studio for the "final."
13. Go to the studio to record the "final."
14. Mix the "final."
15. Send the "final" to the client for approval.
16. Pay the bills for all the preceding.
17. Wait to receive payment from the client.

Some seriously expensive stuff was going on here! It meant that the clients who could afford original music composition and production made up a fairly small and elite group.

Today, the number of steps in the production process is far fewer:

1. Meet with the client at composer's office or project studio.

2. Prepare a computer-assisted demo of the music for the spot.

3. Record the demo at the composer's office or project studio.

4. Play the demo for the client and revise as needed.

5. Mix the demo.

6. Have the computer print out any charts necessary for the "final" version.

7. Book necessary musicians for the "final."

8. Record the "final" in the composer's project studio or, if necessary, book studio.

9. Go to the studio to record the "final."

10. Mix the "final."

11. Send the "final" to the client for approval.

12. Pay the bills for the preceding.

13. Wait to receive payment from the client.

Not only are there fewer steps, but nearly all events take place in the composer's environment, often a project studio, without incurring huge out-of-pocket costs. The result is that the composer can often do the project for a lower dollar fee than previously possible. This means that potential

clients who once could not afford original music compositions now may be able to "buy into" better soundtracks than they once could. This increased volume of work results in an increased demand for composers, producers, and even sound engineers.

The popularity of computers and the seemingly eternal popularity of music combine to create totally new careers. A whole generation of designers and engineers who specialize in the creation of software and hardware for the electronic music industry has come of age.

Some of the early pioneers in the field now own their own companies or serve as consultants to major firms. One of my favorite sections in this book is the Chapter 15 interview with the two

interesting entrepreneurs who own and operate Virtual Entertainment of Walpole, MA (Figure 1.11). Richard Viard and Jeff Pucci served as early pioneers in the development of music software for such companies as Dr. T's and now apply their computer music skills to the exciting world of multimedia.

An area of specialized consulting deals with designing and installing computer music education labs in secondary school and university music departments. For example, Berklee College of Music in Boston (Figure 1.12) provides numerous computer music labs, which are used for experimenting with creative new compositional and arranging ideas and for teaching students of all musical interests.

Figure 1.11. *Richard Viard and Jeff Pucci, owners of Virtual Entertainment.*

In the early days of computer-assisted music, you could find musicians (like the author of this book) struggling all night, sometimes with poorly designed hardware and software, just trying to make deadlines and get better at their craft. (Hmmm…sounds like authoring a book, too!) Now, new authors are writing about how you can become a computer musician, as well (Figure 1.13).

How can computers be used to teach music principles?

Music education is perhaps the best application for the marriage of computers and music. Many nifty, low-cost software programs on the market do an excellent job of teaching music fundamentals. Some of these are available for as little as $30-$40,

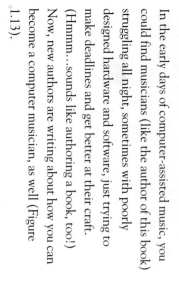

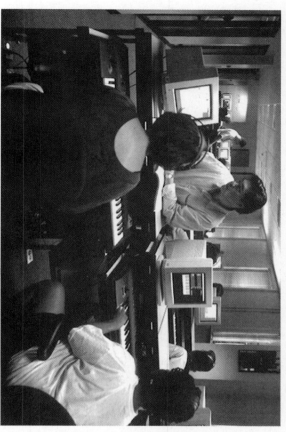

Figure 1.12. *Berklee College of Music. Photo by Bob Kramer, courtesy of Berklee College of Music.*

or they are available on the various computer networks (such as CompuServe) as shareware.[6] A couple of demo versions of this kind of software are included on the enclosed CD-ROM. For a demo, see Appendix A, "Programs That Teach Music." In particular, watch for products distributed by a company named Midisoft Corporation. They have a number of really interesting interactive software titles on the market—some on CD-ROM, which is super-convenient.

Especially helpful are products such as The Miracle Piano system by Software Toolworks (Figure 1.14). This complete, packaged system is pretty much ready to go—right out of the box. It

Figure 1.13. *The author at work at Bowen Music Productions, Indianapolis.*

teaches you how to play the piano while you, your family, and friends are having a ball! It seems that every time I'm in a computer store, someone is plunking around on a Miracle. It's available with either Mac or PC software and includes a basic piano-style keyboard. The system can be purchased for as little as $250 (computer not included) and is available through computer and music stores, as well as chain and mail-order outlets.

[6]*Bear in mind that shareware is not freeware. Shareware is often designed by individuals with great ideas, but without the advertising and marketing power of large companies. Be sure to check out their requested fees before using their programs; they have earned your respect in this area.*

Figure 1.14. *The Miracle Piano System is a nice all-in-one package for use with educational and hobby applications. Photo furnished by The Software Toolworks.*

On a higher and more serious level, you might want to inspect Piano by Musicware, which takes users step-by-step from the basics to an advanced level of two-hand playing competency (Figure 1.15). This piano method (note that I use the word *method* with accuracy) is structured more like actual traditional piano lessons and is widely recommended by educators nationwide. It also features additional supplemental exercise books and is priced at $129 per level.[7]

The market will soon be deluged with complete turnkey hardware/software packages designed for education. The big-name powerhouse manufacturers are just entering this arena, and they're loaded for bear. The new Yamaha CBX-205 system packages a keyboard controller, a sound module, and Trax software by Passport to create a powerful teaching tool.

You shouldn't fully eliminate the influence of a really good human instructor, though. A computer

Figure 1.15. *Musicware's Piano for Windows is used in conjunction with most MIDI piano keyboards and a sound card with a built-in MIDI interface. Photo supplied by Musicware.*

is a great music teacher's aide, but a computer can't teach the most important elements of music: attitude, expression, true dynamics, and feeling. I highly recommend that a music education program or course of private lessons should be based on good instruction by teachers you'll remember forever, and this should be enhanced by Macs and PCs. As multimedia continues to grow and gain influence in the classroom, we should be careful to remember the value of our educators.

What are some multimedia applications for the computer musician?

We are just now seeing the proverbial tip of the multimedia[8] iceberg.

Until recently, multimedia productions were limited to museum kiosks and cute little demos at computer stores. During the past few years, I've had several opportunities to watch fledgling multimedia "producers" struggle to make their

multimedia systems do what they asked them to do. Now, it seems as though the entire multimedia industry has suddenly discovered warp speed! At Christmastime last year, I witnessed cartload after cartload of complete multimedia-equipped computer systems lined up at the checkout counters in a local computer retail store (Figure 1.16). If you want to see something really impressive, take a look at the book I mentioned in the introduction. That book, *Multimedia Madness,* includes about 1,100 pages of information about multimedia...and that's just one book. Chapters 4, 5, and 15 of this book begin to explore computers, music, and multimedia. Current multimedia applications include using sound cards to create digital sound files and MIDI music compositions that can then be "authored into" complete multimedia productions. You can synchronize your own music compositions with the visual elements incorporated into your multimedia productions

[7]*This price does not include the necessary computer, MIDI keyboard, and sound card, but it does include a MIDI adapter cable for use with the Creative line of sound cards.*

[8]*Multimedia productions feature video, graphics, text, sound, and music, all assembled, edited, and authored within the framework of the multimedia computer. Hmm...this is a long enough word to turn into an acronym. How about MPC, for Multimedia Personal Computer? A typical multimedia system might consist of a fairly powerful computer with a fast, high-capacity hard drive and a really good color monitor, a double-speed CD-ROM player, multimedia software, a high-quality video card, a high-quality sound card, and a pair of external speakers. Multimedia systems have been used primarily for business and commercial applications due to their great cost. However, the cost of complete multimedia systems is now dipping under the $2,000 level, and more and more consumers are purchasing multimedia-capable computer systems on both the PC and Mac platforms.*

Figure 1.16. *Computer retail stores feature a surprising number of multimedia-equipped PCs, called MPCs. An MPC usually comes with a CD-ROM drive, a sound card, and a pair of speakers.*

and then use these productions for presentations at your school or business, or for just a plain old great time.

A number of recording artists are exploring unique applications for multimedia-based music video productions.

Rock artists Todd Rundgren, Peter Gabriel, and Thomas Dolby, among others, believe multimedia CD-ROMs will serve as a fresh new medium for music artists in much the same way that MTV and VH-1[9] did in the '80s. Interactive multimedia will enable the viewer to decide what visual effects are shown in the music videos, whether the lyrics of the songs are shown on-screen, and whether the music mix sounds reverberant or dry, while changing the

equalization[10] to match the acoustics of the environment in which they're listening.

This book is fortunate to include some short samples of the CD-ROM *XPlora* by Peter Gabriel on the CD-ROM included with this book. Chapter 15 views this CD-ROM and discusses the making of it.

It is interesting to note that many multimedia experts believe that the best new multimedia applications will be designed by musicians. Some music industry execs are already discussing the creation, production, distribution, and promotion of music-based CD-ROM titles. Their vision is that these CD-ROMs will be available to the public in computer stores, but they also will be sold in stores currently featuring CDs and tapes and will be distributed by companies structured very much like today's record labels.

Here We Go!

Well, I told you this was a "do" book, so let's get with the program (pun intended) and start on the first computer music project.

Oh, yeah. If you forgot to read the introduction, you *must* do so now; it explains how the book is structured. Understanding how the book is structured will make it very useful to you; not understanding will possibly get you lost. We will wait for you to go back and read it now, okay?

Pretty good introduction, huh? I'm glad you read it, because the Sams editorial team and I all worked so hard to get it right.

PC users may now go to Chapter 2.

Macintosh users should skip to Chapter 3.

[9] *The Music Television Network and Video Hits One are music-specific television networks that feature music videos, and they are available in most cable TV package subscriptions.*

[10] *Using an equalizer, or a sophisticated set of audio "tone controls." With an equalizer, the traditional two-band controls of treble and bass are replaced by five to 32 (or even more) narrower bands of tone controls, allowing very detailed sound shaping.*

BASIC
COMPOSITION
WITH WINDOWS

For this chapter you will need the following:

♪ A 386SX, 25 MHz or higher PC running DOS 5.0 and Windows 3.1 or higher

♪ A hard drive with 80MB or more of storage space

♪ At least 4MB of RAM (8MB is faster)

♪ A computer keyboard and a mouse or a trackball

♪ A CD-ROM drive (necessary to use the software provided on the enclosed MusicPower CD-ROM)

♪ The internal sound provided by your computer

♪ A sound card (useful, but not required to use information in this chapter)

Becoming a Computer Musician Features Three PC Tutorials

A unique feature of this book is the inclusion of three tutorial chapters that provide hands-on opportunities to learn to use PC software and create music compositions. Three Macintosh tutorials have also been included, so Becoming a Computer Musician might actually help you decide which computer platform is right for your needs. The enclosed MusicPower CD-ROM includes demo versions of software supplied by some of the finest music-software companies. This software varies greatly regarding features, complexity, and price. Appendix F lists the software titles featured on the MusicPower compact disc. Appendix E tells you how to reach the manufacturers.

Note: Please bear in mind that these demo versions have been stripped of some features and might not save, print, or might even shut down after forty or so minutes. Remember, the licensed versions you might purchase *do* perform perfectly.

Tutorial 1, Chapter 2

This chapter lets you experiment with computer music with *no additional financial investment!* Remember, I have assumed you already know how to work your PC and that you already understand the basic principles of music. You will use the 3.0 demo version of WinSong Composer[1] by Softronics (Figure 2.1).

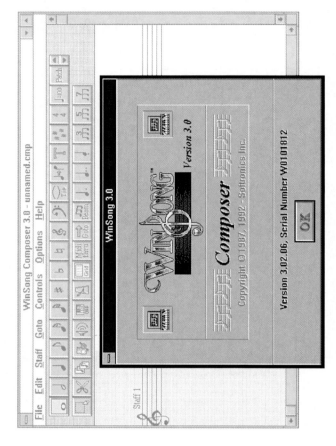

Figure 2.1. *WinSong Composer 3.0 by Softronics.*

[1] *I will refer to this software as "WinSong Composer" for the rest of the book.*

You will place notes onto the music staff and play back your compositions using only the internal sound provided by your computer.

Tutorial 2, Chapter 7: Your First PC-Based MIDI Recording Session

In Chapter 7, you will use MIDI software for the first time. *MusicPower* provides a demo version of Studio for Windows (Figure 2.2) by Midisoft

Figure 2.2. *Studio for Windows by Midisoft Corporation.*

Corporation, one of the leading producers of educational, hobby, and semipro music software.

You will enter notes onto the music staff via computer and MIDI keyboard and play back your compositions using the internal sound provided by your computer, an optional sound card, and an external MIDI sound module.

Tutorial 3, Chapter 12: Professional MIDI Recording with the PC

This is the real deal. A demo version of Cakewalk Professional 2.0 for Windows by Twelve Tone Systems (Figure 2.3) serves as the tool for this

Figure 2.3. *Cakewalk Professional 2.0 for Windows by Twelve Tone Systems.*

chapter, which explores the use of a professional-level MIDI sequencing program.

Chapter 12 describes other pro software, mentioning features you should expect to find in software you might purchase.

Installing the *MusicPower* Software

The first thing you should do is install the software from the *MusicPower* CD-ROM. You will find this CD-ROM in the plastic sleeve inside the back cover of the book.

If you haven't taken the time to install the software from *MusicPower*, you should do this now. Refer to the Introduction to perform this operation.

The Chapter 2 Tutorial

This study uses the sound generated by your computer with *no added hardware*. This sound is called *internal sound*. The internal sound and speaker in your PC are not very powerful in terms of sound quality or volume, and you can play only one note at a time, but will at least get your computer music study underway. Later, you will learn how to improve the sound quality of your music projects. For now, all you need to know is that, as a PC owner, you are ready to get started.

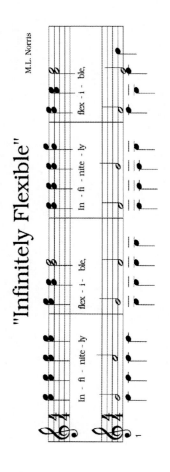

"Infinitely Flexible"

M.L. Norris

In - fi - nite - ly   flex - i - ble,   In - fi - nite - ly   flex - i - ble,

In - fi - nite - ly   flex - i - ble,   Is Norm's mot - to   for suc - cess!

Figure 2.4. *The printed score to "Infinitely Flexible."*

It is likely that you have already installed a sound card in your PC. Good. This will only make working with this chapter more interesting. If you hear no sound when using Composer, don't hesitate to go to the Composer Help menu, select Index, and double-click the MIDI configuration icon. This will open up Help, which provides useful information about configuring your sound card. You will possibly have to create a new MIDI Mapper configuration and save it as a New Configuration. Also, I learned a little trick. When you first open Composer, choose MIDI Mapper under the Options menu and click Edit, then OK, then Cancel. This seems to clear up a lot of problems. Be patient...you know configuring sound cards can be difficult.

Computer Music is "Infinitely Flexible"

For many years my father-in-law, M. L. Norris, has been a member of a university traveling group. A couple of years ago he started thinking it might be fun to create a simple theme song that would be sung by his fellow group members as they traveled from country to country or when they held reunions, dinners, and such. He owned a PC and received an inexpensive software program as a Christmas present. This software enabled him to compose and play back the theme music, add lyrics, and print out his very own sheet music, such as that shown in Figure 2.4. He would then pass this sheet music out to group members and all would sing along.

The idea was a huge success and the tradition continues to this day. The group really has a blast with these songs.

Since the primary idea of this book is to show you how to have fun with computer music, I thought I would use this fun little song, "Infinitely Flexible," by M. L. Norris, as an example for this exercise. Together, you and I will produce a four-part arrangement of this song.

Opening the WinSong Composer Software

Double-click the WinSong 3.0 Demo icon displayed in the Windows Program Manager. Then double-click the icon named "Composer."

Follow the easy-to-understand instructions on the screen. When installation is complete, double-click the Composer icon shown in Figure 2.5. The Composer icon looks like a keyboard with a computer screen full of notes in the background.

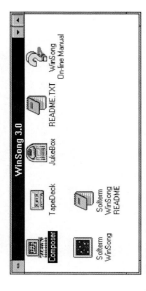

Figure 2.5. *Starting up WinSong Composer.*

Figure 2.6. *The Main window for WinSong Composer.*

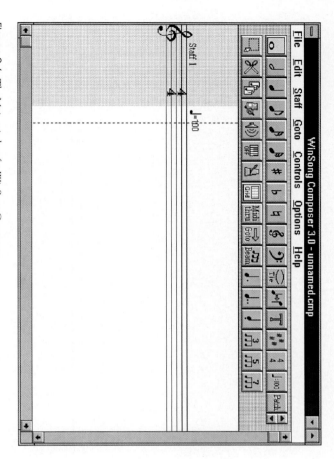

The screen should now feature the WinSong Composer logo. Click OK. You should then see Figure 2.6. This is called the Main window.

Study the Main window in Figure 2.6.[2] Several windows are actually open. The Staff is the primary one. The top row of icon buttons is called the Palette Ribbon, and the icon buttons in the second row make up a group of special function icons that I call the Edit Ribbon. The Staff displays the music elements placed on it.[3] This is the main part of the display. The Palette Ribbon enables you to select music elements, which are added to the Staff. To see the large list of possibilities, select Edit Palette under the Options menu.

This is indeed an impressive display. The Edit Palette Ribbon icons enable you to modify the Palette Ribbon elements placed on the staff. This editing includes cutting, pasting, MIDI playback, triplets, beams, and more.

Many windows in WinSong Composer may be enlarged or reduced, and moved around on the screen, all in the typical Windows fashion. For example, place the cursor over the staff to the left of the 4/4 time signature. Click the right mouse button, hold it down, and you can move the staff up and down on the screen.

Opening a Demo of "Infinitely Flexible"

A good way to get started with any software is by opening a completed work and experimenting with it. Select Open under the File menu. Select your hard drive directories and then double-click the title flexdem.cmp. This title will appear in the left Files window. Double-click it. You will see the first four bars of the music score shown in Figure 2.4. Select Play under the Controls menu[4] and you will hear part one, the first staff of "Infinitely Flexible." Neat, huh?

There are several demo compositions included with WinSong Composer. Just pull down Open in the File menu to load these. They are found in the directory titled winsong3. Take some time to experiment with these selections.

Opening a Template

Let's start with an empty staff and learn how to create a score like "Infinitely Flexible." Click Open under the File menu and open the file comtemp.cmp. This is a template I designed to get you started fast. I call it the Composer Template, and it should look like Figure 2.7.

---

[2] *Softronics provides pop-up help. Select Index under the Help menu and start clicking away.*

[3] *Music elements are time signatures, notes, rests, dynamic markings, repeats, and so on.*

[4] *You can also press P to start and Esc to stop.*

where you want the note on the staff. Do your best to line the note up on the Grid line and click. Bingo…the note appears on the staff and you have just become a computer musician! Or at least you are on your way.

Add a few more notes to the staff in the same way. Moving these notes around with the mouse can be a bit tricky, but mistakes are easy to fix. All you have to do is place the cursor on the errant note, hold the left mouse button down, and drag the mistake off the screen. The computer adds Grid lines as you add notes. You might end up with a few extra Grid lines after correcting mistakes, and this can be confusing. Remove any unused Grid lines by selecting Delete Unused Grids under the Staff menu.

Press P on your computer keyboard to hear your work at any time. Computer musicians call this procedure *playback.* Press Esc to stop. Composer will begin playing the first note that shows on the display, so you might want to use the scroll bar at the bottom of the window to return to the start of the song.

Entering Part 1 of "Infinitely Flexible" into the Score

Reopen the Composer Template and refer to Figure 2.8.

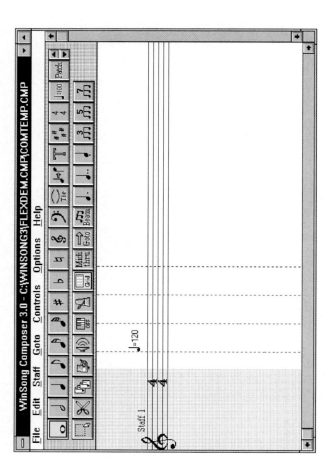

Figure 2.7. *The Composer Template.*

Note: One of the *first* things I do when I get a new piece of software is design a couple of template configurations that will fit *my* most common uses for the software. A template might include things like a certain number of staves[5] and measures, a 3/4 and a 4/4 time signature, and so on. Having templates like this for all music software enables the computer musician to use time more productively…by making music!

My Composer Template is pretty much an empty staff, except that I have selected a 4/4 time signature and a tempo of 120 BPM.[6] WinSong

Composer provides a neat feature, called the Grid, that will help you place music elements onto the staff. The Grid is the set of lines running vertically through the staff,[7] which shows you where to place the music elements. Clicking the Grid icon on the Edit Ribbon (the eighth icon from the left) turns the Grid on and off.

Placing Notes onto the Staff by Click-and-Drag

Click the quarter note icon in the Palette Ribbon window. This means you are going to place a quarter note onto the staff. Move the cursor to

[5]*Remember this is the plural of the word staff.*

[6]*BPM stands for beats per minute.*

[7]*These lines are red when you are working with color.*

"Infinitely Flexible"
Part 1

Staff 1

Staff 1

Staff 1

Staff 1

Figure 2.8. *Part 1 of "Infinitely Flexible."*

Copy the notes from Figure 2.8 using the click-and-drag method I just described. If you make a mistake you can grab the incorrect note with the mouse and drag it off the screen, or you can use the Backspace key as if deleting letters with a word processor. Then place a correct note onto the staff. To clear large numbers of notes, click the Mark icon (the one with the dotted square on it) at the left end of the Edit Ribbon, then move the cursor to the area you want to clear. Click and hold down the mouse button while you drag a box around the offending notes. The notes will highlight. Then select Cut under the Edit menu. Add new notes and corrections so your score looks like Figure 2.8. Note that you will need to return to the Palette Ribbon to select half notes when needed.

Again, press P on your computer keyboard to play back at any time, and Esc to stop. Another way to play back the score is by clicking the Speaker icon on the Edit Ribbon. Click it again to stop.

Warning: The demo software provided with this book does not allow you to save or print. This is to protect the investment the contributors have made in developing their titles.

If this *were* actual software you had purchased, the *very first thing you would do* is save your template under the *new name* of the song you plan to work on. This prevents messing up your template and keeps it in a standard form that is ready to use for the next project. The computer musician always follows one rule religiously:

!!!Save Your Work Often!!!

You can never save it too frequently. If this example were an actual project, I would save to a file named flex1.cmp on my hard drive and to another file named flex1b.cmp on a floppy. I cannot emphasize this double-saving philosophy enough. You will agree the first time you lose eight hours of your best work.

Add another staff by selecting Add New Staff under the Staff menu.

Immediately activate this new staff by positioning the cursor on it and clicking the right mouse button. The staff will highlight. It is now ready for placement of notes, rests, and other music elements.

Remember: You must highlight (activate) any staff before you can perform work on it. Place the cursor on the staff of choice, then click the right mouse button.

Entering Part 2 into the Score

Copy the notes from Figure 2.9, Part 2, using the click-and-drag method as you did before. The notes on the second staff in Figure 2.9 make up Part 2.

If you make a mistake, check how you corrected mistakes before. Continue your work until your score looks exactly like Figure 2.9. Again, you can play back at any time to hear your work. You will now hear Part 1 *and* Part 2 in blissful harmony, provided you have a properly configured sound card installed. If you are using the internal PC sound, you can listen to only one part at a time. To select which part you are hearing, you must first select a track you do not want to hear. Highlight it by clicking the right mouse button. Select Staff Settings under the Staff menu. A new window will appear. This window will look like Figure 2.10.

I am excited for you. You have just completed your first arrangement as a computer musician. If you owned this software, you could print out the score for "Infinitely Flexible" and go practice it on the piano, trumpet, or guitar...or just pass it around to friends for fun, like my father-in-law did.

Or you could start experimenting! Yeah...that's it!

Changing the Tempo

Using computers with music enables you to do some really neat things, such as hearing arrangements with different instruments, or with the parts played in different octaves, or with a few notes changed here and there...and at different tempos!

Changing the tempo (speed) of a song is one basic function of computer music software. Play back any of the versions of "Infinitely Flexible" that you may have open. Locate the Tempo icon toward the right side of the Palette Ribbon. This icon shows that a quarter note equals 100. Click this icon and then click the tempo marking above measure one on the first staff. The window shown in Figure 2.13, labeled Insert Tempo Mark, will appear.

Place the cursor on the up arrow to the left of the Beats Per Minute box. Holding the mouse button down speeds the song up. Placing the cursor on the down arrow and pressing the mouse button will slow the song down. You could insert a tempo change for every measure if you wanted to. This might sound crazy, but some music styles, such as cartoon music, benefit from this kind of feature.

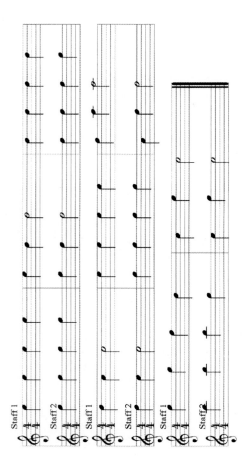

"Infinitely Flexible"

Parts 1 and 2

Staff 1
Staff 2
Staff 1
Staff 2
Staff 1
Staff 2

Figure 2.9. *Four measures of Part 1 and Part 2 of "Infinitely Flexible."*

Now click Mute, then OK. The muted staff will now generate no sound. Repeat this procedure for all tracks you *do not* want to hear.

Entering Part 3 into the Score

Copy the notes from Figure 2.11, Part 3 as you did above. The notes on the third staff make up Part 3.

A PC with a sound card will now play back *three-part harmony!*

If you could save your work, you would be doing this at each step, right? Just a friendly reminder.

Entering Part 4 into the Score

Enter Part 4 of "Infinitely Flexible" into the score. When completed, it will look like Figure 2.12.

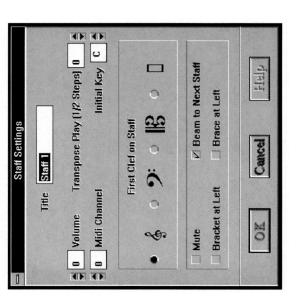

Figure 2.10. *The Staff Settings window.*

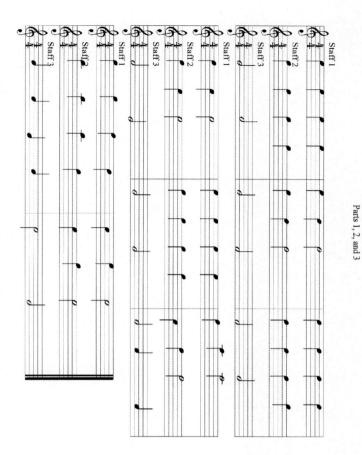

"Infinitely Flexible"
Parts 1, 2, and 3

Figure 2.11. *Four measures of Part 1, Part 2 and Part 3 of "Infinitely Flexible."*

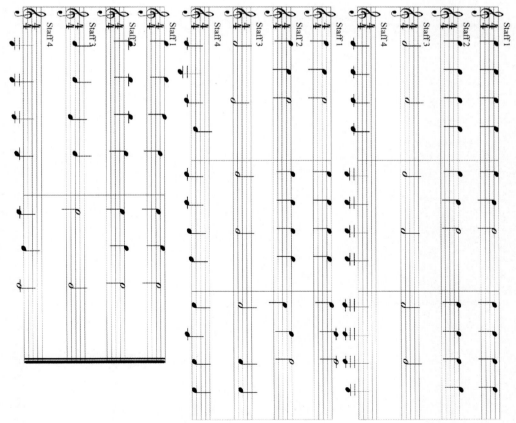

"Infinitely Flexible"
Parts 1, 2, 3, and 4

Figure 2.12. *Parts 1 , 2 , 3, and 4 of "Infinitely Flexible."*

Changing Notes in Parts 3 and 4

Erase all the notes from Part 3, the third staff. You could drag them off the screen one at a time. A much faster way is to "draw" a box around the notes, four measures at a time. Click the Mark icon at the left of the Edit Ribbon. Place the cursor immediately before the first note you want to change. Hold down the left mouse button and drag the mouse. You can see how this enables you to highlight the notes. Clicking Cut under the Edit menu will make the selected notes disappear.[8]

Now look at Figure 2.14. It is an alternate Part 3.

[8] If you want to return to dragging notes off the screen, you must click a note icon in the Composer Palette. That lets you escape the Mark mode of editing.

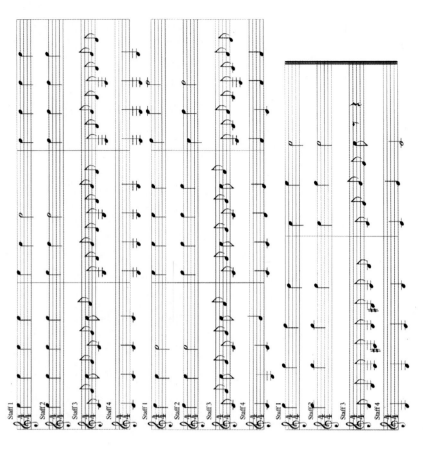

"Infinitely Flexible"
Alternate Part 3

Figure 2.14. *"Infinitely Flexible," alternate Part 3.*

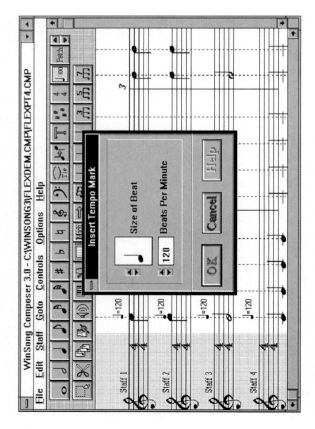

Figure 2.13. *Changing tempo using the Insert Tempo Mark window.*

Enter these new notes to replace the ones erased from Part 3. When you are finished, play back. If you have a sound card you will hear all four parts. If not, mute out all the other parts except this new one. Pretty fun, huh?

Figure 2.15 provides an alternate Part 4 that you can substitute for the first Part 4 used for "Infinitely Flexible." Because this part is full of eighth notes, the energy level of the song is higher.

Transposing the Score

Place the cursor on a staff you want to transpose and click the right mouse button to highlight it. Select the Staff Settings window under the Staff menu. The up and down arrows beside the

Transpose Play box at the upper right will raise or lower the pitch of the notes as they play back. The transposed notes will not move up or down on the staff.[9]

Now you see how to manipulate the notes in your score. When you get good at moving notes up-down-over-under, you can get really creative with your ideas.

[9]There are two schools of thought on this issue. Some computer musicians prefer software that shows these changes on the staff, while others feel that the pitch should change but not the staff notation. Some software enables you to arrange all instrument parts in concert pitch and then apply a transpose function to convert the printed parts into the properly transposed keys required for various musical instruments. Fortunately, there is software for the needs of all of these preferences.

"Infinitely Flexible"
Alternate Part 4

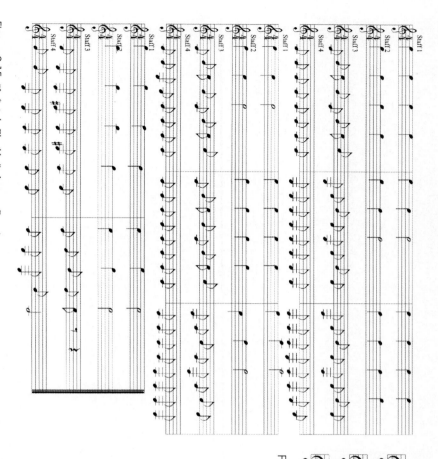

Figure 2.15. *"Infinitely Flexible," alternate Part 4.*

"Infinitely Flexible"
Part 1

Figure 2.16. *The "Infinitely Flexible, Part 1" display.*

Cutting And Pasting Notes

Select Open under the File menu and open the file titled flexpt1.cmp (Figure 2.16).

Figure 2.16 shows what Part 1 looks like. Use the Mark icon and the mouse to draw a box around the notes in measures 1 and 2. The notes will

highlight. Select Copy under the Edit menu. You just created a copy of these seven notes that can be pasted anywhere you want. First, though, you must create a place to put these notes. You can do this using the following procedure. Place the cursor at the start of measure 3, just to the right of the bar

line. Click the right mouse button to position the flashing staff cursor. Select Insert Measure under the Staff menu. The window shown in Figure 2.17 appears.

The lower box enables you to choose how many new measures to insert into your score. You need two, so click the up arrow on the right so the box displays the number 2. Click OK, and two measures are added to the score.

Now you can place the copied notes into the new measures 3 and 4. Click the right mouse button to place the flashing staff cursor at the start of measure 3. Select Paste under the Edit menu (or click the Paste icon on the Edit Ribbon) to place the copied notes at this new location. The seven notes copied from measures 1 and 2 are now pasted into measures 3 and 4!

WinSong Composer "merges" the new notes into any notes already in the two measures where you are pasting. Other software titles move all the

Note: Many famous composers keep different software on hand for different kinds of music productions. Software useful for film work might not be as strong for pop music as other software, and still another title might provide better classical score notation. Careful selection of software, however, will enable *most* computer musicians to find a single software title to fit all or most of their needs fully.

Changing Instrument Sounds

This section will be useful only if you have a sound card installed in your PC. The internal sound in a PC does not enable you to select sound and instrument changes.

Most computer musicians enjoy the ability to change the instrument sounds being played back by the software. This is actually one of the best features of using computers with music, because you can experiment with your orchestrations to hear different versions of your final music productions.

Select Open under the File menu again and open the file titled flexpt1.cmp. It will look like Figure 2.16 again. Now play back the score. Notice the sound is like a piano.[10] The computer musician can change the instrument sound assigned to *any* measure(s) of *any* part of a score. Here's how to do

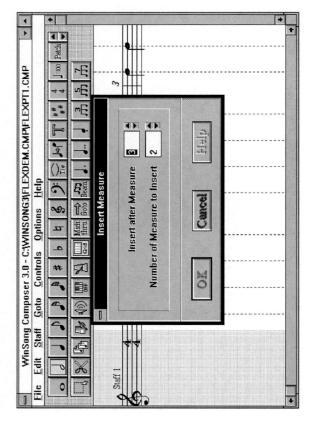

Figure 2.17. *The Insert Measure window.*

other notes past this paste point to the right by two measures. This is called an insert or a splice, and it would leave you with two measures more than your score originally had. You just inserted two extra measures into the "Infinitely Flexible" score, which would make the music timing wrong. You might now remove measures 5 and 6 using the following procedure. Position the flashing staff cursor just to the right of the bar line at the start of measure 5. Select Delete Measure under the Staff menu. A window similar to the one shown in Figure 2.17 appears. Place the number 2 in the Number of Measures to Delete box. Click OK. The extra two measures will be removed.

A point to note. Some software enables you to paste copied notes *over* the old notes, erasing them and keeping the measure count the same. Neither method is better or worse—you just have to know your software and how you prefer to work. Just think of editing a score as being very much like editing a paragraph using a word processor. Hmmm...a music processor, I guess.

Each software title has its own particular set of editing features. It is often the editing that sets a piece of software apart from the rest of the pack, so carefully inspect software for the editing features you want or need when making your selections.

---

[10]*Remember that sound quality varies greatly from sound card to sound card. Unless your card uses wavetable synthesis, you can't expect these sounds to be very realistic. In later chapters I will teach you how to make your computer instruments sound very much like the real thing.*

it using WinSong Composer. Highlight the staff in which you plan to change the instrument. Click the Patch icon on the Palette Ribbon. Position the cursor and click *exactly* where you want the sound to change. Click just to the left of the very first note. A window called Enter a Patch Number will appear. You can insert a program change number into the box. The program change numbers will change the instrument sounds played back by the score.

Now this next part is very cool. Click the Sample button and you will hear a major scale playing the sound number you entered in the box! This enables you to audition several sounds before making a final decision. I really like this feature. Click OK when you have found the sound you like best. The Enter a Patch Number box will close, and the program change number of the selected instrument will appear above the staff where you clicked. You will hear this new sound when you play back the score. You can delete the program change number by dragging it off the screen.

Repeat the above process to change to another instrument sound. Try several. You'll like it.

You can use this method to assign different sounds to Part 1, Part 2, Part 3, and Part 4. Your final selections all save to disk, so you can reload them with the sounds you want to use. This is important, because software like WinSong Composer provides a huge number of choices for you to play...er, uh, work with.

Just for fun, open the file titled chaos.cmp and play back the score. I arranged this file just to show you how wild you can get with sound selection.

More Arranging Exercises

Appendix B contains printed score samples arranged in four parts. You can practice arranging these in the same way that you arranged "Infinitely Flexible." Have fun.

Digging Deeper into WinSong Composer

MusicPower includes four other great demos prepared by the staff at Softronics. Load these up and experiment with them. That's why they are included. Be sure to play with the options under the menus.

WinSong Composer is an infinitely flexible (pun intended) music software title. The software retails for $79 and is loaded with capabilities and features far too numerous to discuss here. Especially noteworthy (another pun?) is the fact that WinSong Composer is *completely* MIDI-capable. Softronics also included demo versions of their MIDI sequencer, called TapeDeck 3.0 and JukeBox 3.0, which enable you to chain WinSong Composer, TapeDeck, and Standard MIDI Files together in any editable order. Could be neat for presentations. Dave Wymer, Greg McAllister, and the Softronics staff are easily accessible and eager to answer your questions at 800-225-8590.

Additional Music Software on *MusicPower*

A DOS-only version of the Laser Music Processor 3.3 by TEACH Services, Inc. is also included on *MusicPower*. You can contact TEACH at 800-367-1844. This is a really nice notation program, doing many of the same things as WinSong Composer. The retail price of LMP 3.3 is $129, and their aggressive rebate program sometimes lowers the price to $70-$100. Literature furnished by TEACH marketing director Timothy Hullquist points out that LMP 3.3 is especially useful for creating choral sheet music and manuscripts. I know this is true because this is the software M. L. Norris originally used to create "Infinitely Flexible." My wife and I bought it for him as a gift.

Expanding Your System

This chapter focused chiefly on using the internal sound of your PC. Most computer musicians elect to expand their hardware (and software, if needed) capabilities. Chapter 4, "All About Sound Cards," will show you how to begin the process of improving the sound quality and flexibility of your computer music system.

PC users should advance to Chapter 4.

BASIC COMPOSITION WITH MACINTOSH

3

For this chapter you will need the following:

♪ A Macintosh Plus or higher computer running System 7.0 or higher (System 7.1 would be best)

♪ A hard drive and a minimum of 4MB or more of RAM

♪ A CD-ROM drive (necessary for use of the software provided on the enclosed *MusicPower* CD-ROM)

♪ The internal sound provided by your computer

Becoming a Computer Musician Features Three Macintosh Tutorials

A unique feature of this book is the inclusion of three tutorial chapters that provide hands-on opportunities to learn to use Macintosh software and create music compositions. Three PC tutorials have also been included, so *Becoming a Computer Musician* might actually help you decide which computer platform is right for your needs. The enclosed *MusicPower* CD-ROM includes demo versions of software supplied by some of the finest music software companies. This software varies greatly regarding features, complexity, and price. Appendix F lists the software titles featured on the *MusicPower* compact disc. Appendix E tells you how to reach the manufacturers.

> **Note:** Please bear in mind that these demo versions have been stripped of some features and might not save, print, or might even shut down after forty or so minutes. Remember, the licensed versions you might purchase *do* perform perfectly.

Tutorial 1, Chapter 3

This chapter lets you experiment with computer music with *no additional financial investment!* Remember, it is assumed you already know how to work your Macintosh and that you already understand the basic principles of music. We will use a brand-new version of DeluxeMusic 3.0[1] by Electronic Arts (Figure 3.1).

You will place notes onto the music staff and play back your compositions using only the internal sound provided by your computer.

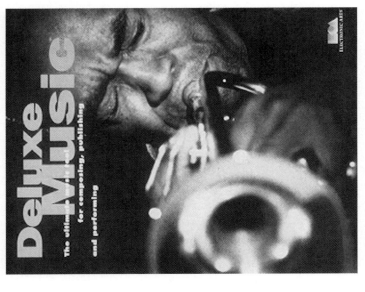

Figure 3.1. *DeluxeMusic 3.0.*

Tutorial 2, Chapter 9: Your First Mac-Based MIDI Recording Session

In Chapter 9, you will use MIDI software for the first time. *MusicPower* provides a demo version of Musicshop (Figure 3.2) by Opcode Systems, one of the leading producers of educational and professional music software.

---

[1] *I will refer to this software as DeluxeMusic for the rest of the book.*

The Chapter 3 Tutorial

This study uses the sound generated by your computer with no added hardware. This sound is called *internal sound*. The internal sound and speaker in your Macintosh are not very powerful in terms of sound quality or volume, but at least they will get your computer music study underway. Later, you will learn how to improve the sound quality of your music projects. For now, all you need to know is that as a Macintosh owner you are ready to get started.

Computer Music is "Infinitely Flexible"

For many years my father-in-law, M. L. Norris, has been a member of a university traveling group. A couple of years ago he started thinking it might be fun to create a simple theme song that would be sung by his fellow group members as they traveled from country to country or when they held reunions, dinners, and such. He owned a PC and received an inexpensive software program as a Christmas present. This software enabled him to compose and play back the theme music, add lyrics, and print out his very own sheet music, such as that shown in Figure 3.4. He would then pass this sheet music out to group members, and all would sing along.

Figure 3.3. *Vision 2.0 by Opcode Systems.*

Installing the Software on *MusicPower*

The first thing you should do is install the software from the *MusicPower* CD-ROM. You will find this CD-ROM in the plastic sleeve inside the back cover of the book.

To install DeluxeMusic, you need only to drag the folder named...well... "Drag Contents to System Folder" into your system folder and restart your computer. The DeluxeMusic program files used for this tutorial do not need installation; they run directly from *MusicPower.*

Note: If you haven't taken the time to install the software from the *MusicPower* CD-ROM, you should do this now. Refer to the Introduction to perform this operation.

Figure 3.2. *Musicshop by Opcode Systems.*

You will enter notes onto the music staff via computer and MIDI keyboard, then play back your compositions using the internal sound provided by your computer, an optional sound card, and an external MIDI sound module. Wow!

Tutorial 3, Chapter 13: Professinal MIDI Recording with the Mac

This is the real deal. A demo version of Opcode's famous Vision 2.0 software (Figure 3.3) serves as the tool for this chapter's exploration of a professional-level MIDI sequencing program.

Chapter 13 also describes other pro software, mentioning features you should expect to find in software you might purchase.

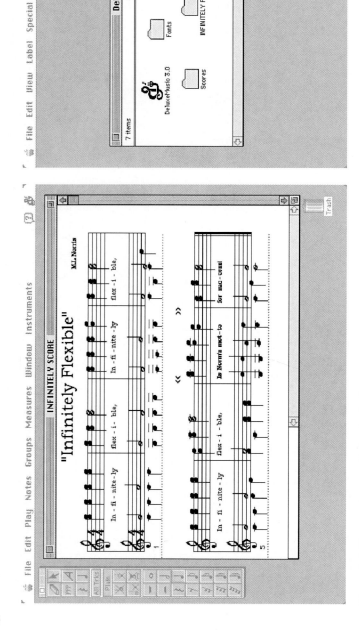

Figure 3.4. *The printed score to "Infinitely Flexible."*

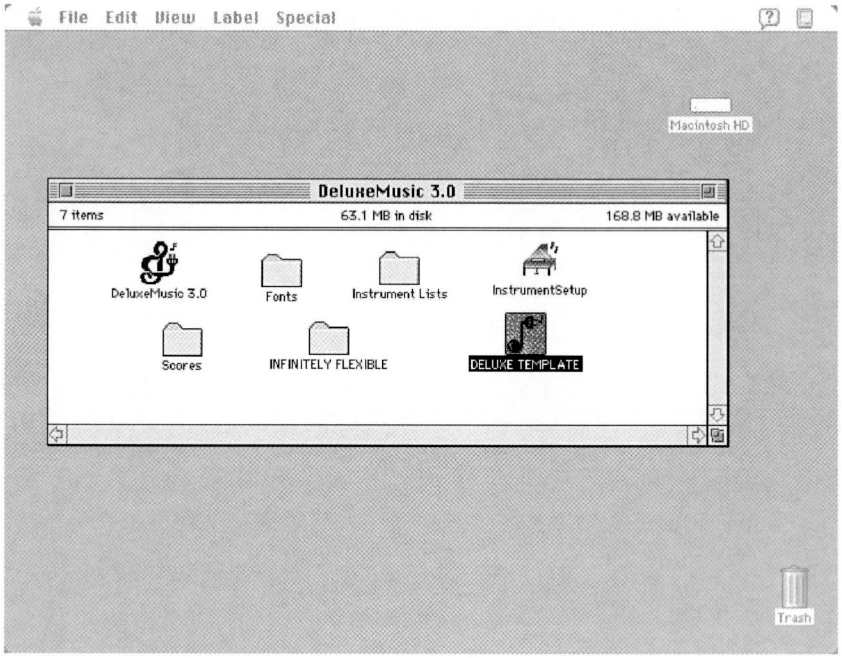

Figure 3.5. *Starting up DeluxeMusic.*

The idea was a huge success and the tradition continues to this day. The group really has a blast with these songs.

Because the primary idea of this book is to show you how to have fun with computer music, I thought I would use this fun little song "Infinitely Flexible," by M. L. Norris, as an example for this exercise. Together, you and I will produce a four-part arrangement of this song.

Launching the DeluxeMusic Software

Select the CD-ROM drive icon for your Macintosh. Double-click. You will see the

DeluxeMusic 3.0 Demo folder. Double-click this folder, then the DeluxeMusic icon shown in Figure 3.5. The DeluxeMusic icon looks like a treble clef with an electric plug.

You should then see Figure 3.6. This is called the Overview window.

Study the Overview window in Figure 3.6. Currently, three windows are open: the Score window, the Keyboard window, and the Note Palette. Close the Keyboard window to create some space. Open the Play Controls under the Window menu, and the Play Controls Panel appears.

The Score window displays the staff. We place music elements onto this staff.[2] The Score window is the main part of the display. The Note Palette enables you to select the music elements you add to the staff. This is the window on the left side of the display. The Play Controls window enables you to play, stop, rewind, and so on, with controls just like those on a tape player. Most good software now provides a control panel like this. This is the window you added. It is located at the bottom of the display.

[2]*Music elements are time signatures, notes, rests, dynamic markings, repeats, and so on.*

Any of these windows may be enlarged or reduced, and moved around on the screen, all in typical Macintosh fashion.

Loading a Demo of "Infinitely Flexible"

A good way to get started with any software is by loading a completed work and experimenting with it. Select Open under the File menu. Double-click the folder "Tutorials." Then double-click "Infinitely Score."[3] You will see the eight bars of the music score shown in Figure 3.4. Click the Play button in the Play Controls window and you will

hear "Infinitely Flexible" in four-part harmony. Neat, huh?

There are several demo compositions included with DeluxeMusic 3.0. They are found in the Scores folder. Take some time to experiment with these selections.

Loading a Template

Let's start with an empty staff and learn how to create a score like this. Click Open under the File menu and open the file "Deluxe Template" (Figure 3.7). This is a template I designed to get you started quickly.

Note: One of the *first* things I do when I get a new piece of software is design a couple of template configurations that will fit *my* most common uses for the software. A template might include things like a certain number of staves[4] and measures, a 3/4 and a 4/4 time signature, and so on. Having templates like this for all your music software enables the computer musician to use time more productively…by making music!

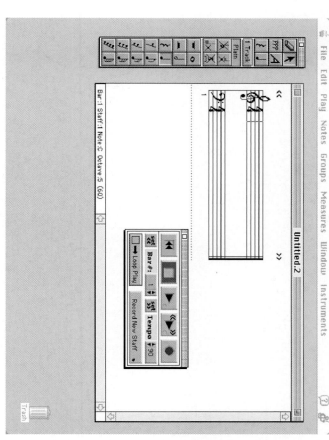

Figure 3.6. *The Overview Window for DeluxeMusic.*

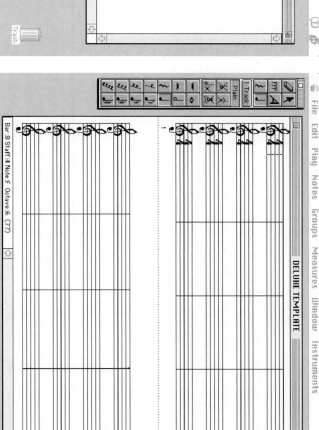

Figure 3.7. *The Deluxe Template.*

[3]*You might want to enlarge the Score window to full screen.*

[4]*Remember that this is the plural of the word staff.*

You will see four measures and four treble clef staves. I could easily have created a template with four bass clef as well, but this template will enable beginners to get started easily.

Placing Notes onto the Staff by Click-and-Drag

Click the quarter note icon on the Note Palette. This means you are going to place a quarter note onto the staff. As you move the cursor with the mouse, notice how it becomes a note of the value you have selected. Move the note to where you want it on the staff and click. Bingo…you have just become a computer musician! Or at least you are on your way.

Add a few more notes to the staff in the same way. Moving these notes around with the mouse can be a bit tricky, but Geoff Brown and the team at Electronic Arts placed a little info box in the lower-left corner of the Score window to tell you the name of the note you are placing on the staff. Clicking the Play button in the Play Controls window will enable you to hear your work at any time.

Reopen the Deluxe Template and refer to Figure 3.8.

Enter the notes from Figure 3.8 using the click-and-drag method just described. If you make a mistake, you can grab the incorrect note with the mouse and drag it where you want it or click the Eraser icon in the Note Palette. The cursor becomes a circle with an "X" through it. Position this "X" over your incorrect note and click. Presto! The mistake will vanish. Then drag a correct note onto the staff. To clear large numbers of notes, click the arrow icon in the upper-right corner of the Note Palette, then move the cursor to the area you want to clear. Click and hold the mouse

button while you drag a box around the offending notes. The notes will highlight. Then select Clear under the Edit menu (or, press Delete). Add new notes and corrections so your score looks like Figure 3.8. Notice that you need to return to the Note Palette to select half notes when needed.

Now click the Play button in the Play Controls window (refer to Figure 3.6) or click Play Score under the Play menu.[5] You will hear Part 1 of "Infinitely Flexible." Computer musicians call this procedure *playback*.

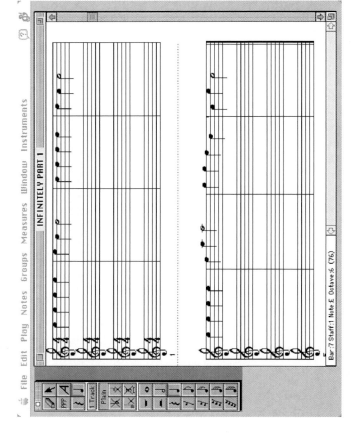

Figure 3.8. *Part 1 of "Infinitely Flexible."*

[5]*There is often more than one way to execute a command when using music software. This allows the software to comfortably fit your specific needs and style.*

Warning: If this were actual software you had purchased, the *very first thing you would do* is save your template under the *new name* of the song you plan to work on. This prevents messing up your template and keeps it in a standard form that is ready to use for the next project. The computer musician always follows one rule religiously:

!!Save Your Work Often!!!

You can never save it too frequently. If this example were an actual project, I would save to a file named "INFINITELY SCORE" on my hard drive and to another file named "INFINITELY SCORE-BU" on a floppy. I cannot emphasize this double-saving philosophy enough. You will agree the first time you lose eight hours of your best work.

Enter the notes from Figure 3.9, Part 2 using the click-and-drag method as you did before. The notes on the second staff make up Part 2.

If you make a mistake, check how you corrected mistakes before. Continue working until your score looks exactly like Figure 3.9. Again, you can click the Play button in the Play Controls window at any time to hear your work. You will now hear Part 1 *and* Part 2 in blissful harmony.

Enter the notes from Figure 3.10, Part 3 as you did above. The notes on the third staff make up Part 3.

Clicking the Play button in the Play Controls window will play back *three*-part harmony!

If you could save your work, you would be doing this at each step, right? Just a friendly reminder.

Placing Notes with the Keyboard Window

You can add Part 4 exactly as you did Parts 1, 2, and 3. But I have another idea. Refer to the Overview window in Figure 3.6. Under the Window menu you will find Keyboard. Let's open that window. Your display should look like Figure 3.10.

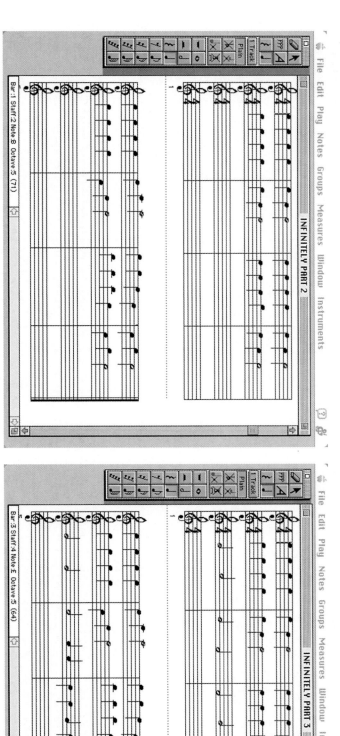

Figure 3.9. *Eight measures of Part 1 and Part 2 of "Infinitely Flexible."*

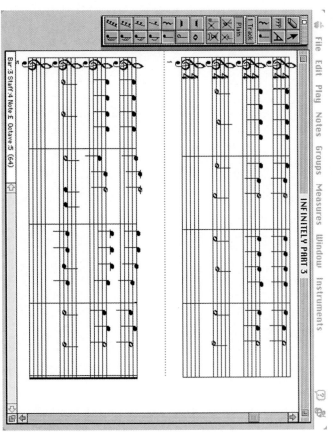

Figure 3.10. *Eight measures of Part 1, Part 2, and Part 3 of "Infinitely Flexible."*

File Edit Play Notes Groups Measures Window Instruments

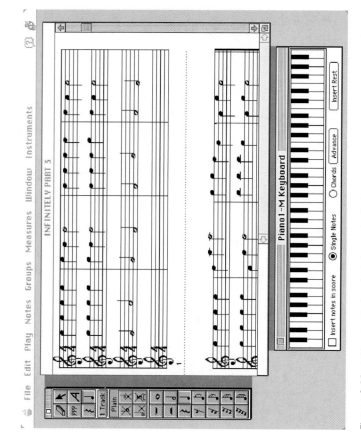

Figure 3.11. *Adding the Keyboard window to the display.*

You might want to click the little square in the upper left of the Play Controls window. That will put the Play Controls window away, which enables the Keyboard window to appear at full length. Then you can drag the Keyboard window to the bottom of the screen.

The Keyboard window enables you to enter notes by using the mouse to "play" the piano keys. Just drag the cursor to the note you want to play on the piano and click. You will hear the note you selected. Experiment freely...you are not harming your previous work.

Click the "Insert notes in score" box on the left side of the Keyboard window. Now when you click the keyboard notes, they will be entered into your work—so be careful and remember how to erase mistakes. Use this keyboard to enter Part 4 of "Infinitely Flexible" into your score. When completed, it will look like Figure 3.12.

Make sure the "Insert notes in score" box has an "X" in it, then use the following procedure to enter Part 4. Go to the Note Palette and click the arrow icon in the upper-right corner of the

window. Now as you move the cursor across the staff, the cursor will *not* turn into a music note. It remains as a cursor. Place this cursor at the beginning of the fourth staff (the one named Part 4), just to the right of the 4/4 time signature. Click. It might take two tries, but the cursor will become a flashing vertical line. DeluxeMusic calls this the Insertion Point. Clicking the keyboard notes now enters them onto the staff, starting at the Insertion Point.

Copy the notes from Figure 3.12, Part 4 onto your blank staff—but this time, "play" the notes on the keyboard slowly and one at a time. You will see each note appear on the staff. Remember, you still need to select note values in the Note Palette. Then place the cursor where you want the new note on the staff and click to place the Insertion Point again. The Insertion Point always determines where you are working on the staff. After you have entered all the notes in Part 4, you are ready for playback. Open the Play Controls window under the Windows menu, and you will see the familiar Play button. You know what to do.

I am excited for you. You have just completed your first arrangement as a computer musician. If you owned this software, you could print out the score for "Infinitely Flexible" and go practice it on the piano, trumpet, or guitar...or just pass it around to friends for fun, like my father-in-law did.

Or you could start experimenting! Yeah...that's it!

Changing the Tempo

Using computers with music enables you to do some really neat things, such as hearing arrangements with different instruments, or with the parts played in different octaves, or with a few notes changed here and there...and at different tempos!

Changing the tempo (speed) of a song is one basic function of computer music software. Play back any of the versions of "Infinitely Flexible" that you may have open. If the Play Controls window is not open, select it under the Window menu. There is a Tempo button on the right side of the window. Placing the cursor on the up arrow while holding the mouse button down speeds the song up. Placing the cursor on the down arrow and pressing the mouse button slows the song down—even while the song is playing back.

Changing Notes in Parts 3 and 4

Erase all the notes from Part 3, the third staff. A fast way is to "draw" a box around the notes, four measures at a time. The notes will highlight or change colors. Clicking Clear under the Edit menu makes the selected notes disappear.[6] Now look at Figure 3.13. It shows an alternate Part 3.

Enter these new notes to replace the ones you erased from Part 3. When you are finished, play back. Pretty fun, huh?

Figure 3.14 provides an alternate Part 4 that you can substitute for the first Part 4 you used for "Infinitely Flexible." Because this part is full of eighth notes, the energy level of the song is higher.

[6]You get one Undo to reverse the process. It is found under the Edit menu.

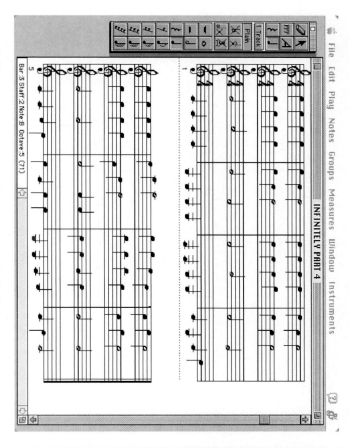

Figure 3.12. Part 1, Part 2, Part 3, and Part 4 of "Infinitely Flexible."

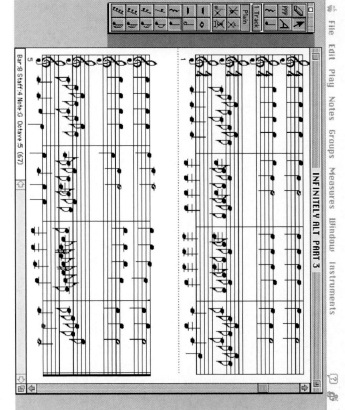

Figure 3.13. "Infinitely Flexible," alternate Part 3.

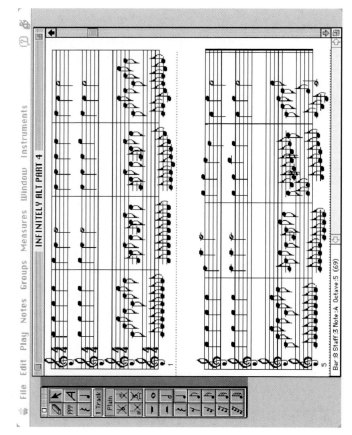

Figure 3.14. *"Infinitely Flexible," alternate Part 4.*

menu. The seven notes copied from measures 1 and 2 are now pasted into measures 3 and 4!

This particular software moves all the other notes past this point to the right by two measures, which will leave you with two additional measures. You might now remove measures 5 and 6 by highlighting the notes in those measures and selecting Cut from the Edit menu. Then you will have the original number of measures again. And remember, you get one shot at an Undo command. Some software might enable you to paste copied notes over the old notes, erasing them. Neither method is better or worse—you just have to know your software and how you prefer to work. Just think of editing a score as being very much like editing a paragraph using a word processor. Hmmm…a music processor, I guess.

Each software title has its own particular set of editing features. It is often the editing that sets a piece of software apart from the rest of the pack, so carefully inspect software for the editing features you want or need when making your selections.

Note: Many famous composers keep different software on hand for different kinds of music productions. Software useful for film work might not be as strong for pop music as other software, and still another title might provide better classical score notation. Careful selection of software, however, will enable *most* computer musicians to find a single software title to fit all or most of their needs.

Transposing the Score

Under the Edit menu is a Select All command. Choose this command. All the notes on the staff will highlight. Under the Notes menu you will find commands that transpose all the highlighted notes. Select the Up Octave command. Play back the score. Then you should select Undo from the Edit menu. Now try the Down Octave command under the Note menu. Play back. Again you should Undo.

Now you see how to manipulate the notes in your score. When you get good at moving notes up-down-over-under, you can get really creative with your ideas.

Cutting And Pasting Notes

Click Open under the File menu and select the file titled "Infinitely Part 1" (Figure 3.15).

Figure 3.15 shows what Part 1 looks like. Here is how you can cut and paste notes on the staff. Use the mouse to draw a box around the notes in measures 1 and 2. The notes will highlight. Select Copy under the Edit menu. You just created a copy of these seven notes that you can place anywhere you want. Place the cursor at the start of measure 3, just to the right of the bar line. Click to activate the Insertion Point. Select Paste under the Edit

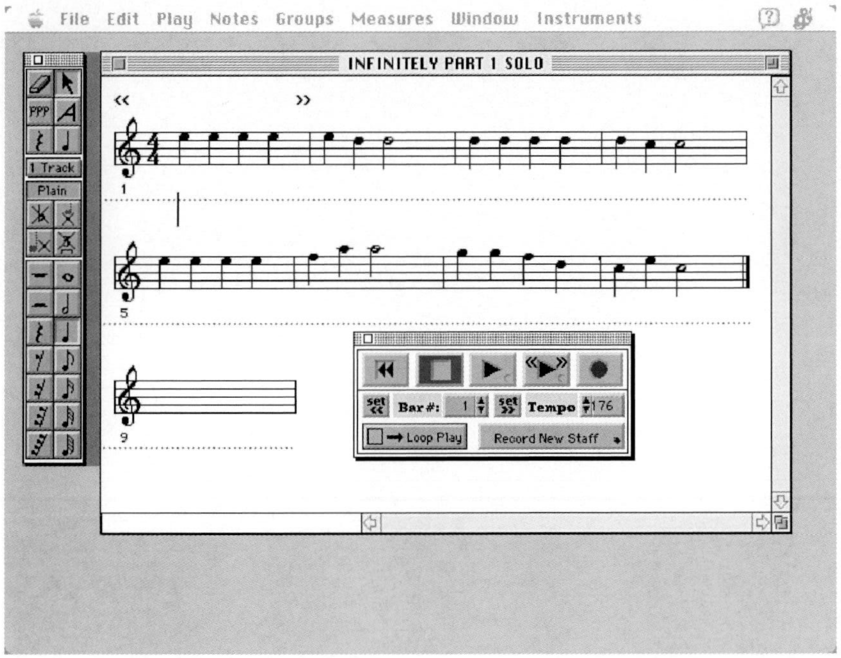

Figure 3.15. *The "Infinitely Part 1" display.*

Changing Instrument Sounds

Most computer musicians enjoy the ability to change the instrument sounds being played back by the software. This is actually one of the best features of using computers with music, because you can experiment with orchestrations to hear different versions of your final music productions.

Again, click Open under the DeluxeMusic File menu and select the file titled "Infinitely Part 1." It will look again like Figure 3.15. Click the Cursor icon in the Note Palette window. Now play back the score. Notice the sound is like a piano.[7] Open the Instruments menu. You will see a list of instruments that you can assign to *any* measure(s) of *any* part of your score. Here's how: Select the instrument you want under the Instruments menu. Let's try Marimba. Place the Insertion Point where you want this instrument to play. Let's select measure 1. Select Set Instrument under the Measures menu. The name of the selected instrument will appear above the staff where you placed the Insertion Point. If you play back now, you will hear a marimba instead of a piano.

Repeat the process to change to another instrument sound. To erase a sound, place the cursor as above. Select Erase Instrument from the Measures menu.

You can use this method to assign different sounds to Part 1, Part 2, Part 3, and Part 4. And your final selections all save to disk, so you can reload them with the sounds you want to use. This is important, because software like DeluxeMusic provides a huge number of choices for you to play...er, uh, work with.

Just for fun, open the file titled "Infinitely Chaos" and play back the score. I arranged this file just to show you how wild you can get with sound selection.

More Arranging Exercises

Appendix B contains printed score samples arranged in four parts. You can practice arranging these in the same way that you arranged "Infinitely Flexible." Have fun.

Digging Deeper into DeluxeMusic

The *MusicPower* CD-ROM is loaded with many other great demos prepared by the staff at Electronic Arts. Load these up and experiment with them. That's why they are included. Be sure to play with the options under the menus.

DeluxeMusic 3.0 is one of the most infinitely flexible (pun intended) music software titles I

[7] *Remember, you are using the internal sound of the computer. You can't expect these sounds to be very realistic. Chapters 4, 11, and 14 teach you how to make your computer instruments sound very much like the real thing.*

have had the opportunity to work with for the price. Especially noteworthy (another pun?) is the quality of the notation printing and the fact that DeluxeMusic is *completely* MIDI-capable. It is loaded with capabilities and features far too numerous to discuss here. It may be the only music software you ever need.

The software retails for $149, but the Direct Sales staff at Electronic Arts has arranged a special offer for those who have purchased this book. You can call 1-800-245-4525 through December 31, 1994, and purchase DeluxeMusic for $89.95 (a super price!). And the Electronic Arts staff is easily accessible and eager to answer your questions at 415-571-7171.

Additional Music Software on *MusicPower*

If you need some help learning the basics of music, there are many educational programs on the market for you to consider. A great resource for Macintosh users is "The Macintosh Product Registry," published by Redgate Publishing at 407-231-6904. All available Macintosh software and hardware is listed by category, complete with pricing and product descriptions. There are so many titles to choose from that I suggest a phone call to your local school music instructor to assist you with a decision.

One program I find especially interesting and useful is Claire, The Personal Music Coach by Opcode Systems. Claire "hears" what is played or sung into the Macintosh and coaches the student with a set of custom-tailored exercises. What I like is that Claire is useful for live instruments—including voice! Opcode has been kind enough to let us include a demo version of Claire on *MusicPower*. I recommend you give it a try.

Expanding Your System

This chapter used only the internal sound of your Macintosh. Most computer musicians elect to expand their hardware (and software, if needed) capabilities. Chapter 4, "All About Sound Cards," will show you how to begin the process of improving the sound quality and flexibility of your computer music system.

Macintosh users should advance to Chapter 4.

ALL ABOUT
SOUND CARDS

4

In Chapters 2 and 3, you discovered how much fun you could have with a personal computer and some basic, inexpensive software. When people start exploring music in this way, something interesting almost always happens—they want to expand the capabilities of their computer music system. The very first hardware upgrade you can make is to add a sound card.[1]

The dings, bleeps, and bonks generated by the computer's sound system may be entertaining, especially for games, but these sounds really don't sound much like music. In fact, using the internal sound capabilities of your personal computer can limit your development as a computer musician in a number of ways:

The computer's internal sound system can generate only a few notes at a time.

You can't get much volume out of internal sound.

Internal sound processors are slow.

The sound is usually monaural.

Internal sound speakers are, in a word, lame. Because they have such a limited frequency rage, they sound a bit like those speakers at fast food drive-up windows.

The increase in the number of computer musicians and the wild popularity of computer games have created a huge new market for better sound-generating products. Several manufacturers saw an opportunity to provide the better sound quality craved by the computer musician and began to manufacture sound cards.[2]

In Figure 4.1, the three sound cards on the left are manufactured by Creative Labs, Media Vision, and Orchid Technologies for the PC. The three on the right are manufactured by Digidesign, NuMedia, and Digidesign, respectively, and are used in Macintosh computers.

Figure 4.1. *Three sound cards for the PC, and three for the Mac.*

Note: The IBM PC platform is the home domain of the sound card industry, especially on the educational and consumer levels. Third-party[3] sound cards do exist for the Mac, but they're few and far between. Authorities in the multimedia and PC worlds attribute this to the fact that Apple's internal audio has historically been superior to that of the PC. Most of the discussion in this chapter centers around sound cards for the PC.

---

[1] *Although product constantly changes, Multimedia World magazine did a nice sound card feature/price comparison chart in its March '94 issue. The address can be found in Appendix E.*

[2] *The folks at Apple actually sensed this public demand and designed their computers to have enhanced sound. They built it into their units, beginning with the 1984 models of Mac and all the IIGS units.*

[3] *This is a term you should know. The manufacturer of a major product such as a computer is the first party, the consumer is the second party, and another manufacturer who makes a product that supports both parties is called a third-party manufacturer.*

The Anatomy of a PC Sound Card

A sound card is a complex beast. The modern sound card boasts features once found only in audio and music equipment costing tens of thousands of dollars. A sound card might consist of the following components:

The software and drivers that operate the sound card

8-bit and/or 16-bit A-D and D-A converters for sampling (recording) and playback of sound

Mono and stereo sound recording and playback

A sound generator or synthesizer[4]

A digital signal-processing chip, called a DSP

A stereo audio amplifier to power speakers or headphones

A stereo line level output to drive a tape deck, audio mixer, or powered speakers

A joystick port that doubles as a MIDI interface

This is all mounted to one small printed circuit board (Figure 4.2)!

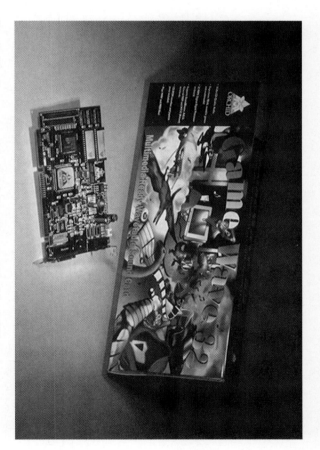

Figure 4.2. *Close-up view of the Orchid GameWave sound card for the PC.*

A PC Sound Card Enables You to Work with Different Kinds of Sound Files

Using a sound card, you can manipulate three basic types of sound files:

CD-quality audio; also known as Red Book Audio

Waveform files; also known as WAVE, WAV, or .WAV in Windows applications[5]

MIDI files; also known as .MID in Windows applications

You can obtain these files on floppy or CD-ROM from a number of third-party sources (often listed in PC magazines), or download them from online services such as CompuServe, America Online, and the Internet.

---

[4] *Most of the PC sound cards include a synthesizer. Very few Mac cards include one. The early music and sound software designers wrote primarily for the Apple line because their chips worked well with music and sound, and because of the easy-to-use, icon-based user interface. Most of the musicians using this software were professionals who didn't care if their computers generated their own sound; they were going to use their own synthesizers anyway. It was the demand from educators and consumers that drove sound card development, not professional demand. Apple and third-party developers still seem to focus on professionals and higher-end product users, for the most part.*

[5] *Creative also uses a sound file formatted as a .VOC file. This file is supported by Sound Blaster-compatible cards, but it's rarely seen these days.*

The best fun of all, though, is when you create your own.

Red Book Audio

These files generate audio of the finest integrity. Red Book Audio is actually the specification for CD-quality sound, just like you hear when you play your CD player at home. The Red Book specification is complex, but basically Red Book audio features 16-bit files with a sampling rate of 44.1 kHz.

.WAV Sound Files

The beeps and bonks you hear when your computer "talks" to you are good examples of .WAV files. These files are commonly used for games, computer prompts, computer voice messages, and lower-quality multimedia applications. These sound files are generally 8- or 16-bit files with a sampling rate of 11 kHz or 22 kHz. Higher quality hardware and software also supports 16-bit files sampled at a rate of 44.1 kHz. This means that some .WAV files can be up to Red Book CD-quality specifications.

Sound File Data and Sampling

Sound files are actually digital recordings.[6] When you record using digital technology, you sort of take "snapshots" of sections of a sound wave. These snapshots are called samples.[7] The number of snapshots per second is called the sampling rate.

All sampling rates are measured in kilohertz (kHz). One kilohertz is 1,000 samples per second, and a sampling rate of 44.1 actually means 44.1 kHz, or 44,100 samples per second. A sampling rate of 11 kHz means there would be only 11,000 samples per second, which is only 25 percent as many as when sampling at 44.1.

If you were photographing your dog catching a Frisbee, you would want to take as many photos as possible in that period of time, so as to catch all of the action. You would be using a high sampling rate. If you took the photos at a slower rate, you would approximate the action of the dog, but some of the details of the action would be lost. You might even miss the most important part—the exact moment the dog caught the Frisbee.

It works exactly the same way when you record digital sound files. If you use the higher 44.1 sampling rate, you get a more accurate digital picture than you would get with a sampling rate of 11 or even 22.

Some camera film seems to capture detail better than other camera film. Film that captures more detail is said to offer higher resolution. This is usually because the film contains more microscopic grains of a chemical that captures the photographic image. The more grains, the higher the resolution of the photos you take.

Sound file recording also features varying degrees of resolution. Generally, a digital sound sample has either 8-bit or 16-bit resolution. An 8-bit digital sample uses 256 sets of binary 1s and 0s to describe its sound. A 16-bit digital sample uses over 65,000 sets! You can see how the increase of 8 bits of resolution leads to much more than a twofold improvement in sound quality.

Figure 4.3 is a visual approximation of what happens to a sound wave that has been sampled during A-D conversion using 11 kHz sampling with 8-bit resolution, and then has been reconverted into a sound wave by the D-A conversion process. Note how much of the original sound wave shape has been lost; the sound also would differ greatly.

Figure 4.4 puts the same sound wave through the same A-D and D-A conversion processes, but uses 16-bit, 44.1 kHz sampling. Notice how faithfully the sound wave is reproduced!

[6]Remember the discussion of A-D and D-A conversion in Chapter 1!

[7]These samples are taken during the A-D conversion process.

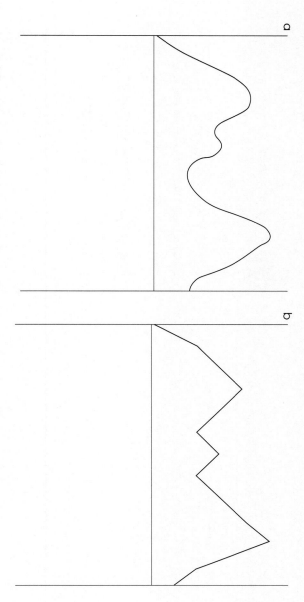

Figure 4.3. *An original sound waveform (a) and the waveform produced by 11 KHz, low-resolution sampling (b).*

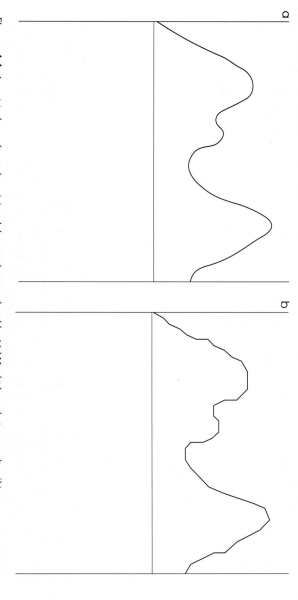

Figure 4.4. *An original sound waveform (a) and the waveform produced by 11 kHz, high-resolution sampling (b).*

If the 16-bit, 44.1 kHz sampling of Red Book audio is so much superior to 8-bit sampling at 22 kHz or 11 kHz, why even use the poorer-quality sound files?

A little simple math will show you.

Table 4.1. Comparing disk space requirements for sound files of different quality.

Number of Bits	Sampling Rate (kHz)	Amount of Data (Bytes/Sec)	Megabytes Required/Sec	Megabytes Required/Min
8	11	11,000	0.011	0.66
8	22[8]	22,000	0.022	1.23
16	22	44,000	0.044	2.64
16	44.1	88,200	0.088	5.28

In computerese, each 8-bit sample is a *byte* of digital computer data. A 16-bit sample is two bytes. Multiply the number of bytes by the number of samples per second (the sampling rate). This gives you the total amount of data eaten up by the sound file. So you can see how a 16-bit, 44.1 kHz digital recording can require about 5MB of disk space per minute! And that's for one-channel or monaural recording only. A stereo recording would require about *10MB of disk space per minute!*

Sure eats up your hard drive quickly, huh? It's to your advantage to use the lower-quality sampling rates whenever you don't absolutely require first-class audio quality.

Playing Back Sound Files on a PC Using the Media Player

To record and play back the sound files in the following exercises on a PC, you must have a sound card that conforms to the MPC[9] or MPC2 specifications with the proper driver installed and configured. To record in these exercises, you also need to have a microphone installed.

If you don't have a microphone or a sound card installed in your PC, you should keep reading anyway. The following information will help you select a sound card.

.WAV and Red Book Audio

Lower-fidelity .WAV files and high-quality Red Book Audio files usually sound different. This is because many .WAV files are recorded using lower sampling rates, often in 8-bit format, and the recorded sound has to be processed by an A-D converter, which might be of questionable quality. If you are using an extremely good sound card with excellent control over recording quality, and you record at 16-bit 44.1 kHz, you can have .WAV files that meet Red Book specs. This is a very rare case, though, so assume there's a difference in the sound quality between .WAV and Red Book sound.

Here's an example. To open the Media Player supplied by Windows[10] and use it to play the CD-ROM enclosed in this book, do the following:

1. Boot the Windows program.
2. In Program Manager, double-click the Accessories icon (Figure 4.5).

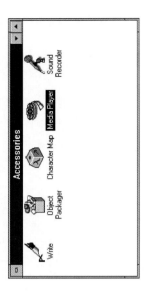

Figure 4.5. *The Windows Accessories window, with Media Player selected.*

3. Double-click the Media Player icon. You'll see the dialog box shown in Figure 4.6.

[8]Note that most sound cards do not support 8-bit sampling with a sampling rate above 22 kHz.

[9]Multimedia Personal Computer. Literature provided by Andrea Bruce from Orchid Technologies explains that MPC is actually an international council that governs the use of the official MPC logo and trademark. The use of the MPC logo on a product indicates that it has met the standards and specifications set by the council. This is done so that software and hardware from different manufacturers has the best chance of being compatible. The MPC2 spec has recently emerged and is quickly dominating the multimedia and sound card field.

[10]The Media Player is an application that controls the sound and video devices in your PC.

Note: If you have run the setup program for *MusicPower*, you will be running a newer version of Media Player than what is shown in Figure 4.6. This new version has some new features and looks neater, but it operates just like the version shown in the figure.

Figure 4.6. *The Media Player from Windows 3.1.*

4. Select Sound from the Device menu. The Open dialog box appears. This is where you select the sound you want the Media Player to play back. In the left box you see .WAV sounds supplied by Windows, as well as any other sounds immediately available for loading.

5. Now load *MusicPower* into your CD-ROM drive, select the CD-ROM drive (usually drive D), select the .WAV sound you want to hear, and double-click the name.

6. The window closes. The sound is now loaded into the Media Player.

7. To play the sound, simply click the Play button. The Media Player's control buttons resemble those found on a tape player. I have included both 8- and 16-bit versions of selected .WAV sound files. You can load and compare both versions if you have a 16-bit sound card. Note how much better the 16-bit versions sound.

You can select and play a number of these sound files. Then do the following:

1. Still using the Media Player, choose CD Audio from the Device menu.[11] Then choose Tracks under the Scale menu. This enables you to select the CD track you want to hear.

2. Select the same sound you selected as a .WAV file above, but now use CD sound. Table 4.2 shows which CD-ROM tracks match the .WAV files. This is a Red Book file. You are now comparing the difference in sound quality between .WAV and Red Book (or CD) sound. You should play back

Note: If you do not hear sound when playing back CD audio, you may not have the audio outputs from your CD-ROM drive connected to your sound card or your speakers. Make these connections, or listen to the CD audio through headphones.

several pairs of sound files. This education will prove useful at several points in the book, so the experiment is worth the time.

Table 4.2. The 8-bit .WAV, 16-bit .WAV, and Red Book versions of PC sound demos on *MusicPower*.

Sound Name	8-Bit .WAV Name	16-Bit .WAV Name	Red Book Track Number
MIDI	MIDI8.WAV	MIDI16.WAV	12
Piano	PIANO8.WAV	PIANO16.WAV	13
Bach	BACH8.WAV	BACH16.WAV	14
Mozart	MOZART8.WAV	MOZART16.WAV	15
To the Stars	STARS8.WAV	STARS16.WAV	
Jesse	JESSE8.WAV	JESSE16.WAV	

[11] *You might need to use a software application that came with your sound card or CD-ROM drive; some Windows systems do not have this option.*

Creating PC Sound Files Using Digital Recording

Remember, you must have a sound card and microphone installed and set up to do this exercise, but you can also just read the information and learn a lot.

Open the Accessories dialog box like you did in the last section.

Double-click the Sound Recorder icon. The result is shown in Figure 4.7. Notice that the buttons resemble the controls on a tape recorder.

Figure 4.7. *The Sound Recorder for Windows 3.1.*

Click the Microphone Button. You instantly start recording. Click the Stop Button when you're finished recording.

Your sound file appears. The Sound Recorder software program gives you a graphic representation of the sound file, so as to give it a shape or form. This is called a *waveform*. You can now play back, name, and save your newly created sound file.

Editing Sound File Waveforms

Now that you've recorded and saved these sound files, you can use software programs to modify the sound file waveform. You can cut, copy, splice, and process the waveform in much the same way you edit sentences with a word processor. This is known as *waveform editing*. You'll find a list of waveform editing programs listed in Appendix F, "Contents of the *MusicPower* CD-ROM," and Microsoft Windows is actually cool enough to provide some basic waveform editing in the Sound Recorder program you just used for recording sound files. Look under the Edit menu on the menu bar. Waveform editing is not the focus of this book, so you may want to refer to the owner's manual or the online help menu included with the waveform editing software you're using to see how this editing is accomplished.

Remember...every waveform you record, import, or save eats up disk space. How much disk space depends on the bit structure and sampling rate used for the sample creation, but any way you look at it, Red Book and .WAV sound files require a significant amount of disk space. To use less disk space, your sample must be recorded with lower sound quality.

The tug-of-war between using the lower sound quality of .WAV files and using the great sound of Red Book may be solved by using a third kind of sound tool provided by the sound card—MIDI.

MIDI for the PC

MIDI stands for Musical Instrument Digital Interface.

> You can't see MIDI.
>
> You can't smell MIDI.
>
> You can't even hear MIDI; it doesn't make a sound.

MIDI generates a set of command data. The commands are very brief and very effective. The synthesizer in your sound card receives this information and generates sounds based on the instructions in the commands.

Figure 4.8 displays some of the command information contained in the MIDI files for a news theme I recently composed for the Fox Network affiliate in Indianapolis, Channel 59 (WXIN). The MIDI software I used for this production was Performer, by Mark of the Unicorn.

MIDI Files Are Very Small

.MID is the Windows file extension for a *standard MIDI file*. A standard MIDI file can be loaded into any MIDI software that supports loading or importing standard MIDI files. Standard MIDI files can even be exchanged between PCs and Macs.

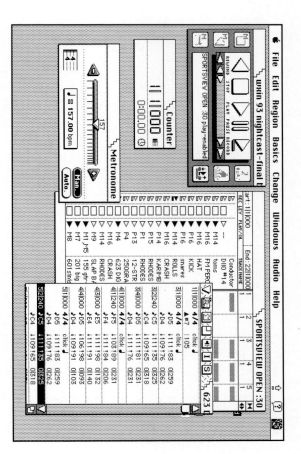

Figure 4.8. *The MIDI event list from a track for Fox TV affiliate WXIN-59's theme music.*

MIDI files do not contain actual sampled sound files, like .WAV and Red Book files; they consist only of this very brief command information and so are very small. A typical MIDI file might take up only 5-20KB of disk space for a music piece that is several minutes long. The Fox 59 news theme is only 60 seconds long. A Red Book file of the finished Fox 59 music would take up about *10 megabytes* of disk space! The MIDI file for the same music would require only about 20KB, or 2 percent as much.

The cost of RAM and hard disk space has certainly decreased in recent years, but it is still quite expensive. So you can easily see the advantage of using MIDI files as a memory- and cost-saving move.[12]

MIDI Is a Super-Interactive Creative Tool

When you use a .WAV or Red Book sound file, you're basically replaying the sound from the original recording. What you record is what you get. Some sound file editing software enables you to cut and paste the digital waveforms and to do some other creative processing to these files. The file still sounds like what you recorded, though. A clarinet is still a clarinet, an explosion is still an explosion, a trumpet is still a trumpet.

MIDI files work in a completely different way. Every sound "played" by a MIDI file can be changed to almost any sound you want it to be. The clarinet can become a flute. The explosion

can become a snare drum. The trumpet can become a violin. This is because the MIDI control data is just that—control data. The sounds are all generated by the device that receives the control commands and enables you to swap sounds around, usually from a synthesizer.

Look at Figure 4.8 again. This is the Track View display for the Performer software. Notice that I'm using kind of a chimey synthesizer sound for the melody in MIDI track 5. Reopen Media Player and select CD Sound from the Devices menu. Play track 5 on *MusicPower* to hear a Red Book version of this arrangement.

If I decide to change the synthesizer melody from the chimey sound to a trumpet, it's easy. All I have to do is click the mouse one or two times and the change is made! Listen to track 6 on *MusicPower* and you'll hear a trumpet playing the melody line. It took me less than two seconds to make this change when I recorded these two versions for the CD-ROM!

Computer musicians really enjoy this ability to customize the sounds and arrangements of music pieces. In Chapters 6 and 7 you'll use MIDI to create your own compositions with the PC. Chapters 8 and 9 show how to create MIDI compositions on the Mac.

[12]*And anytime you work with a smaller data file, your hardware and software systems will work faster as well.*

MIDI is a big deal to the computer musician. Several areas of this book discuss MIDI theory and operation. The preceding was a basic overview of what MIDI is all about. Chapter 5, "The Musical Digital Interface: MIDI," explains in more detail how MIDI operates. Chapter 10, "MIDI In-Out-Thru: The MIDI Project Studio," shows you how to connect the components of a MIDI project studio. Chapter 11, "Is MIDI Black Magic? Or, How Does It All Work?," really digs into all the finer and more complex details of how MIDI works. You're going to love MIDI…I guarantee it.

Comparing the Features of Sound Cards

Sound cards come in many configurations and furnish varied features. Learning about these can help determine which sound card might be right for your needs.

Bit Structure and Sound Quality

The first thing you should realize about sound cards is that there are 8-bit sound cards and 16-bit sound cards. That's the reason I took the time to discuss the .WAV and Red Book sound files. It's important to understand the difference in sound quality between 8-bit and 16-bit sound cards. The 16-bit sound cards simply sound better…much better.

Check the SNR (Signal-to-Noise Ratio) in the specs listings found in the owner's manual. You can think of this as the amount of hiss and other grungy stuff the card mixes into your sound. A SNR of less than 80 is poor. The higher the better—and remember, some manufacturers blatantly lie about their specs. For a true test, plug in a set of headphones or record sound to and from a variety of cards.

Listening with headphones isolates the sound produced by the card from the sounds in the room where you are listening. The noise level in a retail store often will mask poor sound quality, if you just hear the speakers.

Sound Card Software

When you install a sound card, you also install and configure software that enables you to operate it. This is called the *user interface*. All sound card companies refer to their user interfaces by different names, but the software features are usually very similar. Figure 4.9 shows the user interface for the Media Vision Fusion Double CD 16 sound card.

The user interface software usually features the following:

Sound recording and some level of waveform editing. This enables you to record and edit sound, as discussed previously.

The mixer section, which controls the volume levels of the different sound sources.

A synthesizer, which enables you to play MIDI files called *sequences*.

A CD control panel, if you have an optional CD-ROM player.[13]

Sound card software also includes a driver set, which will be discussed during the section on sound card installation in Chapter 6.

Mono-Stereo Sound

A sound card can support mono or stereo sound recording and playback. You want only a stereo card these days; the mono cards, designed to be inexpensive, have pretty much gone the way of the dinosaur. Modern sound cards perform both mono *and* stereo recording and playback.

[13]More and more often, the sound card is installed as part of a complete multimedia kit that includes a CD-ROM drive and a software bundle.

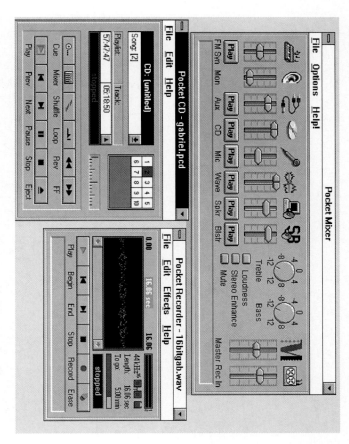

Figure 4.9. *The user interface for the Media Vision Fusion Double CD 16 card enables you to easily access sound accessories.*

The Sound Generator or Synthesizer

A sound generator is found on most sound cards. This sound generator will be called a *synthesizer* or *synth* for the rest of the book.[14] A sound card without a synth is only minimally useful to the computer musician. There are many different kinds of synths built into sound cards. Almost no sound card manufacturer uses its own synthesizer, as really good ones are already made by musical instrument manufacturers. Including a part manufactured by another company in your device is called OEM (Original Equipment Manufacturer)

manufacturing, a very common concept in the sound card industry. The recent buzz in the sound card biz is that sound card companies are buying musical instrument companies, so as to be able to gain access to the sound chips that provide sounds for the synthesizers used by professional musicians. This means the quality of sound produced by sound cards is changing fast.

Yamaha synthesizers were among the first to be used in sound cards, because they were the first ones cheap enough to use on an OEM basis. Yamaha synths are still widely used in sound cards, as you'll see when you start reading the boxes

sound cards come in. Yamaha synthesizers are called FM synths. There are three levels of chips, used to generate three levels of sound quality. The sound quality of the Yamaha chip is determined by how many *operators* the chip uses. Current Yamaha chips used in sound cards include the following:

OPL 2 Two-operator chip; old design

OPL 3 Four-operator chip; newer design

OPL 4 Four-operator chip *plus* wavetable synthesis; the newest Yamaha design

The newer OPL 4 chip uses not only the very synthetic-sounding FM synthesis, but also includes a set of digital sound files of *actual instrument sounds*. This sound set is called a *wavetable*. The FM sounds are generally very thin and work well for instruments that sound bright and chimey, but wavetable synthesis yields far more realistic instrument sounds. Many sound cards using the OPL 3 chip now feature add-on daughterboard expansion that enables you to add a wavetable chip set to the thinner FM sounds. I refer to this use of more than one kind of sound synthesis as *hybrid* synthesis.

[14]*Various synthesizer designs and features are discussed in detail in Chapter 11.*

Wavetable synthesis is catching on fast. Roland uses this technology in the Sound Canvas synth used in its sound cards, and other manufacturers such as Orchid technologies are arranging this use of hybrid sound in their new products. The Proteus by E-mu is a very good pro-level synth that has been used on hundreds of hit recordings. Creative Technologies recently acquired E-mu, so as to have direct access to the Proteus sound chip for use in the optional Creative Labs Wave Blaster daughterboard (Figure 4.10).

The Sound Blaster user now can add this Proteus chip set to Creative cards that support this option, without rendering obsolete the capabilities of the Sound Blaster card. Also, the luxurious, high-quality sounds of Kurzweil instruments are being used by four manufacturers in their new cards.

Watch closely as new card technology enables you to use your own digital sound files as part of the synthesizer wavetable. Just record your own guitar sound as a .WAV file and import the sound directly into the wavetable, where you can play it back through MIDI control. This is the idea behind the Turtle Beach SampleStore synth used in their Monterey card. You used to have to spend thousands of dollars to get this feature on pro-level synths.

Compatibility

This is an area more important to game sound than to music applications. You'll notice the use of the term "Ad Lib-, Sound Blaster-, MT-32-, and MPU-401-Compatible." This refers to the fact

that these hardware formats were among the very first designed, and many computer game authors designed their games to use the sound communications protocols of this hardware. The compatibility refers to MIDI voice assignments and the ability to use .WAV (Windows) and .VOC (Sound Blaster) sound files. As new sound card manufacturers came along, they were smart enough to adopt these protocols as their standards, too.

> **Warning:** Any sound card you buy should support these protocols—especially the MPU-401 protocol, *which determines whether or not your card can be used for MIDI.*

Polyphony

Po(long)-li(accent)-fun-ee. *Poly* means many; *phony* refers to sounds. *Polyphony* tells you how

many sounds the synthesizer can generate at any one instant, and each note played counts as a sound. The number of notes is called the *voice count*. The higher the number, the better. A synthesizer with only 4-note polyphony is said to be a 4-voice synth. Hmmm…sounds like you're getting into the lingo!

Each note played by the instruments you select in your sound card uses up a certain number of "voices." With some instruments, such as the Synthesizer Pad listed in Table 4.3, each note is actually made up of "layers" of voices, and each note played uses one voice per layer per note. Playing a three-note chord using the Synthesizer Pad uses 3 notes × 2 layers, which equals 6 voices in use—even though you hear only 3 distinct notes! This principle is true of all synthesizers.

Figure 4.10. *The Creative Labs Sound Blaster 16 with the attached Wave Blaster card.*

Table 4.3. Voice requirements of a typical MIDI file.

Instrument	Required Number of Notes/Voices
Piano	10
Bass	1
Drums	4
Synthesizer Pad	6
Synthesizer Melody	1
Total Voices Needed	22

You need 22-voice polyphony to play this particular MIDI file. You can see that a sound card with 20 voices wouldn't get the job done. Synthesizer programmers have developed innovative ways to hide the loss of missing sounds, but there's still a limit to what is tolerable. Do yourself a favor and buy a sound card with 28 or more voices.

Note: Fledgling computer musicians often confuse the term *polyphony* with *multitimbral*. The section "MIDI Synthesizers," found in Chapter 11, distinguishes between these two terms.

The Amplifier and Sound Output Connections

Nestled deep within the complex of chips and other stuff on your sound card is an amplifier chip. This chip simply increases the voltage of the sound signal to two higher levels or strengths:

Line Level. This sound output level is used to drive powered external speakers, audio mixers, and tape recorders. This output level is usually about a volt or less.

Speaker Level. This is a much higher power output that drives speakers and headphones directly. Four to six watts of power are common; the more the better.

Figure 4.11 shows the rear panel connections of a Soundwave 32 sound card. This card provides both Line *and* Speaker Level outputs.

The sound boosted by the amplifier chip is sent to the two outputs on the rear panel of the card, one for line level and the other for speaker level. Consumer and semipro sound cards usually feature stereo mini plug audio connections to save space. More professional (and expensive) models enable you to output and input audio in a more substantial, high-quality fashion, as described in later chapters.

Warning: Some sound cards provide only one output jack, usually a speaker level output. This requires you to turn the sound level way down when driving powered external speakers, audio mixers, and tape recorders, in order to prevent distortion. Other cards enable you to select the output level using internal jumpers. You need to make this decision when you install the card. To change levels, you have to take your computer apart again. Selecting a sound card featuring jacks for both output levels is best.

The Sound Input Connections

Some sound cards provide only one sound input, used for both a microphone level input *and* line level inputs, such as from a CD player or tape recorder. This is okay, but I don't like it. Better-quality cards like the Orchid 32 provide a monaural microphone level input and a stereo line level input. This enables you to perfectly match the

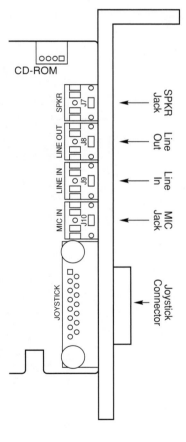

Figure 4.11. *The rear panel of an Orchid Soundwave 32 sound card, showing Audio inputs and outputs and the Joystick/MIDI Port.*

level of the device supplying the sound with the sound card's internal sound processors. Very pro.

A Joystick Port

Another input/output connector, the Joystick/MIDI Port, permits access to the MIDI Interface used when connecting external MIDI controllers and MIDI synthesizers (Figure 4.12). This port was originally designed for game use, but as computer musicians we don't have time for games; we're making music! But those smart people who design sound cards came to realize that the unused connections on this joystick port could be used for a MIDI interface (sure wish this was my invention). Most sound cards require that you purchase an adapter such as that shown in Figure 4.12 to get MIDI into and out of this port.

You'll need the MIDI adapter only if you're going to connect an external keyboard controller or sound module. Be sure the adapter you purchase is compatible with the card you own. They're not all the same.

CD Expansion Capabilities

I didn't believe all the people who told me the value of adding a CD-ROM drive to a computer system. I think you should plan to have one. You can avoid (or at least delay) having your sound card become obsolete by selecting one with CD expansion capability built in. Most cards seem to come this way now, so this is an easy thing to ask.

More About PC Sound Cards

In Chapter 6 you'll configure a sound card and actually do some MIDI recording. I've asked Mac users to read these past few pages, even though the subject has been slanted towards the PC user. Now, the roles will be reversed. If you're using a PC, please read the next sections anyway, as you'll definitely learn something. Besides, all of us at Sams worked really hard to prepare it. Thanks.

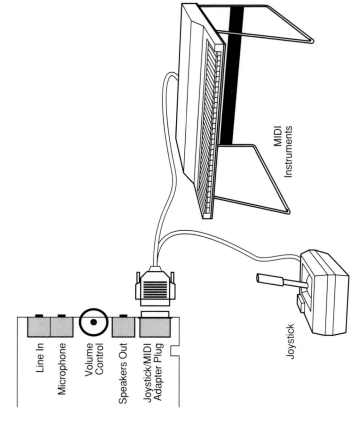

Line In

Microphone

Volume Control

Speakers Out

Joystick/MIDI Adapter Plug

MIDI Instruments

Joystick

Figure 4.12. *The Joystick/MIDI Port found on the rear panel of many sound cards.*

Sound Cards for Macintosh

Apple has always had an interesting approach to design and manufacture of personal computers. They have grown from two brilliant guys in a garage with about $500 to become a huge corporation. They must be doing something right. Their idea is to provide a complete, self-contained, this-is-all-you-need computer system that is super-easy to configure and use. Gary Dauphin from Apple tells me that *all* Macs since 1984 have used the same 8-bit Sony sound chip on their motherboards (the main board in the computer) and the newer models *add* a new 16-bit stereo AT&T chip. 8-bit and 16-bit sound from the Mac family! Macs use 8- and 16-bit sound files in exactly the same way as described for the PC, but the data storage formats are a little different. The sound files for the PC are called .WAV files, and the Mac uses AIFF or .SND files. The end result is the same.

There *are* sound cards for the Mac. They are absolutely awesome in their power. These cards are designed more for professional-level applications than for music education and hobby needs, as reflected by their prices. They cannot be used with all models in the Mac family, as they require a Mac with a NuBus card slot.

These cards are used for recording, editing, and processing sound in high-level music education labs and recording studios around the world. The Audiomedia and Sound Tools cards from Digidesign and the NuMedia and NuMedia^2 cards from Spectral Innovations don't provide a built-in

synthesizer, so they aren't discussed in much detail here. They support a process known as *direct-to-disk recording*, which is discussed in Chapter 14. However, the SampleCell II card from Digidesign and the MacWaveMaker by Morning Star Solutions are monsters for MIDI applications.

Sound cards for the Macintosh are very different from those for the PC. Figure 4.13 shows, from left to right, the NuMedia card from Spectral Innovations, the MacWaveMaker card by Morning Star Solutions, and the Audiomedia II and SampleCell II cards, both from Digidesign. The MacWaveMaker and SampleCellII cards do not sample, but they furnish powerful musical instrument synthesizers. The NuMedia and Audiomedia II cards are superb digital audio cards, but they do not provide musical instrument sound generation.

Figure 4.13. *Mac sound cards by Spectral Innovations, Morning Star Solutions, and Digidesign.*

SampleCell provides a synthesizer that is fully user-configurable...you can load it with any sounds you want![15] The MacWave Maker is loaded with premium sounds from the brand-new Kurzweil MASS chip. For now, let's return to the sound capabilities built into the Mac.

The Built-in Sound Connections

Some Macs (like my Powerbook 165) provide a built-in microphone for routine voice recording. It's well-hidden but faces you directly.

Most Macs require the use of an external mic. Figure 4.14 shows a sound input "port" or jack for the connection of a better-grade external mic or CD sound. The internal mic is automatically bypassed when you connect the external mic,

---

[15] *SampleCell does not let you sample sound files. It plays back sound files that you select from ROM, CD-ROM, hard drives, and floppies. If you want to record your own samples, you must use one of the other cards I mentioned or the internal Mac sound.*

which is the way it *should* work. The mic connector is a monaural mini plug with an icon figure of an old RCA ribbon mic above it, but don't feel like you have to buy a mic with a mini plug attached to the cable. Most of those mics are not very high-quality. Sometimes they're worse than the built-in mic provided by Apple. Better-quality mics come with 1/4-inch or XLR three-pin connectors. You can use one of these mics if you purchase an adapter to convert the connector to a mini. Check your owner's manual to see if the sound input jack is a mic level or a line level input. Connecting a CD player, cassette deck, or synthesizer to a mic level jack will overdrive the input to the point of distortion or damage. Gary Dauphin

suggests a Radio Shack adapter called a *pad*, or attenuator, to cure this problem.

The Mac comes equipped with one internal speaker, and Apple also includes a stereo out jack, in case you want to connect a pair of powered external speakers or send the Mac audio to an audio mixer or tape recorder. In Figure 4.14, note the cute little speaker icon above this jack. This jack accepts a stereo mini plug. This is the kind of jack found on many Walkman-type headphones. P.S. This jack *will* drive headphones.

Playing Back Mac Sound Files

Just as was mentioned for the PC, there are many sources of sound files for the Mac.

Open the Control Panel under the Apple (apple icon) menu in the upper-left corner of your monitor (Figure 4.15).[16]

Double-click the Sound icon. You have now accessed the Sound Control Panel (Figure 4.16). This is where you control the sound functions for the Mac. Notice the Alert Sounds box. This is a list of the sound files currently installed on your Mac.

Click the name of a sound. You instantly hear the sound.

 I have provided a few unique sounds on *MusicPower*. Table 4.4 shows the names of these files, both in 8-bit .SND and Red Book formats. Load some and play them back, comparing the sound quality of the 8-bit and Red Book sounds. If you have a CD-ROM player installed, you can play the Red Book (CD) sounds. You can access the CD Remote or CD Player control panel under the Apple menu, which will enable you to select the CD tracks shown in Table 4.4.

[16] *This procedure is based on Operating System 7.1 or higher. If you are running a version of System 6, your dialog boxes may look slightly different, but this procedure will still work.*

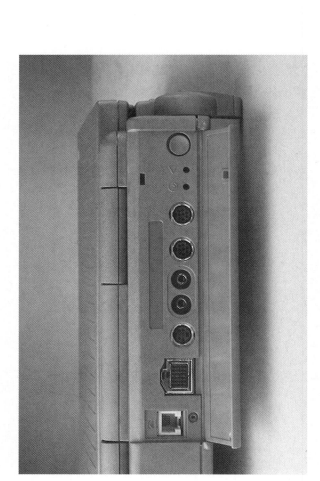

Figure 4.14. *The audio input and output jacks serve as the mini plugs on the rear of this Mac Powerbook 170. Photo by John Greenleigh, courtesy of Apple Computer.*

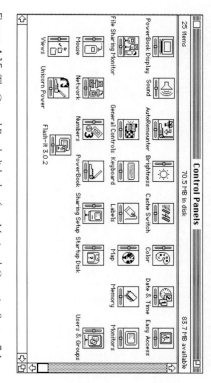

Figure 4.15. *The Control Panels dialog box from Macintosh Operating System 7.1.*

provided. Moving sound around on a Mac is an easy thing to do.

Recording Sound Files on a Mac

You can even record your own sound files, just like with the PC sound card. In fact, all the rules about bits and sample rates and stuff still apply here. But the built-in Mac sound chip can record only at 22 kHz on the 8-bit models. It can record at 22 kHz, 44.1 kHz, and 48 kHz on the 16-bit models.

I hope you left your Sound Control Panel open (Figure 4.16). Double-click the Microphone icon that says "Built-in." This activates the built-in mic.[17] Now click the Add Button.

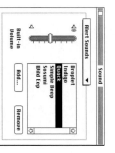

Figure 4.16. *The Macintosh Sound Control Panel.*

A new control panel appears with buttons that emulate tape recorder buttons (Figure 4.17). Recording begins immediately when you click the Record Button, and lasts for ten seconds. To listen to the newly recorded sound, click the Play Button. If the sound is distorted, record it again at a softer level. The Mac Sound Control Panel software doesn't enable you to control the recording level in the nice way permitted by the PC sound card software. Bummer. But it's fun anyway.

Now click the Save Button, name your new sound, and save it.

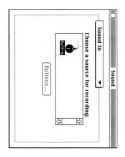

Figure 4.17. *The Macintosh Sound Control Panel recorder functions.*

Table 4.4. 8-bit .SND and Red Book (CD) versions of Mac sound demos found on *MusicPower.*

Sound Name	8-Bit .SND Name	Red Book (CD) Track Number
MIDI	MIDI	12
Piano Riff	Piano Riff	13
Bach	Bach	14
Mozart	Mozart	15
To the Stars	Stars	
Jesse	Jesse	

Hey folks! That last one was Jesse, my golden retriever.

The manual also tells you how to remove sound files from your Mac. This is important, because you'll probably want to get rid of the stuff I

[17]The *Another Source* button is activated if you install a sound card or some other audio device. This enables you to use the sound input on the sound card.

Editing Sound Files on Your Mac

The Mac operating system doesn't supply sound editing, but several third parties produce good sound editors. Demos of some of these are included on *MusicPower*; see Appendix F for a listing. Practice editing some of the sounds you worked with earlier in this section.

The Internal Sound Synthesizer

The Mac provides a polyphonic internal synthesizer, although the sounds are very thin and elementary in nature. Many inexpensive music construction packages enable you to use this sound synthesizer, which certainly saves you money when you are getting started with computer music. The Deluxe Music Construction software you used in Chapter 3 worked this way.

Playing MIDI Files on Your Mac

> **Note:** Be sure you read the section "MIDI for the PC," found earlier in this chapter. MIDI behaves the same on the PC and Mac platforms, with only very minor differences in software terminology.

Actually, Apple made MIDI famous. The icon-based user interface made the Mac the first choice of almost all musicians in the early days of MIDI. However, the operating system and sound cards for the Mac don't support MIDI in the same ways as do PC sound cards. For one thing, there's no MIDI

sequencer supplied with the operating system, as there is with Windows. You have to use a third-party sequencer for MIDI playback. Mac MIDI support isn't worse than PC sound card support, just different. Also, all MIDI interfaces for the Mac are external. Specific MIDI interfaces for the Mac are discussed in Chapters 8 and 11.

Apple has just sent me a hot press release detailing features of their new QuickTime 2.0 application, which promises revolutionary expansion of video, sound, and MIDI playback for multimedia applications. I'm unable to say much about it here, except that it should have a June 1994 release date; if it does everything it says, it will be a huge asset for Mac users. Maybe this book should have a "keep your eyes open for this!" icon.

MusicPower also includes MIDI files for the Mac in a standard MIDI file format. They are represented by the extension .MID. This is actually the Windows extension for a standard MIDI file, but standard MIDI files for the Mac have no standard naming scheme. I have proposed to several of my fellow computer musicians that we adopt the .MID extension for Mac files. If you give standard MIDI files the extension .MID, the names will remain the same if loaded into Windows-compatible MIDI software. I hope other computer musicians will follow this lead.

Any of these .MID standard MIDI files will load or import into the MIDI software demos on *MusicPower*. Feel free to experiment with them after you have explored Chapters 3, 9, and/or 13.

Using Sound from Sound Files and MIDI

This chapter explained the sound capabilities of PC sound cards and Macintosh internal sound. You learned the basics of digital recording (or sampling), and you performed a little bit of waveform editing. The techniques for the recording and editing of digital sound files discussed here have good applications in the area of multimedia production. You can assemble long chains of video files, sound files, graphics, and text to create interesting presentations.

For the computer musician, the star of this chapter is MIDI, the Musical Instrument Digital Interface. MIDI makes the world of the computer musician sing. I can hardly wait to teach you how to work with music using MIDI and sound cards, but first you need to explore MIDI in more detail.

All readers should advance to Chapter 5.

5

The Musical Instrument Digital Interface: MIDI

The single most important tool for today's computer musician is MIDI.

What Is MIDI?

In Chapter 4, I mentioned that MIDI stands for Musical Instrument Digital Interface. MIDI was created in the early '80s and has served as one of the first (and most successful) cooperative ventures ever attempted by an international consortium of electronic music equipment manufacturers. The idea is generally credited to Dave Smith, who at the time headed a company called Sequential Circuits.[1]

MIDI provides a data protocol, or language, that permits the transfer of MIDI data between various electronic devices used for music and audio production. These devices include personal computers, synthesizers, computerized audio mixers, sound cards, and tape machines. MIDI control is even used for some lighting equipment.

MIDI files provide data that *aids* in generating sound. MIDI data doesn't actually *make* any sound until it's received by a MIDI device. Don't expect to hear any sound when you load MIDI data without a properly installed sound card, or without a MIDI interface and external MIDI device.

Why Was MIDI Invented?

MIDI provides the perfect solution to a number of musical problems. Here are some of the reasons why MIDI came to exist.

MIDI Enables You to "Layer" Instruments

In the '70s, musicians who used electronic instruments sometimes wanted to play the same notes on more than one synthesizer to create a "layer" effect. For example, the musician might layer a powerful Yamaha CS-80 string patch[2] with a very synthetic and whispery Oberheim OB-8 patch. Combining these sounds creates a new, richer kind of sound that neither the CS-80 nor the OB-8 could produce alone.

There were two ways to create a layered effect. Method One: The performer, using two keyboards, could play the same notes with each hand, one hand on each keyboard. Musicians such as Rick Wakeman from the band Yes became famous for using this technique. The problem arose when the artist wanted to play more than five notes per hand simultaneously.[3] There was no good solution to this problem for live performances, but the technology of the recording studio provided a way to get it done.

Method Two: Multitrack tape machines (Figure 5.1) enabled the musician to record the sound of one of the synthesizers, using both hands for the performance. That sound was recorded on its own track of tape. As the first performance was played back, the musician reperformed the same notes using the second synthesizer. And you could continue to layer sounds until you ran out of available tracks. This method required a lot of extra time in the studio, and it took up valuable tape tracks that were needed for vocals or other live instruments. As a producer, I've refereed many battles between guitarists and keyboard players over who gets to use the final remaining track. Heads or tails, anyone? (And I don't necessarily mean a coin!)

Several manufacturers tried to solve this problem by designing somewhat proprietary voltage control systems that used converter boxes or interfaces between synthesizers—a system that sort of worked, as long as you played one note at a time. But many interfaces later, electronic musicians were more than ready for something new.

---

[1] These people are famous for inventing and manufacturing the wonderful Prophet line of synthesizers. Some of the best ideas brought to the field of electronic music are credited to these talented pioneers. According to tech editor Larry Fast, Dave Smith and Chet Wood presented a paper about the USI-Universal synthesizer interface at the 1981 Audio Engineering Society Convention. This paper outlined the early design for MIDI Spec 1.0.

[2] It's common to call the sounds generated by a synthesizer a patch. This is a reference to the days when synthesizer sounds were not programmed in software, but rather were created by using patch cables between synthesizer sections or modules. A good place to see this is on the cover of the album Switched on

Bach by W. Carlos, Columbia Records, 1968. Patching is done almost entirely in software in the modern synths we use today.

[3] Some of my friends who were keyboard players used to use matchbooks to pin down extra keys on their B-3 organs and other instruments. I still do this today when I'm playing a keyboard part live and I need a drone or sustained note. My clients get a real kick out of this procedure. Sometimes I do it just to throw a little entertainment value into a session.

It's interesting that the first major concert tour to use MIDI-equipped keyboards was the 1983-84 90125 tour by Yes. Keyboardists Tony Kaye and Jon Anderson made extensive use of new technology and MIDI when recording the 90125 album, and then used much of the same technology, including MIDI, on the concert tour. The new layered sounds generated by this technology helped propel the song "Owner of a Lonely Heart" to a solid number 1 position on the pop-music charts and impressed other musicians enough to guarantee the future and development of MIDI as we know it today.

Other Uses for MIDI

As MIDI hardware and software have become more reliable, more economical, and easier to use, MIDI has also expanded in capability. Today's typical professional computer musician might use MIDI to assist with the following:

- Music composition, recording, and production
- Archiving data for synthesizer sound programs, called *patches*
- Controlling video and audio tape machines
- Designing sound effects for film and video
- Controlling sound-processing devices such as reverbs, delays, and so on
- Managing complex mixing sessions through the automation of audio mixers

Those becoming computer musicians at the home or consumer level could use MIDI for the following:

- Composing music for games
- Creating sing-along songs with printed sheet music
- Music education
- Multimedia presentations for home and business

How Does MIDI Work?

Chapters 10 and 11 explain how MIDI works in great detail,[4] but we'll move on with the easily understandable, basic stuff for now.

Figure 5.1. *The Fostex G-16 is a multitrack tape recorder that enables you to record up to 16 tracks of sound on half-inch recording tape.*

Playing Back MIDI Files

In Chapter 4 you learned that you could double-click a sound file stored on your hard drive or on a floppy,[5] and this would load the file and play it back. This is because the sound file contains all the data needed by the D-A converters to re-create the original sound. MIDI is very different. When you load a MIDI file, the MIDI data file might load perfectly, but you'll hear no sound when the file is played back.

 The first rule of MIDI: MIDI files do not make sound. Period. Music-store salespersons tell me this is *the* most misunderstood part of the whole computer-music scene.

Okay. Okay. Okay. So now that you know that rule, how *does* MIDI data become a sound you can hear?

MIDI Event Data

The data used in the digital communications language of MIDI is called *MIDI event data.*[6]

[4] If all that information were covered here, it would be a long time before you could start more fun computer music activities. So if you just can't wait to fully understand MIDI, you can be insubordinate and skip to Chapter 10 after you finish this chapter.

[5] If you're using a PC, you must have a sound card installed.

[6] Other kinds of MIDI data are supported by MIDI Spec 1.0. These are discussed in Chapter 11.

The Hardest-Working Drummer in America

Photo by Jay Wiley

An Interview with Drummer Kenny Aronoff

Kenny is best known for his fourteen years of drumming, both live and in the studio with John Mellencamp. He has been featured on literally *hundreds* of famous recordings by such artists as Elton John, Jon Bon Jovi, Bob Dylan, Bob Seger, Iggy Pop, B.B. King, Bonnie Raitt, Meat Loaf, Waylon Jennings, Hank Williams, Jr., Vince Gill, and Cinderella. Kenny studied classical percussion at the Indiana University School of Music, where he is presently an associate professor. He has worked under the baton of such great conductors as Leonard Bernstein, Aaron Copeland, Siege Ozawa, and Arthur Feidler. Kenny authors a regular column for *Modern Drummer* magazine and occasionally can be seen filling in as the drummer on *The Late Show with David Letterman.* I had the opportunity to talk with Kenny between his recent sessions in Italy, L.A., and Nashville, and we discussed ways in which he integrates computer-assisted music technology into the recording process. The following are excerpts from that conversation:

"…we recorded a record called *Scarecrow* in 1985, and the sounds on that record were very powerful and unique. We had created a new type of drum sound, which is never an easy thing to do. When it was time to go on tour I wanted to re-create that powerful and unique sound live. I heard about an electronic drum company called d-drum, who could take my sampled sounds from tape and put them into 'sound packs,' or EPROM cartridges. Each cartridge, which held one or two sounds, could then be put into a slot in the d-drum brain.

Every time I hit one of my drums, I would trigger one of my sampled sounds. The challenge was to get the d-drum brain to trigger every time I hit the acoustic drum so as to emulate all of my dynamics. On this particular tour, the engineer blended the sounds from my acoustic drums with my sampled sounds in the d-drum brain."

"After the Scarecrow tour, I decided to get involved with computers. I started to fool around with writing my own music on a Mac SE with a music program called Performer. As time went on, I just got more and more involved with electronic music and computers. I started using MIDI instruments and I eventually built a little MIDI studio, where I would spend days building wild and exotic drum and percussion tracks. Today, I have a Powerbook 160 and a Mac SE-30. I have a MIDI studio at home and one at Indiana University. Ideally, I like to incorporate both the MIDI stuff and real drums and percussion...both in the studio and live."

"In the studio I usually create a click track for me and the other musicians to follow when we're recording basic tracks. Instead of programming only one sound as a click, such as a cowbell or a clave, I prefer to create a more involved program, using as many as six to eight individual tracks with many different sounds. I'll either use a drum machine as my sound source or will use MIDI to get sounds from two, three, or even four different sound sources. On

a Corey Hart record called *Attitude and Virtue* (1991), I made a pretty involved click track, using four different modules for sound sources. I tried to make the click track as musical as possible by programming dynamics, pitches, and pannings. When I programmed the click track I tried to make it sound like a musical part of the song and not just a way to keep steady time while recording. Basically, I created a drum loop that worked as a click track."

"I like to integrate my electronic sounds with my acoustic drums and acoustic percussion whenever possible. So, sometimes on a session I'll record my click track or sequence first, and then, I'll record my acoustic drums as the other musicians and I record the song. Finally, I might add acoustic percussion to the existing tracks."

"Sometimes I'll do a session where we print the SMPTE on one of the tracks and then have the SMPTE run a [sequencer] program such as Performer, Cakewalk, or Vision. The SMPTE synchronizes the recording tape and the computer. On the Jefferson Airplane reunion album *Jefferson Airplane* (1989) I used Cakewalk to write eighteen different percussion tracks for a song called the 'The Wheel.' SMPTE made it possible for us to combine the tracks recorded on analog tape with the MIDI tracks recorded on the computer."

"On the Chris Isaacs album *San Francisco Days*, the engineer recorded all of my acoustic drums

to analog tape and at the same time he also recorded all of my drum parts on his computer [workstation]. They spent weeks or even months editing different sections, different measures, and even different beats of the takes we recorded until they had created what they thought was a perfect take. Because all of my parts were recorded into a computer, it was much easier to do all the edits. They even had the flexibility to change my kick or snare pattern in the computer."

"On Jon Bon Jovi's *Blaze of Glory*, we integrated my real drum sounds with a very involved sequence written by Aldo Nova. The sequence was made up of lots of percussion sounds, with many additional sound effects. I used his sequence as [a] click track. Then I had to play perfectly with his sequence, because Jon wanted to keep both the sequence and the acoustic drums in the final mix."

"I integrated a drum-machine part with my drum kit on the Elton John boxed set *To Be Continued....* Elton had fallen in love with the sounds and the parts programmed on a drum machine. So, we used the kick and snare from the drum machine and I overdubbed all of the cymbal parts [hi-hat, ride, and crashes]. Then I overdubbed my drum fills."

"I have a MIDI studio at Indiana University and I not only provide private instruction on drum set, tympani, and marimba, but I teach my students how to program a drum machine, how to use MIDI, and how to use a computer to write music. I also record their lessons and occasionally have them play along with a drum machine, CDs, or tapes, to help develop their time and groove on the drum set. I try to teach them how to incorporate electronics with their acoustic instruments."

Author's note: *MusicPower* features opening sections of Kenny's *Power Workout* tutorial videos. Be sure to view this section now: Drummers will also want to check out the following educational materials, all authored by Kenny and available from CPP/Media Group, 1-800-628-1528, extension 215.

Laying it Down: The Basics of Rock Drumming—Video, $39.95

Power Workout 1—Video, $24.95

Power Workout 2—Video, $24.95

Power Workout 1+2: Powerpack—2 Videos, $39.95

Power Workout 1—Book (with cassette, $21.95; with CD, $24.95)

Power Workout 2—Book (with cassette, $21.95; with CD, $24.95)

Lessons with the Greats—Book (with cassette, $22.95; with CD, $24.95)

Kenny's PowerPlay signature drumsticks by Vic Firth (617-326-3455)

MIDI event data can be generated by the following sources:

A MIDI-capable keyboard, wind instrument, guitar, or percussion controller

A sequencer that has recorded the MIDI event data generated by one of the above

A sequencer playing back a file of previously recorded event data, such as a .MID file

The MIDI event data tells devices in the MIDI system what to do. An example of a MIDI event would be *Key On*, which is generated when you press a key on a keyboard controller or hit a MIDI percussion pad. Key On tells a sound-generating MIDI device (such as a synthesizer) to make a sound, and it even tells the device which note to play. An extensive list of MIDI events and what they do is presented in Appendix D. MIDI event data is most commonly generated by MIDI computer software or by a MIDI-equipped keyboard controller. These MIDI events are said to be "transmitted" to another MIDI device, which is said to "receive" the MIDI information.[7] How does it get there? Through the *MIDI channels*.

The MIDI Channels

The MIDI data is transmitted from one MIDI device to another through a MIDI channel. MIDI Specification 1.0[8] states that MIDI devices exchange MIDI data through 16 basic MIDI channels.[9] These channels can *all* be contained in one serial data stream, which means MIDI gear can transmit or receive all 16 MIDI channels

through a single wire. This makes for a wonderfully integrated and interactive system that is inexpensive, reliable, and easy to install and use.

The MIDI Sequencer

MIDI event data is most useful when used with software designed to record it and play it back. The software programs used to play MIDI files are called *sequencers*.

Figure 5.2 shows the Track Overview screens from two popular MIDI sequencers: Cakewalk Professional for the PC on the left, and Performer 5.0 for the Mac on the right. These are two of the most popular sequencers used by serious computer musicians. Notice how they both feature control buttons that mimic or "emulate" tape recorder buttons. This makes them easy to use.

Windows has a MIDI sequencer built right in!

[7] *Think of it this way: MIDI is a little like a telephone system. When you pick up your telephone to make a call, you must select the destination that will receive the data representing your voice. Dialing someone's phone number enables you to determine which phone is the destination or receiver. When you speak, your telephone transmits your voice data only to the phone number you dialed. The phone on the receiving end generates sound based on the digital information sent by the transmitting phone.*

[8] *All MIDI applications are still based on MIDI Specification 1.0, which is the standard protocol approved by the International MIDI Association. Call them at (818) 598-0088 for all the brutal details concerning MIDI code. Although many enhancements have occurred since the mid-80s, there's no serious discussion concerning a revision of the 1.0 specification.*

[9] *Chapter 11 explores ways to expand these 16 basic channels to the 512 channels that are now available.*

MIDI Playback in Windows

MIDI playback in Windows is another subject that really applies to the PC platform and works best with a sound card. You should understand these PC applications even if you're a Mac user, because the two platforms are quickly moving closer in style of operation. Many products, such as the Cubase sequencer by Steinberg-Jones, are appearing for both platforms and the two versions look and operate almost identically.

If you have run the Setup program for *MusicPower*, you will be running a newer version of Media Player than what is shown in Figure 5.3. This newer version has a few new features and a nifty new look, but it operates just like the version shown in the figure.

Open the Windows Media Player. Just double-click the Accessories icon in the Program Manager dialog box, then double-click the Media Player icon. Figure 5.3 shows what you see on your screen.

Open MIDI Sequence under the Device Menu. You will again see the Open dialog box. To play one of the MIDI files provided on *MusicPower*, select any of the .MID files in the directory named MIDI.

The screen returns to the Media Player dialog box, and you're ready to play the sequence. You may need to be sure that the MIDI Mapper has *all* MIDI channels 1-10 mapped to your sound card synthesizer. Otherwise, the sounds may not play back properly.

a

Figure 5.3. *The Media Player in Windows 3.1 is actually a play-only MIDI sequencer. It can play back Standard MIDI files with the .MID suffix.*

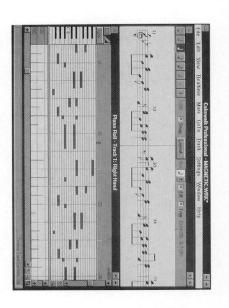

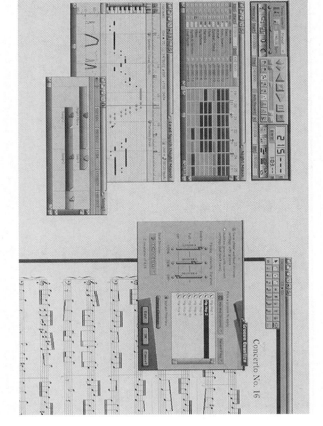

b

Figure 5.2. *The track overviews of two popular professional sequencers: (a) Cakewalk Professional, and (b) Performer 5.0.*

MIDI File Formats and Configurations

There are two kinds of MIDI file formats: proprietary MIDI file formats, and the Standard MIDI file format.

Notice when I used the phrase "proprietary MIDI File formats" that I used the plural, "formats." This is because there is no standard for MIDI files of this type. Let me explain. If I create a MIDI sequence using the Mac sequencer Opcode Vision 2.0 and then save the file, I'll probably save the file in an Opcode Vision format. If I try to open the same file in Performer 5.0 by Mark of the Unicorn, the Vision file will not even be recognized, much less loaded successfully. The same thing happens if I try to load the file into Master Tracks Pro by Passport. I'm not criticizing these companies...all MIDI sequencer files used to have this problem, just like different word processors couldn't load each other's files. Fortunately, software developers learned quickly (???) to work together and invent a standard file format that could be read by all sequencing software, regardless of whether it's on the PC or Mac platforms. This great invention is called the Standard MIDI file.

Notice in Figure 5.4 that you can save your MIDI files in either the Performer format or Standard MIDI file format. These files can then be reopened by any sequencer supporting the Standard MIDI file format, and most decent sequencers do exactly that.

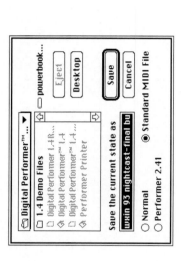

Figure 5.4. Many sequencers enable you to save your work as a Standard MIDI file format, which means the file can be loaded or imported by other sequencer application software...regardless of the computer platform you are using at the time. This option is selected in the Digital Performer Save File dialog box.

The real winner is the multimedia programmer. With the Standard MIDI file format, a musical sequence can be composed and produced on any sequencer and played back on nearly any other sequencer. The only remaining problem is that of MIDI mapping, or sound assignment.

MIDI Configurations or MIDI Routing

You've learned how a MIDI channel delivers event data from a source to a destination through a channel. After the source event data is recorded, it no longer matters where it was generated. It's just a bunch of digital 1s and 0s waiting for something to do. What matters now is the device receiving the event data and generating the sounds we hear. Perhaps when I recorded the aforementioned sequence using Performer, I

intended for Track One to be received by a device set up to generate a bass sound. If I send that recorded event data through MIDI channel 1, and if the device receiving on channel 1 is generating a bass sound, all is fine. However, if the device receiving this data on channel 1 is set up to generate a quacking duck sound, I'm in real trouble. You would say my MIDI configuration is incorrect...that I have a problem with my MIDI channel assignments.

This was a bit of a problem with early game sounds: The MIDI files didn't play the right sounds on all cards. That's why some games were compatible only with certain sound cards. Again, a few standards arose, such as compatibility with Sound Blaster, AdLib, and MT-32. But the MIDI files began to grow more complex, and computer musicians began to want less-confusing MIDI setups, so Roland introduced a new MIDI standard called the General MIDI specification.

General MIDI

Roland learned early on that it could use a new version of its MT-32 voice arrangement or MIDI configuration in other keyboards it designed, and make it easy for its customers to add synthesizers to their MIDI setups. Other manufacturers also found this to be true, and in the late '80s several manufacturers began to use the same channel and key assignment for drums as found in the MT-32. Roland started the push toward General MIDI (GM) with its Sound Canvas sound module, which implemented the proposed GM spec. But because GM was not "officially" adopted, those early Sound Canvas units didn't have the GM logo screen printed on them! Now they do bear the official GM logo, as do dozens of other GM products.

This new standard assured the MIDI user that the sounds she was composing with would be the sounds re-created when his MIDI file was played back by any synthesizer supporting GM, regardless of who manufactured the synthesizer. Some MIDI sequencers for the Mac and the PC include GM templates complete with prenamed track, channel, and voice assignments, which makes for a tidy, efficient package.

The General MIDI template specifies 128 preset instrument sounds and 47 percussion sounds. GM voice configurations are found in Appendix C. It's a good idea to get a photocopy of the two charts you'll find there, so you can have them on hand when you're composing. You can send me $25.95 plus $7.50 postage and handling for a photocopy of Appendix C, or do it yourself for 4 cents.

The MIDI composer enters a MIDI event called Program Change in each MIDI track. This command selects which of the GM sounds is "played" by the other MIDI events.

Correcting MIDI Problems with the MIDI Mapper

Sometimes MIDI voice assignments still don't work properly. It has taken computer musicians 10

years to figure this subject out…and we still get stumped sometimes!

A typical MIDI composition uses several sources (such as sequencer tracks), channels, and destinations for MIDI data. The MIDI event data is *transmitted* through a channel, and the device *receiving* the data on the *same* channel generates the sound. If this assignment is not made correctly, one of two bad things can happen:

♪ Nothing at all. Remember—MIDI makes no sound of its own! A receiving or destination device must convert MIDI events into sound.

♪ The wrong sounds play the wrong notes, creating a jumble.

Incorrect channel assignment is usually the area where fledgling computer musicians first encounter intense confusion. *Channel-assignment problems should be corrected in your sequencing software!*

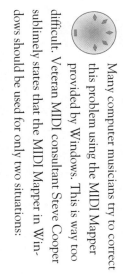

Many computer musicians try to correct this problem using the MIDI Mapper provided by Windows. This is way too difficult. Veteran MIDI consultant Steve Cooper sublimely states that the MIDI Mapper in Windows should be used for only two situations:

1. To fix configuration problems when Standard MIDI files are being played back by the Media Player or some other multimedia authoring program.

2. To fix configuration problems caused by poorly designed sequencers. The best solution here is to select another sequencer.

So basically, don't mess with the MIDI Mapper unless you have a problem.

Real MIDI Recording

The best way to really grasp the wild world of MIDI is to roll up your sleeves and actually use it. Thanks to the gracious attitudes of several software manufacturers, the enclosed CD-ROM supplies you with demo versions of some of the best and most popular MIDI sequencers on the market. Just as in Chapters 2 and 3, there are both Mac and PC versions. Use Chapter 7 or 9 to record, edit, and play back some of our very own MIDI music creations.

PC-platform users may now go to Chapter 6.

Macintosh-platform users should skip to Chapter 8.

SETTING UP
6
YOUR PC FOR
MIDI RECORDING

For this chapter, you will need the following:

- 386SX, 25 MHz or higher, running DOS 5.0 and Windows 3.1 or higher
- 4MB of RAM (8MB is faster)
- A hard drive and a mouse or trackball
- A CD-ROM drive (to use the software provided on the *MusicPower* CD-ROM, included with this book)

Hardware for PC MIDI Recording

I assume that you have a PC that's configured as I just recommended. Let's move on to learning about some hardware you may not know about.

The essential pieces of hardware required for MIDI recording are as follows:

A MIDI controller, usually a keyboard instrument

A MIDI interface, which connects the controller to the computer

A synthesizer, which generates *all* the sounds in a MIDI system

The MIDI Controller

The MIDI controller is the primary source of the MIDI event data (MIDI events) that drives the entire MIDI system. The MIDI controller provides the main user interface to the MIDI system, and is the instrument you actually play and use to record MIDI event data into the computer software.

Your MIDI controller might be a keyboard instrument, guitar, wind instrument, or percussion pads.[1] I will use the word *controller* for the rest of this chapter to represent any of these types of controllers. Most computer musicians use a keyboard controller, which features a keyboard like the one found on a piano. Figure 6.1 shows a popular MIDI controller.

You can use the same controller instrument with the PC, Mac, Amiga, or Atari platforms.[2] Any controller you purchase should have the following:

A MIDI OUT jack

A MIDI IN jack (if your controller has a built-in synthesizer)

The MIDI Interface

The MIDI interface converts MIDI data to PC computer data and vice versa. Without a MIDI interface, you can't use an external controller for MIDI recording. You *can* still play back MIDI files with your sound card, and you can assemble MIDI soundtracks with the click-and-drag method described in Chapter 2. Without a MIDI interface, you can't use external synthesizers for sound generation. You instead have to use the internal PC sound (yuk!) or a sound card.

The MPU-401 Interface Protocol

The computer "language" used by an interface is called its protocol. Roland invented the first successful MIDI interface for the PC in the middle '80s and based it on their MPU-401 protocol. For a long time the MPU-401 protocol was the only interface available for the PC, and thus it became the standard for all other popular PC interfaces.

Figure 6.1. *The Roland A-30 MIDI keyboard controller.*

[1]We will discuss all these types of MIDI controllers in detail in Chapter 11.

[2]You can also use the controller to play MIDI sound modules directly, without having a computer involved at all.

This is what is meant by the phrase *MPU-401-compatible*.

The importance of MPU-401 compatibility is not to be underrated! There's no reason for you to purchase a sound card or other MIDI interface that is *not* MPU-401-compatible.

There are two modes of operation with the MPU-401 protocol. Intelligent (or "smart") mode allows the processing and manipulation of data *within the interface*. This enables you to use complex MIDI functions, such as event filtering and remapping, MIDI THRU or echoing, tape synching, and timing clock conversion, all without tying up the CPU of your computer. This is very useful for certain professional applications.

UART (or "dumb") mode doesn't actually furnish any onboard data processing, but simply transmits and receives MIDI data to and from the computer. UART mode doesn't support some of the more advanced MIDI features that are supported by "smart" mode. These functions must be handled by other software (such as your sequencer) if your interface is a UART model. Most interfaces are based on the UART mode and will work fine for most computer musicians.

PC interfaces exist in two forms:

Interfaces built into the MIDI/joystick port connector on your PC's sound card

Interfaces that you can install into an expansion slot inside your PC

Many sound cards on the market today feature a built-in MIDI interface. This is a nice cost-saving feature for the music educator, student, or hobbyist, or for the person working with basic multimedia music tracks. The serious computer musician will find these interfaces too inflexible and complex to use for any kind of day-to-day, dead-line-governed productions. Let's take a look at both interface types.[3]

MIDI Interfaces Included on Sound Cards

The MIDI interface provided with a sound card is accessed through the MIDI/joystick port on the back of the sound card (Figure 6.2).

Figure 6.2 shows the rear panel illustration of a typical PC sound card. Note the multipin connector on the lower-right corner of the card. This multipin connector is the MIDI/joystick port. It will be called the MIDI port for the rest of this book. A MIDI adapter cable like the one shown in Figure 6.3 provides another multipin connector that plugs into this MIDI port.

The MIDI adapter cable also furnishes two MIDI connectors. You can see these on the left side of Figure 6.3. They should be labeled MIDI IN and MIDI OUT.

The MIDI IN attaches to the MIDI OUT of your controller. The MIDI OUT attaches to the MIDI IN of any external synthesizer you use.

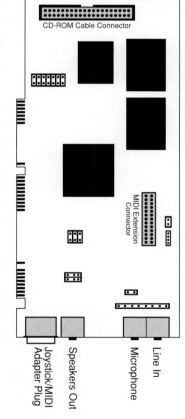

CD-ROM Cable Connector

MIDI Extension Connector

Line In

Microphone

Speakers Out

Joystick/MIDI Adapter Plug

Figure 6.2. *A drawing of a typical PC sound card. Note the multipin MIDI/joystick port.*

³*This is a good time to read through Chapter 8, which discusses interfaces for the Mac. Interfaces for the two computer platforms are not interchangeable, and are installed, configured, and used in very different ways.*

Figure 6.5. *If you try installation yourself, you might end up like this. Better get help.*

interfaces are designed like this. MIDI controllers and synthesizers then connect to these interfaces in various ways, depending on the manufacturer. Some of these cards might connect to your MIDI gear with an adapter cable, as with a sound card MIDI port. The PC MIDI Card provides MIDI IN-OUT connectors on a hardware adapter that mounts directly to the card. You can see this clearly in Figure 6.4.

Installing Software for MIDI Interfaces

Just as installing a sound card involves the hassles of configuring IRQs, DMAs, jumpers, and drivers, so too does the installation of a PC-based MIDI interface (Figure 6.5).[6]

There's no substitute for a local dealer who will assist you with installation. I think it's simply better to pay the extra $35 or so and let the seller perform the installation for you. But if you're a purist who wants to totally absorb the MIDI experience, here are a few tips I have learned from well-known MIDI consultant Steve Cooper:

♪ Back up. Back up. I know you're in a hurry, but go to the Windows directory and copy all .INI files to a new directory with a different name from the original.

Figure 6.3. *The MIDI adapter cable for a sound card.*

MIDI Interface Cards

The better MIDI interfaces for the PC are units that generate no sound. These interfaces dedicate their functions exclusively to interfacing outboard MIDI controllers and synthesizers with the PC.[4] Figure 6.4 shows one of these stand-alone MIDI interfaces.

Notice that the PC MIDI Card featured in Figure 6.4 is designed to be installed directly into an expansion slot inside your PC.[5] Many PC

Figure 6.4. *The PC MIDI Card, made by Music Quest, is one of the most widely recommended MIDI interfaces for the PC.*

[4] Hmmm…not exactly. Some interfaces can perform many additional functions. These are discussed in Chapter 11.

[5] During my 1994 visit to the Music Educators National Conference in Cincinnati, Ohio, I noticed that many distributors of educational music materials included listings for this interface in their catalogs. Talk on the street says that this card is actually more reliable and bug-free than even the original Roland

MPU-401 that it emulates! The unit is very reasonably priced, as well.

[6] You can love Apple or hate it, but this is the area where Mac users win big. Apple and the manufacturers of Mac-based music products virtually eliminated these headaches early in the history of MIDI.

- Also, back up your registration database (REG.DAT), a file in the Windows directory that determines screen layout and icon arrangement.

- Back up MIDIMAP.CFG (located in C:\WINDOWS\SYSTEM). Adding new peripherals can really fool with your system, so just do it.[7]

Don't forget to install a new MIDI driver that's MCI-compatible.

Use the MIDI driver that comes with the interface. Remove other MIDI drivers from the system. Configure all of your applications to use the new MIDI driver.

Even if the interface is MPU-401-compatible (I hope so!), don't use a preinstalled MPU-401 driver. Use the new one. It may have different features that are important.

Remember, the PC has never been especially MIDI-friendly, but it can work just great if you're careful about installation details.

Single-Port Interfaces

The single-port MIDI interface is the only interface many computer musicians will ever need. A sound card interface is usually a single-port version. Another single-port interface is the PC MIDI Card, shown in Figure 6.4.

Features common to many single-port interfaces include the following:

One MIDI IN connector. This connects to the MIDI OUT on your controller.

One or more MIDI OUT connectors. You need these to transmit MIDI event data to synthesizers in your MIDI system. Interfaces with more than one MIDI OUT can make it easy to connect more than one synthesizer.

A single-port interface handles up to 16 channels of MIDI recording and playback. No matter how many MIDI OUT connectors are on the interface, *a single-port unit will support only 16 MIDI channels*—which is actually a lot of channels![8]

Multiport Interfaces

There's a huge misconception about MIDI. Many computer musicians believe there are only 16 MIDI channels. True, but computer music manufacturers have found ingenious ways to reliably coax up to 512 channels of MIDI out of a single computer and interface!

A dual-port interface provides two MIDI OUT connectors. Each MIDI OUT provides access to 16 MIDI channels, which gives you a total of 32 MIDI channels!

There are MIDI interfaces with even more ports, each providing 16 channels of MIDI information. The MIDI Express by Mark of the Unicorn (Figure 6.6) is one of these powerful interfaces.

Multiport interfaces are very popular in professional MIDI studios. Chapter 11 discusses the useful features offered by these units.

 A multiport interface will not allow these additional MIDI channels to work unless your software also supports the additional MIDI channels.

You might be asking, "Why would I ever need more than 16 channels? I would certainly never use 512?!" This subject is discussed in Chapter 11. For now, trust me...you'll need at least a dual-port, 32-channel interface for semipro and professional MIDI recording. Most educational, multimedia, and hobby needs can be filled perfectly by a single-port interface.

MIDI Synthesizers

In Chapter 5 you learned that the sound in our MIDI system is actually generated by the MIDI synthesizer. Your MIDI synthesizer might be built into one of the following pieces of hardware:

A MIDI sound module (Figure 6.7)

A sound card (Figure 6.8)

Or, most commonly, a keyboard instrument (Figure 6.9)

[7] *PC consultant Sue Hardesty suggests using a de-install program when removing applications. This is a great idea, and it is the only way to get rid of all unwanted files and drivers. De-install software is available at most software stores.*

[8] *Especially if you consider that the monster soundtrack to the TV show Miami Vice was produced at a time when all we had available were single-port units with only 16 channels of MIDI.*

Some newer MIDI sound modules combine a MIDI interface with a MIDI synthesizer. The idea is so new that manufacturers are just now releasing these products. One that is very popular is the Roland SC-55mkII Sound Canvas (Figure 6.10).

Roland actually pioneered the idea of low-cost MIDI modules for home and educational use, areas where the Sound Canvas continues to excel. And this unit works with both the PC and the Mac! I find the built-in headphone jack very useful for late-night MIDI experimenting. All of these two-in-one units make MIDI recording and playback of hobby, multimedia, and educational applications much easier.

I will use the word *synthesizer* for the rest of the book to describe all of these types of MIDI synthesizers. A MIDI synthesizer must at least have a MIDI IN to be useful to the computer musician. See Chapter 11 for more information about MIDI synthesizers.

Figure 6.6. *The MIDI Express PC offers the user up to six ports supporting as many as 96 MIDI channels.*

Figure 6.7. *The Proteus FX from E-mu Systems is a MIDI sound module with 6MB of rock, pop, jazz, and symphonic sounds.*

About the Sequencer Software

The computer is a powerful tool if the proper application software, designed to accomplish a particular task, has been installed. Without this, the computer is useless. The "brain" of the computer music system is the MIDI sequencer. Without the MIDI sequencer, we wouldn't have computer music as we know it today.

Figure 6.8. *The Roland RAP-10 sound card uses the same sound set as the Roland Sound Canvas synthesizer.*

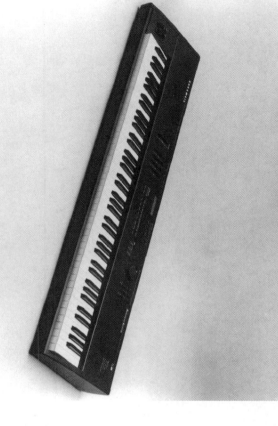

Figure 6.9. The Kurzweil PC88 Performance controller has a powerful built-in synthesizer.

Figure 6.10. The Roland Sound Canvas SC-55mkII provides a MIDI interface and a synthesizer in one efficient package. The SC-55mkII works with both the PC and the Mac.

MusicPower provides a demo version of Studio for Windows, by Midisoft Corporation of Redmond, WA, one of the leading producers of educational and hobby-level music software (Figure 6.11).

Studio for Windows is a MIDI sequencer that's easy to understand and use. The graphics and color are very nice, so it's fun to work with as well.

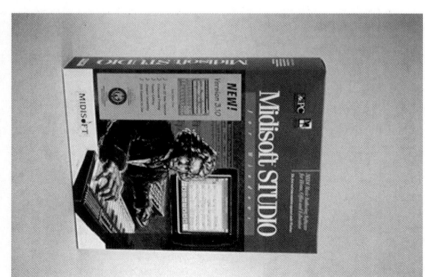

Figure 6.11. Studio for Windows, by Midisoft Corporation, is used for the Chapter 7 MIDI recording tutorial.

Opening the Studio for Windows Software

Find the Studio for Windows icon in Program Manager and double-click it. You'll see the Studio for Windows icon shown in Figure 6.12.

Figure 6.12. *The Studio for Windows icon.*

Double-click the Studio for Windows icon. You are asked if you want to play demo songs provided by Midisoft Corporation. Click the Cancel button.

You now see the Score View and Mixer View windows (Figure 6.13).

 Midisoft Corporation provides a Help menu at the end of the menu bar. It's one of the best-written Help utilities included with a MIDI software application that I've seen. This further reinforces my opinion that Midisoft Corporation provides good educational software. Take some time and explore the different categories listed under this menu. The text will help reinforce the teachings of this book in a really fun way.

One of the most important MIDI events to know about is the Panic, All Notes Off, or MIDI System Reset command. Notes played by any piece of MIDI equipment can occasionally get "stuck" and continue to play, which can be obnoxious. The Panic, All Notes Off, or MIDI System Reset command sends a Note Off event to all MIDI devices on all MIDI channels, which stops all sound in the MIDI system.

You should immediately find which menu this command is under when you open any new MIDI software. Studio for Windows handles this with the MIDI System Reset command under the Help menu.

Study the Score View and Mixer View windows in Figure 6.13.

1. The Transport controls are located in the lower-right corner of the Mixer View window. Click these buttons to play, stop, rewind, and so forth, just as you would do with a tape player. Remember, most good software now provides a control panel like this.

2. The Score View window displays the staff and the musical events you record into the software.

3. The Track Module enables you to select which track is record enabled, control instrument volume levels, and add effects processing to the music composition.

4. The Toolbox contains controls for recording and editing your MIDI recordings.

5. The Counter Display tells you what measure and beat you're on and enables you to select the tempo.

Preparing Your Hardware and Software for MIDI Recording

Here's a checklist you can use when you're preparing for your MIDI recording session. Not doing these things will make your session either impossible or awkward.

> **Warning:** Always make your MIDI and audio connections with the equipment turned off. Making these connections with the equipment powered up can initialize the memory on MIDI devices, and in some cases can blow output amp chips on synthesizers!

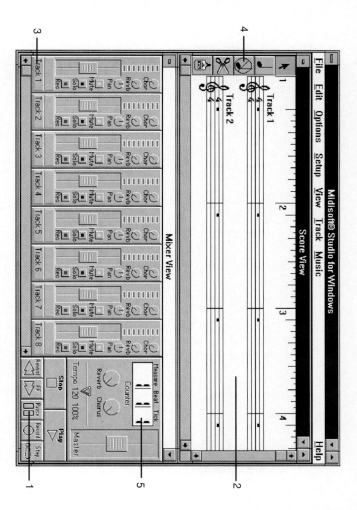

Figure 6.13. *The Score View and Mixer View windows from Studio for Windows.*

Setting Up the Interface and Controller

☐ Be sure the MIDI OUT on your controller is connected to the MIDI IN on your interface.

☐ The MIDI OUT on the interface should be connected to the MIDI IN on your synthesizer.[9]

☐ Be sure your interface has the proper drivers installed. Because this procedure is very dependent on the type of interface you have, you're on your own here. The best bet is to use a MPU-401 driver if at all possible.

☐ If there's a synthesizer built into your controlling instrument, you must turn its local control off. Your owner's manual tells you how to do this. When you turn the local control off, *your keyboard makes sounds only when it's properly patched through the interface and sequencing software.* You have to turn the local control on when you're not using the interface and sequencing software, or your instrument won't make sound.

[9]*For most people, the synthesizer is the same instrument as the controller.*

Setting Up the Studio for Windows Sequencing Software

Select MIDI Drivers under the Setup menu. A window appears like the one in Figure 6.14.

This box enables you to determine which MIDI driver is being used by Studio for Windows. It must be set up properly for you to have any sound. You must select Multimedia Drivers if you plan to use any other MIDI software (I am certain that you will), or if you use any sound card other than one made by Roland. So, in other words, select Multimedia Drivers and General MIDI Setup (channels 1-16) and the MIDI Drivers Setup window will look exactly like Figure 6.14.

 You will use only 16 channels of MIDI with Studio for Windows, so you need to have only one port available for this exercise.

Now you can proceed with the software setup for Studio for Windows.

1. Open Studio for Windows. Select MIDI Thru under the Options menu. This allows the MIDI event data from the controller to pass "thru" the sequencer and interface to the synthesizer. The synthesizer will not generate sound without Thru turned on unless MIDI events are recorded and then played back by Studio for Windows.

2. Most sequencers enable you to record MIDI information in more than one mode. Sequencer designers use different names for these modes; the results of recording in these modes are as follows:

Studio for Windows Name	Generic Name	Result
Record Mode	Record	Records MIDI events
Punch	Punch-in	Allows the recording in only a user-specified track area
Overdub	Merge	Combines the in-coming MIDI events with those already recorded

Studio for Windows lets you make this selection in the Studio Panel View window under the View menu. Click a listing in the column beneath the heading Track Mode and the record mode will change for the Track numbered directly to the left. Keep clicking to cycle through the possible

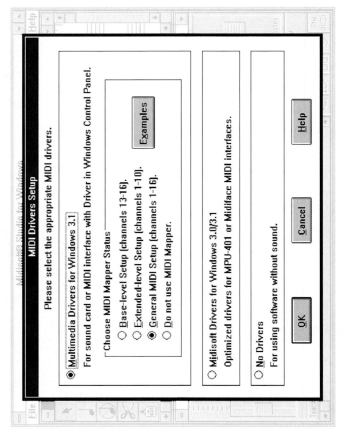

Figure 6.14. *The MIDI Drivers Setup window.*

choices. You will make a Record Mode selection immediately before you begin to record.

Setting Up the Synthesizer

Make sure your synthesizer is set up in a GM configuration.[10] These exercises should sound perfect if you are using a GM-compatible synthesizer. If not, you will have to refer to the owner's manual for your synthesizer and set the Receive Mode to Multi or Multitimbral. Then, assign the MIDI Receive channels and patches as shown in Table 6.1.

Make sure that all of these MIDI channels are properly assigned in your MIDI Mapper to the synthesizer you are using. If not, you will not hear all of the sounds being used.

If you do not have one of the pieces of hardware necessary for the Chapter 7 tutorial, you should consider reading Chapter 10 and perhaps even Chapter 11 before you make a purchase. And don't forget Appendix E, "The Resource Guide."

PC users should advance to Chapter 7, "Your First PC-Based MIDI Recording Session."

Table 6.1. MIDI channel and patch assignments for the Chapter 7 tutorial.

MIDI Channel Number	Sound Type	GM Program or Key Number
1	Clavinet	7
2	Synth Bass	39
3	Off	
4	Off	
5	New Age Pad, Fantasia	66
6	Off	
7	Off	
6	Off	
9	Off	
10	Open and Closed Hi-Hat	46, 44[11]
	Kick Drum, Snare	36, 40
11	Off	
12	Off	
13	Off	
14	Off	
15	Off	
16	Off	

[10]This includes the synthesizer furnished by your sound card, if that is what you are using.

[11]All sounds in the GM percussion bank are "played" by a single patch on Channel 10, but each key in this patch has one of sound assigned to it. Thus, the number 1 have listed for each percussion sound is a Key number. A list of the Standard GM percussion key assignments is included in Appendix C.

YOUR FIRST PC-BASED MIDI RECORDING SESSION

7

For this chapter you will need the following:

- A 386SX, 25 MHz or higher PC running DOS 5.0 and Windows 3.1 or higher
- 4MB of RAM (8MB is faster)
- A hard drive, a computer keyboard, and a mouse or trackball
- A CD-ROM drive (necessary to use the software on the enclosed *MusicPower* CD-ROM)
- A MIDI interface for the PC, and two MIDI cables

You must have *one* of the following setups to generate MIDI event data and sound:

- A MIDI controller *and* a multitimbral MIDI sound module
- A multitimbral MIDI-equipped keyboard synthesizer
- A MIDI controller and a MIDI-capable (preferably General MIDI-compatible) sound card

Tip: Before you start this chapter, be sure to read Chapter 6, "Setting Up Your PC for MIDI Recording." We will more thoroughly discuss *connecting* computer-music hardware in Chapter 10. Chapter 11 provides details about the functions of MIDI event data, with explanations of how these MIDI events affect computer-based music.

The present chapter's study shows how to actually use the information learned in Chapters 4 and 5. Make sure you understand that information before you start on this new material.

The "Dino Disaster" Exercise

In the spring of 1993 I was commissioned by the Discovery Center in Amarillo, Texas, to create an original music score for their planetarium show, titled "The Dinosaur Disaster." The score featured very diverse music styles, ranging from high-energy pop-rock sections to elegant orchestral passages. I really enjoyed working on this production, and it makes very good use of MIDI recording techniques. Let's use "Dino Disaster" for the tutorial.

Loading a Demo of "Dino Disaster"

As stated in Chapter 2, a good way to get started with any software is to load a completed work and experiment with it. Open the Studio for Windows software as you learned in Chapter 6. Select Open under the File menu, and double-click the directory DINO.MID. Then double-click the file DINSCGM.MID. You will see several bars of the music score shown in Figure 7.1.

Warning: I have included versions of these exercises with no Program Change events. These files do not contain the letters *gm* in their names, and you *should* use these if using a synthesizer that is not GM-configured. For example, loading and playing the file DINSCOR.MID instead of DINSCGM.MID will allow your non-GM synthesizer to remain set up as you configured it in Chapter 6. Playing the file DINSCGM.MID will constantly change your MIDI channel-to-patch assignments. This will probably make you quit this exercise, so just don't do it. Please?

Click the Play button in the Transport Controls window to hear "Dino Disaster," a complete multitrack MIDI production.

Select Studio for Windows Panel View under the View menu. Clicking this window shows you a list of the track-to-MIDI channel assignments and GM Program Changes for instruments used in MIDI composition. You will learn how to change this information later in this chapter.

Loading a Template

Let's open up an empty staff and learn how to create a score like "Dino Disaster." Click Open under the File menu and select the file STUTEMP.MID. This is a template I designed to get you started fast. It looks like Figure 7.2.

The MIDI Track and Channel Assignments

You can change the track-to-MIDI-channel assignments on nearly all sequencers. Until you understand how to do this correctly, you could create some real trouble for yourself. Midisoft Studio for Windows defaults to a standard template of one MIDI channel per track: Track 1 = MIDI Channel 1, Track 2 = MIDI Channel 2, and so on.[1] This can be configured differently, and I have elected to assign MIDI Channel 10 to Tracks 4 and 5.[2] I did this so you could see all the parts in the Score View window at one time.

[1] *A professional will soon need to alter these assignments.*

[2] *The popular General MIDI (GM) configuration dedicates MIDI Channel 10 to drums and percussion.*

Notice how the Mixer View window displays a row of Track Modules showing the instrument name of each track. There is also a Fader for control of the volume level of each instrument, and a Pan control to move the instrument sound to and from the left or right speaker.

But most importantly, there is a red button named Record. Click this button, and the track is now ready to record MIDI events from your controller.

Recording MIDI Event Data in Step-Time Mode

Now you are ready for the real thing. Let's record Part 1 of "Dino Disaster" as shown in Figure 7.3. This is a busy eighth-note melody that features a Clavinet sound and might remind you of the composition style of Alan Parsons or Jan Hammer.

In Chapter 2, you entered the notes onto the staff by the click-and-drag method. Entering music events one note at a time is also called *Step-Time* recording.

You can also enter notes in Step-Time mode using a controller instrument:

1. Click the red Record box in Track Module 1, named "Clav." That record box enables Track 1.

Figure 7.1. *A section of the score from "Dino Disaster."*

"Dino Disaster"

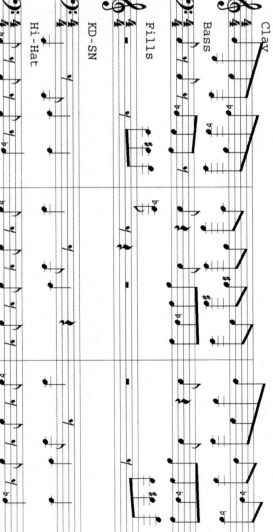

"Dino Disaster"

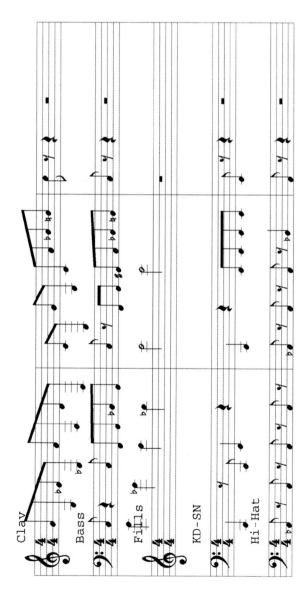

Figure 7.1. *continued*

2. Be sure that MIDI THRU is active under the Options menu. Click the box at the bottom of the Track Module. The Track Settings dialog box appears. This enables you to change the instrument assigned to this track. It should be set for Clavinet, so just click OK. This procedure allows the MIDI THRU command to pass your controller performance to the Clavinet patch in the synthesizer.[3] Now you can rehearse using the Clavinet sound.

3. Locate the Step Time record icon in the lower-right corner of the Transport Controls. Click this button and the footprint (step, footprint—get it?) is highlighted.

4. Click the quarter-note icon in the Toolbox. The Toolbox expands as shown in Figure 7.4.

5. Click the eighth-note icon in the expanded Toolbox. The Toolbox is where you select the note value for each entry in Step-Time recording. Leave the eighth note selected for now. This means that every note played on the controller enters an eighth note into the score.

6. Click the large Record button in the Transport Controls. Be sure the Record button in the Track Module is still red. You are now fully record-enabled.

7. Play the first note of Part 1 on your controller. It magically appears on the staff!

Play the notes from Figure 7.3 using the Step-Time method just described. To erase an incorrect note, find the Note Delete icon in the Toolbox. This icon is a quarter note in a circle with a line through it. When you click this icon, the cursor takes on the shape of the Note Delete tool. Position this tool directly on top of your incorrect note and click. The mistake will vanish. Then play or drag a correct note onto the staff. To clear large numbers of notes, select the Arrow icon in the Toolbox, hold down the mouse button, and drag a box around the offending notes. They will become highlighted. Then select Cut under the Edit menu. Continue your work until your score looks like Figure 7.3.

Click the Stop button in the Transport Controls window (refer to Chapter 6 if necessary), then click the Play button. You will hear Part 1 of "Dino Disaster."

[3]*This is an unusually quirky way to activate a MIDI THRU feature. Normally, the controller-generated MIDI event data is passed through automatically when you enable recording on a track. The Midisoft Corporation techs promised they would modify this in the Fall 1994 version.*

Also, Studio for Windows may behave unpredictably if you have more than six Windows drivers in operation. The solution is to remove drivers so as to allow Studio for Windows to function properly. For assistance, call Midisoft tech support at (206) 881-7176. If you have more than one MIDI interface installed, you might also have problems with Studio for Windows. Again, call Midisoft tech support for solutions to these possible problems.

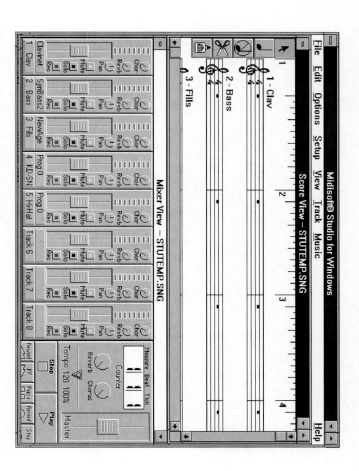

Note: You must again click the Step Time record icon, just as you did with Step 2. Then enable recording by clicking the Record button in the Transport Controls.

Copy the notes from Figure 7.5 using the Step-Time method as you did before. Notice that you will need to return to the Toolbox to select quarter, eighth, and half notes when needed. To enter rests, assign the value for the rest by clicking a corresponding note value in the Toolbox, then pressing the Spacebar on your PC keyboard.

If you make a mistake, check how you corrected mistakes earlier. Continue your work until your score looks exactly like Figure 7.5. Again, you can click Play in the Transport Controls window at any time to hear your work.

Figure 7.2. *The Studio for Windows template.*

You can now record Part 2 of "Dino Disaster" (Figure 7.5). This is the bass line.

First, you must select a new track to record on. Just click the little Record box in Track Module 2, named "Bass." It will highlight. Then repeat Step 2 from the previous list using the controls in Track Module 2. Make sure the sound Syn Bass 2 is highlighted in the Track Settings dialog box. Click OK.

Figure 7.3. *Part 1 of "Dino Disaster."*

"Dino Part 1"

Clav

Clav

Clav

The fully licensed version of Studio for Windows enables you to save your work. If you *could* save your work, you'd be doing this at each step, right? I thought so.

Real-Time Recording

Most MIDI sequencers default to Real-Time recording, and Studio for Windows is no exception. Real-Time recording enables you to record much as if you were recording with a tape machine, so you must be able to actually "play" your controller to some degree. The advantages of Real-Time recording are that the recording session moves along much faster and the music has a more human feeling and expression.

Let's use Real Time to record Part 4 of "Dino Disaster" (Figure 7.7). Part 4 is a drum track featuring kick and snare drums.

Here is an outlined procedure for Real-Time recording with Studio for Windows:

1. Set up for recording exactly as you did for Step-Time recording, but don't click the Step Time record icon.

2. This time, click Record in Track Module 4.

3. Your sense of rhythm and time is crucial when recording in Real Time, so you need a metronome or click track to help stay in rhythm. Select Metronome Enable under the Options menu. Then select Metronome under the Setup menu. The dialog box shown in Figure 7.8 appears.

Next, copy the notes from Figure 7.6, Part 3 as you did before. This part is a set of fills, which are the musical equivalent of a sprinkle of nuts on an ice cream sundae.

The notes on the third staff make up Part 3. Clicking the Play button in the Transport Controls window plays back your first three parts.

Figure 7.4. *The Toolbox displays note values for Step-Time recording.*

"Dino Part 2"

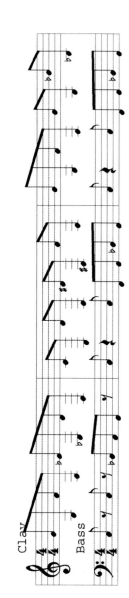

Figure 7.5. *Part 2 of "Dino Disaster."*

"Dino Part 3"

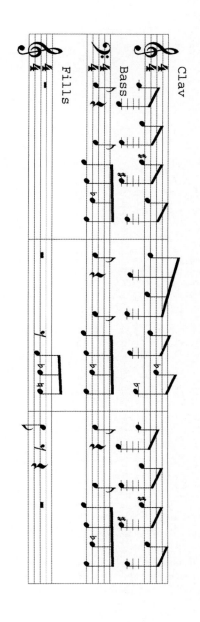

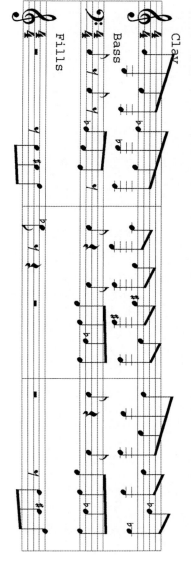

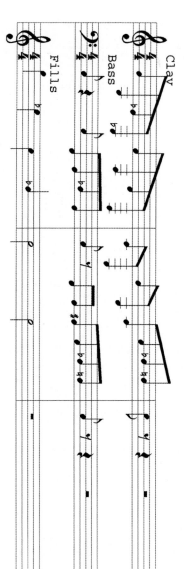

Figure 7.6. Part 3 of "Dino Disaster."

Most good sequencers like Studio for Windows enable you to customize your click, and that is what the Metronome Settings box allows. Two options are to have the click played by your synthesizer or by your PC computer speaker. Let's keep things simple and select Internal for now. Then click OK. Now if you click the Record (Rec) button in the Transport Controls window, you will hear your click track. The click track will be heard *only* when you click the Record button. This is because you set the click up in the Metronome Settings box so it will not play during playback. Change this if you want...after all, you *are* becoming quite a computer musician!

4. Select Lead In Measures under the Options menu. This will let the click play for two measures before the recording actually begins. This is often called the Countoff. A Countoff gives you time to get ready for the big moment—your first Real-Time recording!

If Studio for Windows and your synthesizer are properly configured, you can now play the notes in Part 4 on your controller and hear the sound of a kick drum and a snare drum. The kick is on the note C and the snare is on the note E. You might have to test different octaves on your controller to find which C and E respond properly. Try the ones on the left end of your keyboard first.

Get ready! Set! Click Record…wait for the first eight clicks to go by and you're off. Play your fingers off. I can tell you are really getting warmed up now. Stop whenever you feel like it, but remember: You do have to stop sometime, no matter how much fun you are having.

Here is a great tip: Always let the first two measures of your score go unrecorded. That way you can later add pick-up notes or an extra one-measure phrase to lead into your score. I find myself making these additions on most of my MIDI recording projects, and using this little trick saves me the hassle of editing in an extra two bars later.

Click Play and listen to your work. This might be a case of the good, the bad, and the ugly. But hey, you're just getting started. I didn't quit 10 years ago when I was at the same stage as you are right now, and you have me to help you now.

Step-Time Recording Versus Real-Time Recording

The first sequencers many of us used recorded in Step Time. Step Time enables you to enter a music event…wait…wait…enter the next note perfectly…wait…add a rest…wait. This is really helpful for the computer musician who has limited performance skills, and it can provide an easy way to record blindingly fast strings of notes, but Step Time is a slow process. And Step Time is by nature a rather mechanical process. In fact, if I want to arrange a very "techno" or "industrial" feeling piece, I often begin with a track or two of Step Time passages, as in "Dino Disaster."

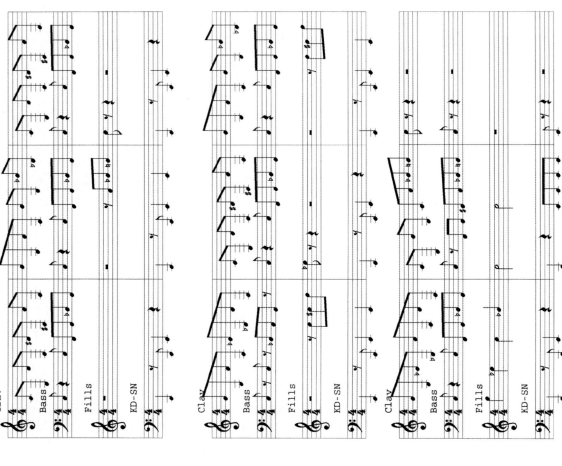

"Dino Part 4"

Figure 7.7. *Adding Part 4, drums, to "Dino Disaster."*

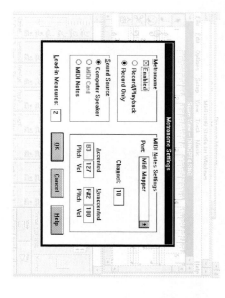

Figure 7.8. *The Metronome Settings window enables you to customize your click track.*

Step-Time recording has sort of a "computer programmer" feel about it, while Real-Time recording has more of the feel of traditional tape-based recording. Computer musicians say that Real-Time recording has a friendly "user interface"—not a piece of hardware, but how comfortable it is to record. That is why the Transport Control buttons resemble those on a tape machine. Software designers have worked hard to make the MIDI recording process as much like working with tape as possible, while retaining the editing and correction features that only a digital medium can provide. I think they have done very well at perfecting this user interface.

By the way, I really dislike the term *sequencer*. I prefer to call sequencing software a MIDI recorder. I usually run my software the same way I would a multitrack tape machine, doing punch-in recording on the fly and trying to add as many dynamics as possible to the music as I record. Of course, my keyboard chops have their limit, so I really benefit from being able to edit, quantize, and so on. The main thing is to use the hardware and software to enhance, not hinder, the creative process.

Quantizing the Recording

Quantizing can be thought of as error correction. When you quantize your recording, you move the occurrence of the MIDI events to the nearest beat or fraction of a beat. This can make up for errors in your sense of timing or make the recording easier to edit. Christopher Brown writes in the Opcode Musicshop reference manual that this is much like the way a CAD or graphics program does a "snap-to" grid. Good analogy.

Here is a sample of a recording where I performed badly (Figure 7.9). You will notice how chaotic the performance is.

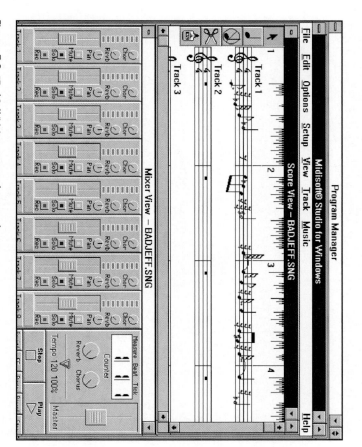

Figure 7.9. *"Bad Jeff." My very own sloppy performance.*

Now I quantize the recording. First I select Quantize under the Music menu. Then I choose the track I want to quantize (in this case Track 1) by clicking the blue box just below the heading "Track" and scrolling. If I didn't want to quantize the whole track, I could use the Start Point and End Point to define a specific region to quantize. I then repeatedly click the Note icon in the Resolution box to select the note value that the notes in "Bad Jeff" will round off or "resolve" to. I choose eighth-note resolution, then click OK. The notes in "Bad Jeff" shift around and become eighth notes, eighth rests and multiples of these. You can see the result in Figure 7.10.

Try quantizing your own "bad" performance. Some of the results may be startling. And useless, too. The most commonly used values for quantization resolution are the sixteenth note, the eighth note, and the eighth-note triplet. Studio for Windows offers the opportunity to auto-quantize as you are recording. This is the way many of us used to program drum machines, and many computer musicians still like to record this way.

Whoo-Whoo!: I hear the sound of a train wreck about to happen! Studio for Windows does *not* provide Undo for some of the editing functions. If your licensed software doesn't enable Undo commands, be sure to save your latest copy *before* you perform editing functions!

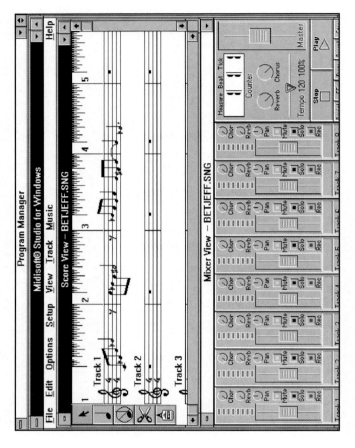

Resolve recordings to the smallest note value that you think you recorded. If I recorded quarter and eighth notes, I would quantize in eighth notes, for example.

Figure 7.10. *"Bad Jeff" is improved by quantizing.*

What, a Controversy?

I just heard the boos and hisses of a number of my colleagues. Many of them believe strongly that quantizing the recording makes it sound like Step Time. And to a degree, they are correct. You will eventually learn when to quantize your work and when not to. That is a creative decision to be left in the hands of each computer musician. As Los

Angeles-based recording engineer Michael Jay recently told me, there often is not a technically right or wrong computer-recording method—just a different set of opportunities for the creative musician. I think Michael's opinion is valuable: He used Digital Performer by Mark of the Unicorn to record the *Talk* CD by the powerhouse group Yes, released in the spring of 1994.

Changing the MIDI Channel Assigned to a Track

The easiest way to use Studio for Windows and other MIDI recorders is to use the "one track per MIDI channel" configuration used for this study.

Most computer musicians find they can enhance their MIDI system's flexibility and ease of use by reconfiguring the MIDI channel-to-track assignments. Studio for Windows makes this easy to do (Figure 7.11).

Reopen the file named DINSCGM.MID. Next, open the Studio for Windows Panel View window by selecting Studio Panel under the View menu. The Studio Panel shows the complete overview of all track-to-MIDI-channel and MIDI-channel-to-patch assignments. The leftmost column shows the track names. The second column shows the track numbers. The third column enables you to select the record mode for overdub, punch-in, and other types of recording. The MIDI Port column would be useful if you were using a multiport interface. The fifth column, however, is the one you are most interested in at the moment. This column enables you to change the MIDI channel assigned to any track!

Just click repeatedly on any of the numbers in this column to enter a new MIDI channel assignment for any track or tracks. Look at Track 5. Notice that I changed this track's MIDI channel to Channel 10—the same channel that Track 4 is assigned to. Why?

Remember that Track 4 plays back drum sounds. All the drum sounds in a GM configuration are assigned to MIDI Channel 10. If I used only one track (Track 4) to record drum parts, I would have to record all the drums and percussion in a single pass. That would be pretty rough if I wanted to use lots of percussion instruments. Another method would be to merge or overdub record all of my recorded performances onto a single track (Track 4), using the Overdub function under the Track Mode column. But that would merge all the MIDI events together and make editing the individual events very difficult.

I rarely use overdub or merge record modes.

I would rather record each percussion instrument onto its own individual track and then assign all those percussion tracks to the same MIDI channel. In the case of the GM percussion configuration for "Dino Disaster," this would be Channel 10. That is how I recorded the hi-hat part into Track 5, and assigned Track 5 to MIDI Channel 10. If you made this change as I did, you could record the following hi-hat part (Figure 7.12) onto Track 5.

It is not uncommon for me to use a *dozen* tracks for drums and percussion, with many or all of those tracks then assigned to the same MIDI channels. This gives me maximum flexibility in re-recording and editing these percussion recordings.

Transposing the Score

Oh, by the way. Remember the fills we recorded on Track 3? I think those would sound much better an octave higher.

The Transpose window, which can be selected under the Music menu, enables you to transpose a track or section of a track up or down. Choose the

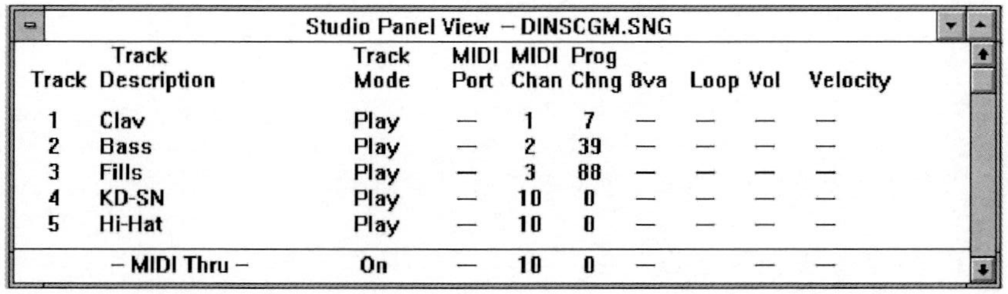

> **Warning:** Just because this is one of my favorite tools doesn't mean you have to try it. You can totally confuse your entire MIDI recording system with a couple of "small" changes in this window. Used properly, however, this tool can open terrific new possibilities for your MIDI recording sessions.

Track Description	Track	Track Mode	MIDI Port	MIDI Chan	Prog Chng	8va	Loop	Vol	Velocity
1 Clav		Play	—	1	7	—	—	—	—
2 Bass		Play	—	2	39	—	—	—	—
3 Fills		Play	—	3	88	—	—	—	—
4 KD-SN		Play	—	10	0	—	—	—	—
5 Hi-Hat		Play	—	10	0	—	—	—	—
— MIDI Thru —		On	—	10	0	—	—	—	—

Studio Panel View — DINSCGM.SNG

Figure 7.11. *The Studio for Windows Panel View window for the "Dino Disaster" recording titled DINSCGM.MID.*

track you want to transpose (in this case, Track 3, "Fills") by clicking the blue box just below the heading "Track" and scrolling. If you didn't want to transpose the whole track, you could use the Start Point and End Point to define a specific region. Then, click the number in the Octaves or Half-Steps box to select the degree of transposition. Choose one octave, then click the Up button. Transposition of the selected track is immediate. Play back the score and look at the notes on the third staff. Transposing improves the sound of this "fills" part greatly.

Cutting and Pasting Notes

You learned how to cut-and-paste edit with WinSong Composer in Chapter 2, so we won't repeat the details here. Studio for Windows provides many ways to cut-and-paste edit, so refer to the Help menu to explore which is best for you. One method uses the Arrow cursor in the Toolbox for cut-and-paste editing. This is easy if you follow these steps:

1. Click the Arrow cursor in the Toolbox.

2. Place the mouse cursor just before the first note you choose to edit. This works best in the Score View window, where the measures and beats are displayed.

3. Click, and the Arrow cursor becomes a crosshair. Holding down the left mouse button while dragging the mouse highlights a group of selected events.

"Dino Part 5"

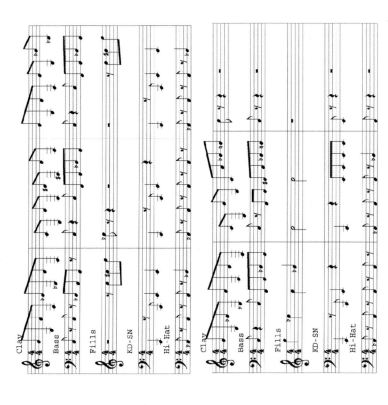

Figure 7.12. *The hi-hat part for "Dino Disaster."*

4. You can now select Cut or Copy under the Edit menu.

5. After you select Cut or Copy, the cursor turns into a "paste bottle" cursor, which you can reposition on the staff. A helpful vertical red line helps you position the tip of the paste cursor perfectly. Clicking again pastes the events into the selected region.

Remember that you can choose to edit all tracks or as few as one, depending on the area you highlight with the crosshair cursor.

Warning: This pasting procedure merges the pasted notes with any that might already be on the staff in the pasting location. What a mess!!! Be sure to first clear any notes from areas where you plan to do a paste.

Another option is to select Splice/Paste under the Edit menu. A dialog box asks where to paste the edited material, and the set of Paste Style buttons enables you to select one of three Paste modes: Combine (merge), Splice (insert new material between the edit point and existing material), and Replace (overwrite existing material).

Changing Instrument Sounds

It is super-easy to change the instrument assigned to a track in Studio for Windows. Let's reopen the demo of "Dino Disaster," the file DINSCGM.MID. Reopen the Studio Panel View under the View menu. You will again see Figure 7.11. The sixth column has the heading Prog Chng. Click the first number in the column (it should be the number 7). A long list of names fills a new window, called the Program Change window (Figure 7.13).

These are the patches utilized by the General MIDI Standard. These same names and numbers are designed into any GM synthesizer. As you click and drag the cursor down this screen, the instrument names highlight. Stop the cursor on item 42, "Cello." Click OK. The window disappears and the patch name "Cello" appears in Track Module 1. This Program Change event is sent to MIDI Channel 1 of your synthesizer when you play back your recording. The synthesizer then changes its sound on that MIDI channel to item 42, "Cello." Each MIDI channel can have its own set of Program Changes without affecting the sounds selected on other MIDI channels. To erase a Program Change, just select any other instrument in the same way, or select "none" at the top of the list.

Enter a zillion Program Changes and listen to how the instrument sounds change. The Program Changes I placed in the "Dino" demo will reset your GM system to the proper configuration when you reload and play the demo again.

Note: This is a good time to refer back to the segment about General MIDI in Chapter 5. I think you will better understand the importance of the GM standard now that you have actually worked with it in Studio for Windows.

Digging Deeper into Studio for Windows

The list of Studio for Windows features goes on and on. There are many ways to perform the same tasks, so explore this software thoroughly. You can view all the MIDI events in the MIDI List View window under the View menu. Chapter 12 explores editing individual MIDI events, through a study of Cakewalk Professional. I suggest you return to work with Studio for Windows after studying Chapters 10, 11, and 12.

MusicPower is loaded with many other great Studio for Windows demos prepared by the staff at Midisoft Corporation. Load those up and experiment with them. That's why they are included. Be sure to edit, and transpose, and cut and paste, and...well, you get the idea.

Studio for Windows is one of the most disaster-free (pun again intended) MIDI sequencers you will find at this price point. The software retails for $249.95, although special discounts can save you $50-$60, and Studio for Windows is loaded with more capabilities and features than can be discussed here.

Although it is not really notation software, Studio for Windows will print a score. In fact, it was used to print the score shown in Figure 7.1. The Midisoft Corporation sales and technical support staffs are easily accessible and eager to answer your questions at (206) 881-7176.

Where Do We Go from Here?

This book is designed to help computer musicians reach the level of expertise that *they* want to achieve. Mastery of the materials that have been presented up to this point will enable you to produce many incredible music projects. You will be able to accomplish many of the educational, hobbyist, and home-recording goals discussed in the Introduction and Chapter 1.

This is a good time to explore the Appendices. Appendix A will help you develop your musical skills. Appendix B provides several more printed scores, which you can use with the software featured in your Chapter 2 and Chapter 7 studies.

Many of You Have Only Just Begun

Now that you are MIDI-literate, we can talk about a completely integrated MIDI studio. Many computer musicians would call this a *MIDI project studio*. You will learn how to design and assemble one in Chapter 10, "MIDI In-Out-Thru: The MIDI Project Studio." The following chapters feature studies of the newest recording and editing methods used by today's professionals. And don't forget Chapter 12, the third PC software tutorial, featuring Cakewalk Professional 2.0.

PC users should advance to Chapter 10.

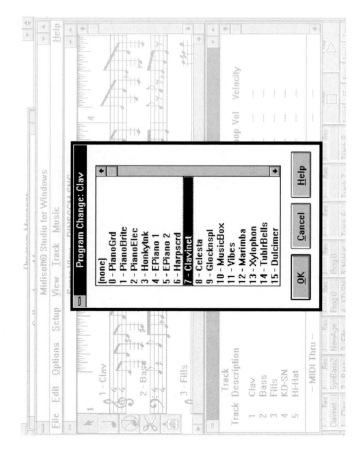

Figure 7.13. *The GM Program Change list.*

Additional Music Software on *MusicPower*

Completion of this chapter qualifies you to freely try some of the other demo software included on *MusicPower*. Appendix E lists these software titles and tells you how to contact the manufacturers who have kindly furnished demo versions of their sequencing software. Launch this software and open or import the various *.MID standard MIDI files of "Dino Disaster" included in the DINO.MID directory. Work with them in the same way that you worked with Midisoft Studio.

It's a great opportunity to experiment without additional financial investment.

One demo I really like is SuperJAM! by Blue Ribbon Soundworks, which actually uses some artificial intelligence to create accompaniment tracks for you to play along with. It's great for a guitarist, bassist, sax player, or any musician to use for practice. Be sure to check out the demo!

And remember, the WinSong Composer software used in Chapter 2 is fully MIDI-capable. You can use it with the preceding exercises, too.

SETTING UP YOUR MAC FOR MIDI RECORDING

8

For this chapter you will need the following:

♪ A Macintosh Plus or higher computer running System 6.03 or higher

♪ A hard drive and 4 or more megabytes of RAM

♪ A CD-ROM drive (necessary for use of the software provided on the enclosed *MusicPower* CD-ROM)

Hardware for Mac MIDI Recording

I assume that you have a Mac configured as recommended at the head of this chapter, so let's move on to learning about hardware you may not know about.

The essential pieces of hardware required for MIDI recording are the following:

A MIDI controller (usually a keyboard instrument)

A MIDI interface, which connects the controller to the computer

A synthesizer (synthesizers generate *all* the sounds in a MIDI system)

The MIDI Controller

The MIDI controller is the primary source of the MIDI event data (or MIDI events) that drive the entire MIDI system. The MIDI controller provides the main user interface to the MIDI system and is the instrument you actually "play" or "record" into the computer software.

Your MIDI controller might be a keyboard instrument, a MIDI guitar, a wind controller, or MIDI percussion pads.[1] I will use the word "controller" for the rest of this chapter to mean any of these types of controllers. Most computer musicians add a keyboard controller that features a keyboard like the one found on a piano. Figure 8.1 shows a popular MIDI controller.

You can use exactly the same controller instruments for any of the Mac, PC, Amiga, or Atari platforms.[2] Any controller you purchase should furnish the following:

A MIDI OUT jack (essential!)

A MIDI IN jack (if your controller has a built-in synthesizer)

The MIDI Interface

The MIDI interface converts MIDI data to Mac computer data.

Mac interfaces connect to the serial printer and/or modem ports found on the rear of the computer. There are two broad categories of interfaces: single-port and multiport.

[1]*Chapter 11 discusses all these types of MIDI controllers in detail.*

[2]*You can also use the controller to play MIDI sound modules directly, without having a computer involved at all.*

Single-Port Interfaces

The single-port MIDI interface is the only interface many computer musicians will ever need. Single-port units are usually small boxes similar to the interface shown in Figure 8.2.

Refer to the illustration in Figure 8.3, which shows features common to many single-port interfaces. These features include the following:

♪ A serial port connector. The MIDI STRIP (Figure 8.3) has a connected cable that you plug into a Mac's 8-pin mini-DIN serial port (usually the modem port is recommended), but more commonly there is a detachable cable used to connect the interface to the Mac port.

♪ One MIDI IN connector. This connects to the MIDI OUT on your controller.

♪ One or more MIDI OUT connectors. One of these is connected to the MIDI IN on each synthesizer in your MIDI system. Interfaces having more than one MIDI OUT can make it easy to connect more than one synthesizer.

A single-port interface will permit up to 16 channels of MIDI recording and playback. No matter how many MIDI OUT connectors are on the interface, *a single-port unit will support only 16 MIDI channels*—which actually is a lot of channels.

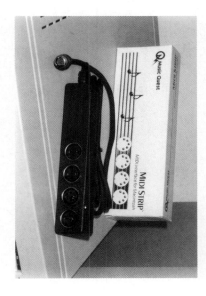

Figure 8.1. *The Roland A-30 MIDI keyboard controller.*

Figure 8.2. *The Music Quest MIDI STRIP interface is a single-port unit.*

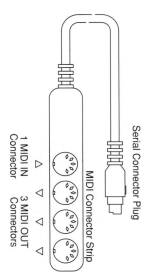

Serial Connector Plug

MIDI Connector Strip

1 MIDI IN Connector   3 MIDI OUT Connectors

Figure 8.3. *Illustration of the MIDI STRIP interface.*

Figure 8.4. *The rear view of a Sync-Link dual-port MIDI interface.*

Multiport Interfaces

There is a huge misconception about MIDI: Many computer musicians believe there are only 16 MIDI channels. True, but computer-music manufacturers have found ingenious ways to reliably coax up to 512 channels of MIDI out of a single computer and interface!

Dual-port interfaces are becoming very common. Figure 8.4 shows the rear of a Sync-Link dual-port interface made by J. L. Cooper Electronics.

A dual-port interface provides *two* connections to the Mac: one for the modem port and one for the printer port. A dual-port unit will allow for up to 32 channels of MIDI: 16 channels for the modem port and another 16 channels for the printer port.

A multiport interface will allow these additional MIDI channels to work only if your software also supports the additional MIDI channels.

You may be thinking, "Why would I ever need more than 16 channels? Certainly I would never use 512!" That exact subject is discussed in Chapter 11. For now, trust me: You will need at least a dual-port, 32-channel interface for semipro and professional MIDI recording. Most educational, multimedia, and hobby needs will be filled perfectly by a single-port interface.

MIDI Synthesizers

You will recall from Chapter 5 that MIDI synthesizers actually generate the sound in a MIDI system. Your MIDI synthesizer might be built into one of the following pieces of hardware:

♪ A MIDI sound module (Figure 8.5)

♪ A sound card (Figure 8.6)

♪ Or, as is usually the case, a synthesizer built into a keyboard instrument (Figure 8.7)

An interesting new breed of product is emerging that combines a MIDI interface and a MIDI sound module.

The idea is so new that several manufacturers are just now releasing these products, but three that have really caught my attention are the Yamaha Hello Music module, the MacWaveMaker sound card from Morning Star Solutions, and the brand-new SoundEngine from E-mu Systems. I foresee big futures especially for the SoundEngine and the MacWaveMaker, as their synthesizers are based on all of those terrific E-mu and Kurzweil sounds, respectively. And I love the built-in 1/4-inch headphone jack on the SoundEngine! All of these

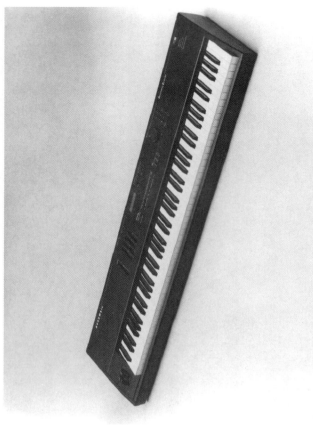

Figure 8.7. *The Kurzweil PC88 Performance Controller has a powerful built-in synthesizer.*

Figure 8.5. *The Proteus FX, from E-mu Systems, is a MIDI sound module with 8MB of rock, pop, jazz, and symphonic sounds.*

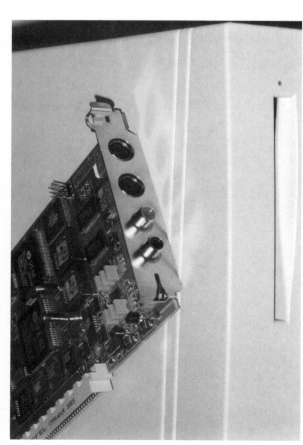

Figure 8.6. *The MacWaveMaker sound card, from Morning Star Solutions.*

two-in-one units will make MIDI recording and playback for hobby, multimedia, and educational applications much easier.

I will use the word *synthesizer* for the rest of this chapter to mean any of these types of MIDI synthesizers. Any MIDI synthesizer must at the very least have a MIDI IN jack in order to be useful to the computer musician. See Chapter 11 for more information about MIDI synthesizers.

About the Sequencer Software

The computer is a powerful tool if the proper application software has been installed, but a computer is simply useless without application software designed to accomplish the task at hand. The "brain" of the computer music system is the MIDI sequencer. Without a MIDI sequencer, we really wouldn't have computer music as we know it today.

MusicPower provides a demo version of Musicshop (Figure 8.8) by Opcode Systems, one of the leading producers of educational and professional music software.

Musicshop is a MIDI sequencer that is easy to understand and use. The graphics and color are very nice, making it fun to work with, too.

Figure 8.8. *Musicshop, by Opcode Systems, is used for the Chapter 9 MIDI recording tutorial.*

Launching the Musicshop Software

Select the CD-ROM drive icon for your Mac. Double-click the Musicshop Demo folder, then double-click the Install Musicshop Demo icon. When the installation program starts, click the Install button and follow the directions. When the installation is complete, you will see the Musicshop Demo folder on your hard drive.

Double-click the Musicshop icon (Figure 8.9). If you are launching Musicshop for the first time, you will see a dialog box that looks like Figure 8.10.

This box enables you to determine which port is being used by your MIDI interface. It must be set up properly for you to have any sound. Let's assume here that you are using the modem port. Set the interface patching *exactly* as shown in Figure 8.10.

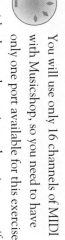

You will use only 16 channels of MIDI with Musicshop, so you need to have only one port available for this exercise. You *might* also need to activate the printer port if you want Musicshop to run in sync with another sequencer or drum machine. Those applications are explored in Chapters 10 and 11.

The next window to appear is the Musicshop Edit window. Select Open under the File menu. Open the file entitled Dino Disaster Score - GM (found on the CD-ROM, in the Dino Disaster Files folder). The Edit window will now look like Figure 8.11.

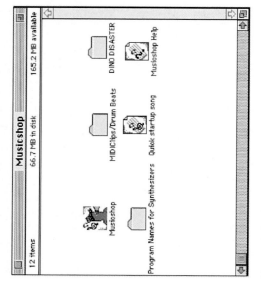

Figure 8.9. *The Musicshop icon.*

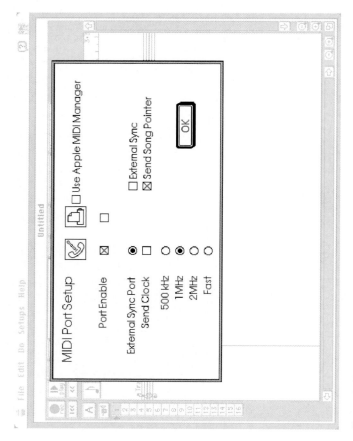

Figure 8.10. *The MIDI Port Setup dialog box.*

Note: Opcode provides a pop-up help feature in Musicshop! Hold down Shift+Option+Command (the key with the little apple), and the cursor turns into a small question mark. Then place the question mark on the display item of your choice. When you click and hold the mouse button, a window will appear explaining the selected feature. Take some time to explore the display. It is really fun, and you will get a good idea of what the windows will enable you to do with Musicshop.

One of the most important MIDI events to know about is the Panic or All Notes Off command. Notes played by *any* MIDI equipment can occasionally get stuck "on" and will continue to play obnoxiously. The Panic or All Notes Off command sends a Note Off event to all MIDI devices on all MIDI channels, which stops all sound in the MIDI system.

You should immediately find which menu this command is under when you launch any new MIDI software. Musicshop handles this with the Turn Stuck Notes Off command under the Setups menu.

Let's study the Edit window in Figure 8.11. We will begin by using the following controls and boxes in this window:

1. The Transport Controls are located in the upper-left corner of the Edit window. Click these buttons to play, stop, rewind, and so on, just as you would use them with a tape player. Remember, most good software now provides a control panel like this.

2. The Staff displays the musical events you record into the software. This is the main part of the display.

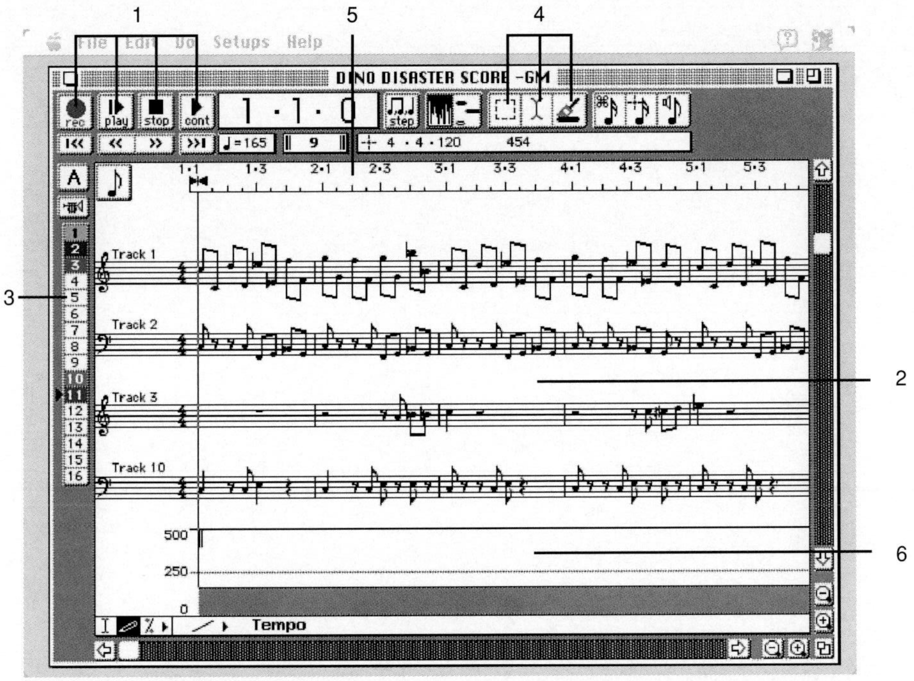

Warning: Always make your MIDI, computer, and audio connections with the equipment turned off. Making these connections when powered up can initialize the memory on MIDI devices—and in some cases can blow output amp chips on synthesizers!

Setting up the Interface

The MIDI interface must be set up correctly if the MIDI system is to work. This is a common problem area, but follow these steps carefully and you'll do just fine:

1. Be sure the MIDI OUT on your controller is connected to the MIDI IN on your interface.

2. The MIDI OUT on the interface should be connected to the MIDI IN on your synthe-sizer.[3]

3. The interface must be connected to the modem port of your Mac. This is true even if your interface also provides a printer port connection. Do not connect the printer port for now.

4. The MIDI Port Setup dialog box must look like Figure 8.10.

Figure 8.11. *The Musicshop Edit window.*

3. **The Track Bar.** This strip enables you to select which track is in record, and which tracks appear in the Staff display.

4. **The Edit Bar.** These are controls for editing your MIDI recordings.

5. **The Edit window Header** tells you what measure and beat you are on.

6. **The Strip Chart** displays MIDI events other than notes and rests.

Preparing Your Hardware and Software for MIDI Recording

Here is a checklist for you to use when preparing for your MIDI recording session. Not doing these things will make your session either impossible or awkward.

[3]*For most people, this is the same instrument that is being used as a controller.*

Musicshop Name	Generic Name	Result
Replace	Record	Records over and erases existing MIDI events.
Punch	Punch-in	Enables the recording only in a user-specified track area.
Overdub	Merge	Combines the incoming MIDI events with those already recorded.

Setting up the Controller

If there is a synthesizer built into your controlling instrument, you must turn its Local Control OFF. Your owner's manual will tell you how to do this. When you turn Local Control OFF, *your keyboard will make sounds only when properly patched through the interface and sequencing software*. You will have to turn Local Control ON for your instrument to make sound when not using the interface and sequencing software.

Setting up the Musicshop Sequencing Software

1. Launch Musicshop. Select Keyboard Thru under the Setups menu. This allows the MIDI event data from the controller to pass through the sequencer to the synthesizer. The synthesizer will not generate sound without Keyboard Thru turned on.

2. Most sequencers enable recording of MIDI information in more than one mode. Sequencer designers use different names for these modes. Here are some modes and the results of recording in them:

You will make a Record mode selection immediately before you begin to record.

Setting up the Synthesizer

1. Make sure your synthesizer is set up in a GM configuration. The exercises should sound perfect if you are using a GM-compatible synthesizer. If not, you will have to refer to

the owner's manual for your synthesizer and set the Receive Mode to Multi or Multitimbral.

2. Assign the MIDI Receive channels and patches as shown in Table 8.1.

If you do not have one of the pieces of hardware necessary for the Chapter 9 tutorial, you should consider reading Chapter 10 and perhaps even Chapter 11 before you make a purchase. And don't forget Appendix E, "The Resource Guide."

 Mac users should advance to Chapter 9, "Your First Mac-Based MIDI Recording Session."

Table 8.1. The MIDI-channel-to-GM-patch assignments for "Dino Disaster."

MIDI Channel Number	Sound Type	GM Program or Key Number
1	Clavinet	7
2	Synth Bass	39
3	Off	
4	Off	
5	New Age Pad, Fantasia	88
6	Off	
7	Off	
8	Off	
9	Off	
10	Open and Closed Hi-Hat	46, 44[4]
	Kick Drum, Snare	36, 38
11	Off	
12	Off	
13	Off	
14	Off	
15	Off	
16	Off	

[4] All sounds in the GM percussion bank are "played" by a single patch on Channel 10, but each key in this patch has one sound assigned to it. Thus, the number listed for each percussion sound is a key number. A list of the standard GM percussion key assignments is included in Appendix C.

YOUR FIRST MAC-BASED MIDI RECORDING SESSION

9

For this chapter you will need the following:

♪ A Macintosh Plus or higher, running System 6.0.3 or higher

♪ A hard drive and 4 or more megabytes of RAM

♪ A CD-ROM drive (for use of the software provided on the enclosed *MusicPower* CD-ROM)

♪ A MIDI interface for the Mac and two MIDI cables

You'll also need one of the following setups to generate MIDI event data and sound:

♪ A MIDI controller and a multitimbral MIDI sound module

♪ A multitimbral MIDI-equipped synthesizer

♪ A MIDI controller and a MacWaveMaker sound card by Morning Star Solutions

♪ A MIDI controller and a SampleCell sound card by Digidesign

Tip: Before you start this chapter, be sure to read Chapter 8, "Setting Up Your Mac for MIDI Recording." Chapter 10, "MIDI In-Out-Thru: the MIDI Project Studio," contains a more thorough discussion of connecting computer music hardware. Chapter 11, "Wow, Is MIDI Black Magic? Or, How Does It All Work?" provides details about the functions of MIDI event data, with explanations of how these MIDI events affect computer-based music.

This chapter teaches you how to actually use the information you learned in Chapters 4 and 5. Make sure you understand this information before you start on any new material.

The "Dino Disaster" Exercise

In the spring of 1993, I was commissioned by the Discovery Center in Amarillo, Texas to create an original music score for their planetarium show, titled "The Dinosaur Disaster." The score featured very diverse music styles, ranging from high-energy pop/rock sections to very elegant orchestral passages. I really enjoyed working on this production. It makes good use of MIDI recording techniques. You'll use my composition "Dino Disaster" for your tutorial.

Loading a Demo of "Dino Disaster"

You learned in Chapter 3 that a good way to get started with any software is to load a completed work and experiment with it. Launch Musicshop, as you learned to do in Chapter 8. Select Open from the File menu. Double-click the file named Dino Disaster Score-GM. You will see several bars of the music score (Figure 9.1). Your screen will not display all of the information shown in the figure—only one track of information.

Take a look at the Track Bar.[1] Notice that some of the boxes show highlighted numbers. This indicates that these tracks contain MIDI event data. As you click each highlighted track number, the staff changes to show the notation for the selected track. Clicking a number that isn't highlighted activates an unrecorded staff.

To view the staves for more than one track at a time, you can hold down your Shift key while you click the track numbers. In fact, go ahead and Shift+click the boxes numbered 1, 2, 3, 10, and 11. Now your screen should look exactly like Figure 9.1. You might want to use the scroll bar on the right side of the window to scroll through the tracks from top to bottom. Notice that the staff for each track displays its instrument name.

Click the Play button in the Transport Controls window to hear "Dino Disaster," a complete multitrack MIDI production. Musicshop gives you two ways to play the file. The play button with the vertical bar on the left side returns the composition to the beginning before playback begins. The play button labeled Cont starts playback at the point where the vertical line cursor (I call this the event cursor) is positioned on the staff. Note that the event cursor flashes continuously.

A small arrow can be found just to the left of the track bar. Click this arrow to see a list of the MIDI

[1] *If you can't find the track bar, refer to Chapter 8, Figure 8.11.*

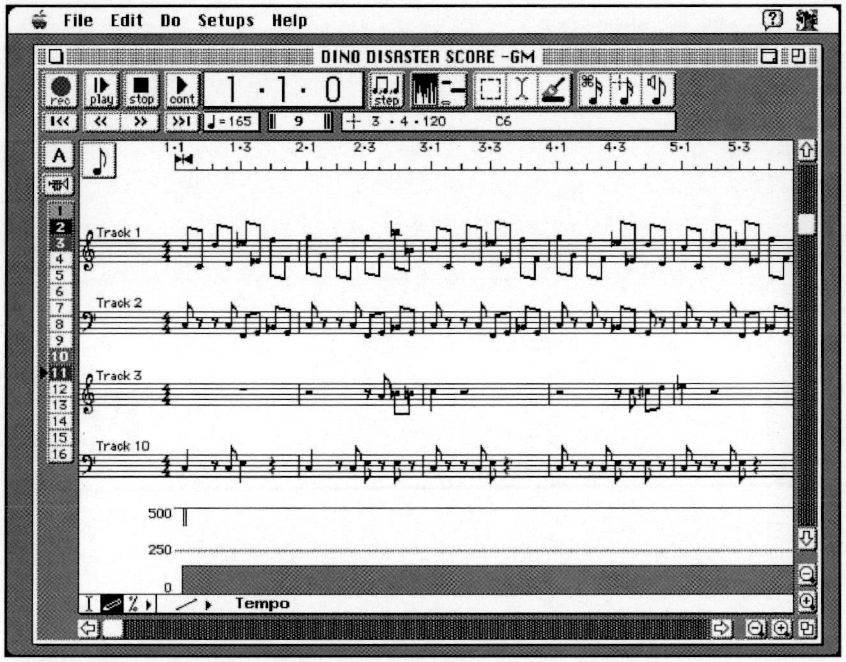

channel and instrument assignments used in your MIDI composition. You will learn how to change these instruments later in this chapter.

Loading a Template

Now you'll learn how to create a score like "Dino Disaster," starting with an empty staff. Click Open in the File menu and select Musicshop Template. This is a template I designed to get you started fast. It looks like Figure 9.2.

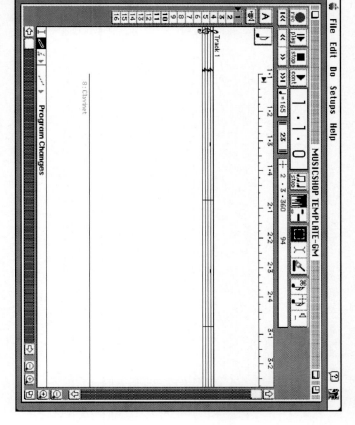

Figure 9.1. *A section of the score from "Dino Disaster."*

Figure 9.2. *The Musicshop template.*

You will find a command titled Select All Tracks in the Do menu. Select this now. All the track number boxes in the track bar become high-lighted.

The MIDI Track and Channel Assignments

You can change the track-to-MIDI channel assignments on nearly all sequencers. If you don't understand how to do this, you can create some real trouble for yourself. Musicshop defaults to a standard template of one MIDI channel per track. Track 1 = MIDI Channel 1, Track 2 = MIDI Channel 2, and so forth. You can change the configuration, but the preceding is the best template configuration for most computer musicians.[2] You'll use this configuration in the following exercise.

[2] A professional will soon need to alter these assignments.

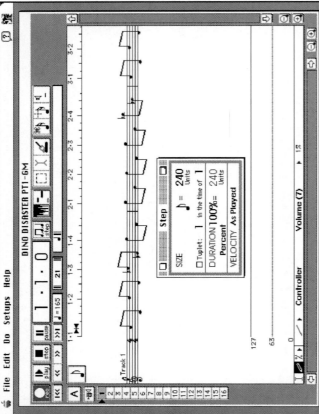

Figure 9.3. *Part 1 of "Dino Disaster."*

Recording MIDI Event Data in Step-Time Mode

Now you're ready for the real thing. You'll record Part 1 of "Dino Disaster" as shown in Figure 9.3. This is a busy eighth-note melody that features a Clavinet sound, and might remind you of the composition style of Alan Parsons or Jan Hammer.

In Chapter 3 you entered the notes on the staff by using the click-and-drag method. Entering music events one note at a time is also called *step-time recording*. You can also step-time record notes with a controller instrument. Here's how:

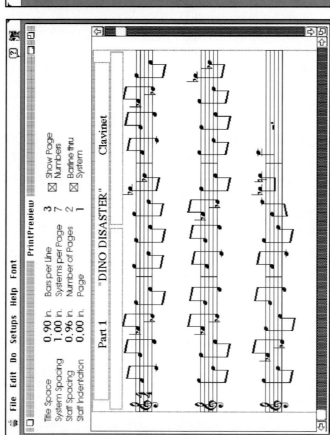

Figure 9.4. *The Step Record window.*

1. Click the Track 1 box in the track bar to enable Track 1.

2. Find the Setups menu on the menu bar. The top three commands determine the record mode, discussed in Chapter 8 under the heading "Setting up the Musicshop Sequencing Software." Select Replace for this exercise. Be sure that Keyboard Thru is also active.

3. Locate the Step Record icon in the center of the top row of icons. It looks like two eighth notes and a quarter note, with the word "step" under them. Click this icon to bring up the Step Record window (Figure 9.4).

4. There's a (♩) =480 Units area toward the upper-right side of the Step Record window. Place the cursor on the quarter note and hold down the mouse button. Move the mouse. Various note values become highlighted. This area is where you select the note value for each entry in step-time recording. Select the eighth note icon and release the mouse button. The dialog box changes to (♪) =240 Units. This means that every note you play on the controller causes an eighth note to be entered into the score.

5. Play the first note of Part 1 on your controller. It magically appears on the staff. To
enter rests, assign the value for the rest in
the Step window and hit the space bar on
your Mac keyboard.

Play the notes from Figure 9.3, using the step-time
method I just described. Erase mistakes by using
the Delete key. To clear large numbers of notes,
hold down the mouse button, drag a box around
the offending notes, and select Clear from the Edit
menu. Continue your work until your score looks
like Figure 9.3. Notice that you need to return to
the Step Record window to select quarter and half
notes as needed.

Click the Stop button in the Transport Controls
window (refer to Figure 8.11 if necessary) and then
click the Play button. You will hear Part 1 of
"Dino Disaster."

You can now record Part 2 of "Dino Disaster," the
bass line (Figure 9.5).

You must first select a new track to record on. Just
click the Channel 2 box in the track bar to
highlight it. Note: You must again click the Step
Record icon, just as you did in Step 3 of the
preceding list.

Copy the notes from Figure 9.5 with the step-time
method, just as you did before. If you make a
mistake, check how you corrected mistakes before.
Continue your work until your score looks exactly
like Figure 9.5. Again, you can click the Play
button in the Transport Controls window at any
time to hear your work.

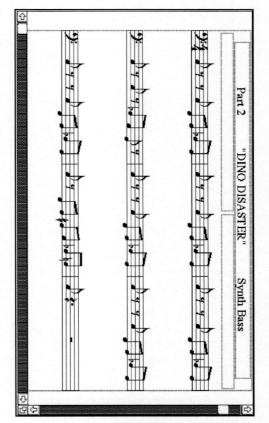

Figure 9.5. *Part 2 of Dino Disaster.*

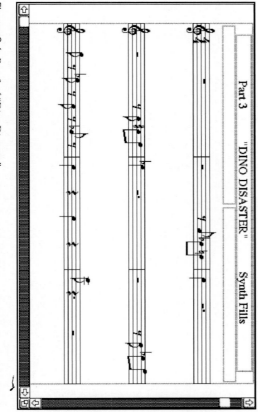

Figure 9.6. *Part 3 of "Dino Disaster."*

Copy the notes from Part 3 (Figure 9.6) in the
same way. This part is a set of "fills," the musical
equivalent of a sprinkle of nuts on an ice cream
sundae.

The notes on the third staff make up Part 3. Click
the Play button in the Transport Controls window
to play back your first three parts.

The demo version of Musicshop will not save or print, but the copy you might purchase certainly will. If you could save your work, you would be doing this at each step, right? I thought so.

Real-Time Recording

Most MIDI sequencers default to real-time recording. Real-time recording is similar to recording with a tape machine, so you must be able to actually play your controller to some degree. The advantages of real-time recording are the following:

> The recording session moves along much faster.

> It gives the music a more human feeling and expression.

You'll use real-time to record Part 4, a drum track featuring kick and snare drums (Figure 9.7).

Here's the procedure for real-time recording with Musicshop:

1. Set up for recording exactly as you did for step-time recording, but don't click the Step Record icon.

2. This time record enable Track 10 on the track bar.[3]

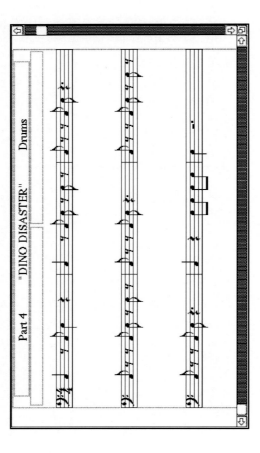

Figure 9.7. Adding Part 4, drums, to "Dino Disaster."

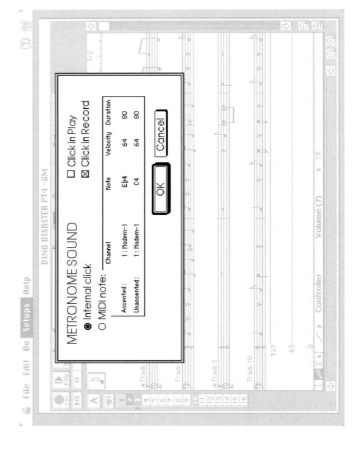

Figure 9.8. The Metronome or "Click" window.

[3]The widely popular General MIDI (GM) configuration dedicates MIDI Channel 10 to drums and percussion.

3. Rhythm and timing are crucial when you're recording in real-time, so you need a metronome or "click" track to help you stay in rhythm. Select Metronome from the Setups menu. The dialog box in Figure 9.8 appears.

   Most good sequencers, like Musicshop, enable you to customize your click track, and that's what the Metronome Sound box does. One choice you have is whether you want the click track to be played by your synthesizer or by your Mac. Keep things simple and select Internal click for now.[4] Then click OK. Now if you click the Record (Rec) button in the Transport Controls window, you'll hear your click track. The click track will be heard only when you click the Record button. This is because you set the click track up in the Metronome Sound box so it will not play during playback. Change this if you want. After all, you *are* becoming quite a computer musician!

4. Select Countoff from the Setups menu. This will cause the click track to play for two measures before the recording actually begins. This gives you time to get ready for the big moment…your first real-time recording!

If your synthesizer is properly configured, you will hear the sound of a kick drum and a snare drum when you play the notes in Part 4 (recorded on Track 10) on your controller. The kick is on the note C and the snare is on the note E. You might have to test different octaves on your controller to find which C and E will respond properly. Try the ones on the left end of your keyboard first.

Get ready! Set! Click Record, wait for the first eight clicks to go by, and you're off. Play your fingers off. I can tell you're really getting warmed up now. Stop whenever you feel like it, but remember: You do have to stop sometime, no matter how much fun you're having.

Here's a great tip. Always let the first two measures of your score go unrecorded. That way you can later add pick-up notes or an extra one-measure phrase to lead into your score. I find myself making these additions to most of my MIDI recording projects, and using this little trick saves me the hassle of adding an extra two bars later.

Click Play and listen to your work. This might be a case of the good, the bad, and the ugly. But hey, you're just getting started. I didn't quit ten years ago when I was at the same stage as you are right now. And you have me to help.

Step-Time Recording Versus Real-Time Recording

The first sequencers many of us used recorded in step-time. Step-time enables you to enter a music event, wait, enter the next note perfectly, wait, add a rest, wait, and so on. This is really helpful for the computer musician who has limited performance skills, and it can provide an easy way for you to record blindingly fast strings of notes, but it's a slow process. It's also mechanical. In fact, if I want to arrange a very "techno" or industrial-feeling piece, I often begin with a track or two of step-time passages, like in "Dino Disaster."

Real-time recording has much of the feel of traditional tape-based recording. Computer musicians say that software like this has a user-friendly interface. In this case, "interface" refers not to a piece of hardware, but to how comfortable it is to record with the software. That's why the Transport Control buttons resemble those on a tape machine. Software designers have worked hard to make the MIDI recording process as much like working with tape as possible, while retaining the editing and correction features that only a digital medium can provide. I think they've done very well at perfecting this user interface.

I explained in Chapter 8 that I really dislike the term "sequencer." I prefer to call a piece of sequencing software a MIDI recorder. I usually run my software just like I would a multitrack tape machine, doing punch-in recording on the fly and trying to add as many dynamics to the music during recording as I can.

---

[4]*Some Macs don't allow Musicshop to use an internal click. In this situation, a click count will be sent on a MIDI channel to your synthesizer. You can assign a cowbell or other percussion sound to the channel on which the click is sent. Make your selection in the Metronome window.*

Of course, my keyboard chops have their limit, so I really benefit from being able to edit, quantize, and so on. The important point is to use the hardware and software to enhance, not hinder, the creative process.

Quantizing the Recording

Quantization can be considered error correction. When you quantize your recording, you move the occurrence of each MIDI event to the nearest beat or fraction of a beat. This can make up for errors in your sense of timing and make the recording easier to edit. Author Christopher Brown wrote in the Musicshop reference manual that this is much like the way a CAD or graphics program does a "snap to grid." Good analogy.

Figure 9.9 shows a sample of a recording where I performed badly.

Notice how chaotic the performance is. Now I'll quantize the recording. First I select the notes I want to quantize by choosing Select All from the Do menu. The notes are all highlighted. Then I click the Command-8th Note icon (third from the right in the edit bar) and hold the mouse button down. I can drag the mouse around to select the note value that the notes in "Bad Jeff" will round off or "resolve" to. I choose 8th note "resolution." Then I choose Quantize Selection from the Do menu. The notes in "Bad Jeff" shift around and become 8th notes, 8th rests, and multiples of these. You can see the result in Figure 9.10.

Try quantizing your own "bad" performance. You can always choose Undo from the Edit menu, so

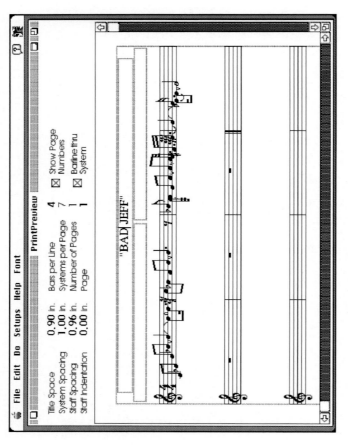

Figure 9.9. "Bad Jeff," my very own sloppy performance.

Figure 9.10. "Bad Jeff" becomes "Better Jeff" through quantizing.

experience the effects of choosing various resolutions of quantizing. You'll want to use Undo, because some of these results may be startling and possibly useless. The most common values for quantization resolution are the 16th note, the 8th note, and the 8th note triplet.

Musicshop offers several different modes of quantization. Hold down Shift+Option+Command and click each of the icons on the right end of the edit bar. Pop-up help will appear concerning other quantizing possibilities.

Resolve recordings to the smallest note value that you think you recorded. If you recorded quarter and 8th notes, you would quantize in 8th notes, for example.

What? A Controversy?

I just heard the boos and hisses of a number of my colleagues. Many of them believe strongly that quantizing the recording makes it sound like step time. They're correct, to a degree. You'll eventually learn when to quantize your work and when not to. It's a creative decision that should be left in the hands of each computer musician. As Los Angeles-based recording engineer Michael Jay recently told me, there's seldom a technically right or wrong computer-recording method; there's just a different set of opportunities for the creative musician. I think Michael's opinion is valuable; he used Digital Performer by Mark of the Unicorn to record the *Talk* CD by the powerhouse group Yes, released in the spring of 1994.

Changing the MIDI Channel Assigned to a Track

The easiest way to use Musicshop and other MIDI recorders is to use the "one track per MIDI channel" configuration you used for this chapter. Most computer musicians find they can enhance their MIDI system's flexibility and ease of use by reconfiguring the MIDI channel-to-track assignments. Musicshop enables you to do this easily.

Figure 9.11 contains the Track Setup window, which you call up by pressing Option+T. The left column shows the track numbers. The next two columns indicate that the tracks are assigned to the modem port of your interface. The fourth column is very interesting: *It enables you to change the MIDI channel assigned to any track!*

Just click any of the boxes in the fourth column to enter a new MIDI channel assignment. Look at Track 11. Notice that I changed the MIDI channel to 10—the same channel as Track 10. Why?

Remember that Track 10 plays back drum sounds. All the drum sounds in a GM configuration are assigned to MIDI Channel 10. If I use only one track (Track 10) to record drum parts, I have to record all the drums and percussion in a single pass. That will be pretty rough if I want to use lots of percussion instruments. Another method is to merge all of my recorded performances onto a single track (Track 10) by using the Overdub function from the Setups menu. However, this merges all the MIDI events together and makes editing the individual events very difficult.

I rarely use Overdub or Merge record modes.

I would rather record each percussion instrument onto its own individual track and then assign all those percussion tracks to the same MIDI

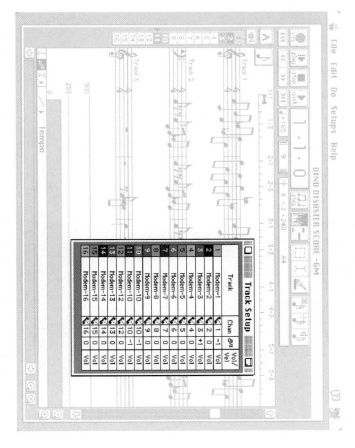

Figure 9.11. *The Track Setup window.*

channel. In the case of the GM percussion configuration for "Dino Disaster," this would be Channel 10. I recorded the hi-hat part onto Track 11, and assigned Track 11 to MIDI Channel 10. If you made this change as I did, you could record the hi-hat part in Figure 9.12 onto Track 11.

It's not uncommon for me to use a dozen tracks for drums and percussion, with many or all of those tracks then assigned to the same MIDI channels. This gives me maximum flexibility in re-recording and editing these percussion recordings.

Warning: Just because this is one of my favorite tools doesn't mean you have to try it. You can totally confuse your entire MIDI recording system by making a couple of "small" changes in this window. However, knowing how to use this tool properly can open terrific new possibilities for your MIDI recording sessions.

Transposing the Score

The Track Setup window also enables you to transpose a track up or down. Just click the appropriate box in the 8va column and enter a positive or negative number. Transposition of the selected track is instantaneous.

Cutting and Pasting Notes

You learned how to cut and paste with DeluxeMusic in Chapter 3, so I won't repeat the

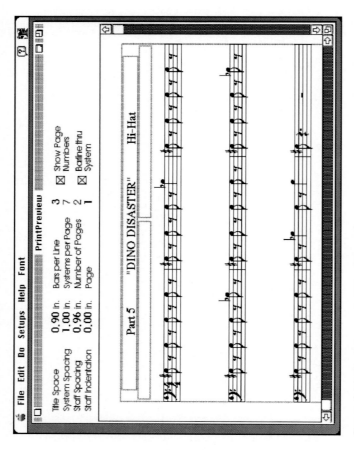

Figure 9.12. *The hi-hat part for "Dino Disaster."*

details here. Musicshop uses the flashing event cursor for cut-and-paste editing. This is easy if you follow these steps:

1. Select the track(s) you want to edit by highlighting their track number boxes in the Track Bar. The staves for these tracks appear.

2. Place the mouse cursor just before the first note you want to edit. This works best in the Edit window Header, where the measures and beats are displayed.

3. Click the mouse button. The flashing Event Cursor moves to the selected position.

4. Hold down the mouse button while dragging the mouse to highlight a group of selected events. You can select Cut, Copy, or Clear from the Edit menu. If you choose Cut or Copy, you can move the Event Cursor to a new position and choose Paste Selection at that point. Remember, you can choose to edit all tracks or as few as one, based on your selections in the track bar.

Changing Instrument Sounds in the Strip Chart

It's easy to change the instrument assigned to a track in Musicshop. Reload the demo of "Dino Disaster." If you look closely at Figure 9.13, you'll notice that "8: Clavinet" appears just below the line that runs across the bottom of the screen. This area is called the Strip Chart. Notice that the bar across the bottom says "Program Changes." A Program Change is a MIDI event that asks your synthesizer to change the sound it's generating; "8: Clavinet" is a Program Change command, for example. You can have a program change in any track and at any place, just as when you changed

the instrument sounds with DeluxeMusic in Chapter 3.

Click the Pencil tool to the left of "Program Changes." When you move the cursor into the area near the "8: Clavinet" program change, the cursor becomes a pencil. Click and hold the left mouse button down. A huge list of names fills the window (Figure 9.14).

These are the patches utilized by the general MIDI standard. These names and numbers work with any GM synthesizer. As you drag the cursor across this screen, the instrument names are highlighted.

Stop the cursor on "43: Cello" and release the

mouse button. The window disappears and the program change "43: Cello" appears in the strip chart. This program change event is sent to your synthesizer when you play back your recording. The synthesizer then changes its sound to Cello.

To erase a program change, click the Beam tool (to the left of the Pencil icon), hold the mouse button down, and drag the cursor across the program change that you want to erase. It becomes highlighted. Press the Delete key on your Mac keyboard to erase this MIDI event.

Enter a zillion program changes and listen to how the instrument sounds change. The program changes I placed in the "Dino Disaster" demo will

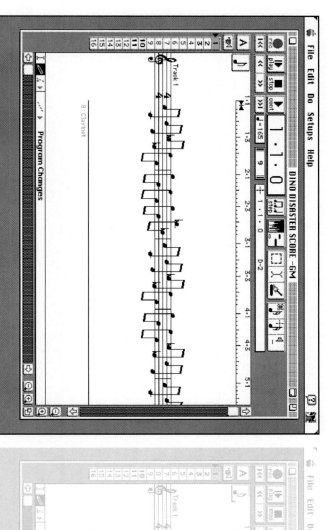

Figure 9.13. The Strip Chart is at the bottom of the Edit window.

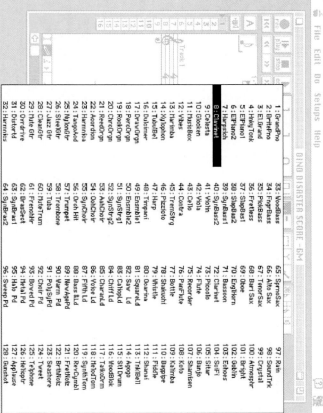

Figure 9.14. The GM Program Change list.

reset your GM system to the proper configuration when you reload and play the demo.

> **Tip:** This is a good time to refer back to the segment about General MIDI in Chapter 5. I think you'll understand the importance of the GM standard now that you've actually worked with it in Musicshop.

Digging Deeper into Musicshop

The list of Musicshop features goes on and on. Explore this software thoroughly. You can view all of the control events in full color in the strip chart, and there's a "piano roll" type of viewing that enables you to enter and edit notes by drawing lines with your mouse. You will learn about working with Piano Roll in Chapter 13 when you study Opcode Vision. I predict you'll return to work with Musicshop after you study Chapters 10, 11, and 13.

The *MusicPower* CD-ROM is loaded with many other great Musicshop demos prepared by the staff at Opcode. Load those up and experiment with them. That's why I included them. Be sure to edit, and transpose, and cut, and paste, and... well, you get the idea.

Musicshop is one of the most "disaster"-free (pun intended) MIDI sequencers you'll find at this price point. The software retails for $149.95 and is loaded with more capabilities and features than I

can discuss here. It's not really notation software, but it will print a score. You used it to print the score in Figure 9.1. The Opcode staff is easily accessible and eager to answer your questions. You can call them at (415) 856-3333.

Additional Music Software on *MusicPower*

Todd Souvignier at OSC in San Francisco (415-252-0367) sent me a demo version of their sequencer, Metro. Metro provides many professional features at a very reasonable price ($225 in the United States), and the editing software is superbly designed, especially the event editing. Metro works with the internal Mac sound synthesizer, which lets you start MIDI recording without having to purchase a synthesizer. Todd explained that Metro was designed for compatibility with Apple QuickTime, so it's very useful for multimedia movie authoring. Launch Metro and work with it the same way you worked with Musicshop. It's a great opportunity to experiment without additional financial investment.

Don't forget *The Macintosh Product Registry*, which was mentioned in Chapter 3. Other Mac software and hardware is listed by categories, complete with pricing and product descriptions. And remember, the DeluxeMusic software you used in Chapter 3 is fully MIDI-capable. You can use it with the preceding exercises, too.

Where Do You Go from Here?

This book is designed to help computer musicians reach the level of expertise that they want to achieve. Mastery of the materials I've presented up to this point in the book will enable you to produce many incredible music projects. You'll be able to accomplish many of the educational, recreational, and home-recording goals discussed in the Introduction and Chapter 1.

This is a good time to explore the Appendices. Appendix A helps you develop your musical skills. Appendix B provides several more printed scores that you can use with the software featured in Chapters 3, 9, and 13.

Many of you have only just begun.

Now that you're MIDI-literate, you can learn about a completely integrated MIDI studio. Many computer musicians would call this a MIDI project studio. I'll teach you how to design and assemble one in Chapter 10. The subsequent chapters feature studies of the newest recording and editing methods used by today's professionals. And don't forget Chapter 13, the third Mac software tutorial, featuring Vision 2.0.

Mac users should advance to Chapter 10.

10

MIDI In-Out-Thru: The MIDI Project Studio

MIDI systems have grown up. They started out as simple two- or three-device systems and have now grown to a level where entire studios, featuring dozens of MIDI channels and racks of sound modules and synthesizers, can be designed. This chapter explores this modern type of studio, called a *MIDI project studio*.[1]

MIDI Studios Are a Hot Item!

For a number of years, music trade journals have been reporting steady increases in the sales of MIDI studio hardware, software, and support periphery.[2] In fact, national surveys of retail stores indicate that MIDI studios are far and away the fastest-growing sector of the entire music industry!

MIDI Is Fun

Well, as you've discovered, being able to compose and record with MIDI on even a simple level is a real blast. Yeah, sure, it can get a little confusing at times, and occasionally when you change hardware or software you think your system will never, ever work properly again, but when all the bugs are worked out, MIDI is marvelous.

Computers and Music Have Grown Up with Us...

It is indeed amazing to visit your local museum and notice how even very young children seem to operate the kiosks and interactive exhibits with ease, often as their parents peer over their

shoulders wearing painfully confused expressions. This is a result of the explosive success of the personal computer in the elementary school environment. Almost all schools now provide some type of computer lab where young people can get their hands on some basic computer hardware and software. The best methods for teaching computer skills to these age groups involve lots of entertainment value, with as much energy and excitement as possible. And of course, one of the most popular and entertaining activities for young people is music. Educators have responded by incorporating many sound and music activities into their computer labs, and the result is that electronic music activities have become the norm for children at an early age. This familiarity sticks with young people because it's supported by other computer-based studies, hobbies, and games.

Students at the high-school level often have the opportunity to work in some sort of computer music lab, usually serving as a part of the school music program. These music labs are often fully equipped with MIDI (another factor contributing to increased overall sales of MIDI gear) and provide an environment where students can interactively study the works of the great composers in history, learn the theory of music composition and arranging, and bang out a few original tunes to impress their friends with.

By this age, many students have a seriously developed case of MIDI Madness, preferring to save their hard-earned cash to purchase a new synthesizer, and then happily loading it into a car

with no matching tires and the rear seat removed so as to get all the PA gear in for band rehearsal (Figure 10.1).

Warning: A serious infection known as "MIDI Madness" can quickly consume your time, your patience, and especially your wallet. There's no reason to fight this "disease" because it's usually permanent, and you'll actually feel better as the infection gets worse...did I say that?

The serious student at the collegiate level finds a similar musical experience waiting. Some universities and recording arts schools maintain digital recording facilities that are far better-equipped than most commercial studios.[3] But a student who mastered the tools available in the high-school music lab will find the transition to Electronic Music 101 to be a breeze. This is because MIDI was brilliantly designed to be easily expanded after the basic principles are understood.

---

[1]*On a controversial note, major battles are being fought in some cities regarding project studios. Many project studios operate in violation of local zoning ordinances. Inspect your local zoning ordinances carefully before committing lotsa dollars and work to installation.*

[2]*See music industry publications such as NAMM Report, MIX magazine, Electronic Musician, EQ, Keyboard, and others.*

[3]*Each year MIX magazine prints a directory of recording arts schools. This is a comprehensive listing and includes such information as addresses, contact names, phone numbers, fax numbers (hmm...another way musicians use computers!), curriculum descriptions, and equipment lists. Students trying to select a recording school will have great success using this directory as their first step. The address for MIX is listed in Appendix E, "The Resource Guide."*

So you can see how the methods and tools used to teach music are consistent from a very young age through adulthood; the learning curve is smooth and well structured—and most importantly, learning is a lot of fun at all levels. Computer-assisted music education has solved a traditional music education dilemma—what does a student do with her instrument when she has graduated and there's no band to play in anymore? For example, unless you're going to play clarinet as a career, it's frankly not much fun at nineteen years old to be playing Klasé scales on your B-flat tenor sax in your room. But a student with computer music skills can compose and arrange at will, with full orchestral arrangement, and even create MIDI arrangements of background tracks to accompany live solo instruments such as the sax. Now you're getting somewhere!

The MIDI Customer Base Is Self-Perpetuating

As a new crop of computer musicians is educated, a new crop of potential MIDI studio customers is developing. Many of you reading this book were teenagers when MIDI was developed in 1984. Some of you may have children who are noodling around with computer music programs in their first years of school...a new generation ready to become computer musicians.

Figure 10.1. *No sacrifice is too great for some young electronic musicians. Have to get that new keyboard you saw on MTV!*

MIDI Equipment Prices Are Decreasing Fast!

So many consumers are now purchasing MIDI gear that the prices are crashing fast. This means that more consumers can afford to purchase, which in turn means the prices will continue to drop.

As a case in point, when I purchased my Kurzweil K250 in 1989, the list price was about $12,000 (Figure 10.2). Kurzweil recently introduced the exciting K2000, which does many of the things my K250 does—some of them even better. List price for the base model is around $3,000. I rest my case. And now many manufacturers that produce what is considered to be high-end MIDI gear are providing their excellent hardware and software to other companies on an OEM[4] basis. This means that these OEM companies will use technology from the big guys to manufacture dynamite MIDI products at much lower prices.[5]

[4]Short for Original Equipment Manufacturer.

[5]As an example, Barr Tupper from Kurzweil informs me that Kurzweil ROM sound chips will soon be appearing on the sound cards of four OEM manufacturers. American electronic music innovator E-mu Systems was acquired by Creative Technology Limited (which owns and operates the famous Creative Labs), primarily to give Creative access to the terrific sound ROM chips developed over the years by E-mu. Creative will feature E-mu Proteus-level sounds in their next generation of audio products.

New MIDI Customers Emulate Celebrity MIDI Musicians

I clearly remember the British music invasion of the '60s. One result of it was that young American musicians began to dress like the Brits, wear their hair like the Brits, walk like the Brits, and talk like the Brits.

But the most significant effect was that these American musicians sacrificed almost anything to own the same models of instruments as Clapton, Beck, and Page (Figure 10.3). It was a time that proved how much influence major music stars have on their fans. That influence continues to this day, as young musicians race out to buy the same keyboards used by such artists as Paul

Shaffer, Rick Wakeman, and Prince. The enthusiasm for electronic music is the modern equivalent of the guitar craze of the '60s.

The MIDI Project Studio

Well-equipped MIDI project studios are appearing in the homes and offices of professional musicians around the world. The professionals who use such a setup include the following:

♪ Orchestral composers who need to hear approximations of major works before taking them to orchestra rehearsal

♪ Film composers who work out very complex click tracks[6] before they go to the studio to record live instruments

Figure 10.3. The famous Gibson Les Paul guitar became the must-have dream item in the late '60s. Photo courtesy of Gibson Guitar Corporation.

[6]A click track, also known as a metronome track, provides the tempo for conductors and musicians to follow during recording. This kind of work is now assisted by SMPTE time code so that selected measures and beats in the click tracks "hit" the action in the film perfectly. Chapter 15 describes this kind of production, as does the Chapter 5 interview with Kenny Aronoff.

Figure 10.2. The vintage Kurzweil 250.

- Jingle writers preparing demos for advertising clients
- Teachers who use notation software to print out exercises for student choirs, bands, and orchestras
- Many major recording artists, some of whom compose, rehearse, record, and produce their album masters entirely in their own home MIDI studios

And what the pros do, so emulate the semi-pro or amateur musician:

- Hobby musicians who just want to have fun
- Songwriters hoping to sell songs to major recording artists
- Bands and solo artists who produce their own demos, hoping to get a record deal
- Serious music students who use MIDI arrangements for rehearsal accompaniment

What You Will Need for a Basic MIDI Project Studio

The amount of hardware you can install in your MIDI project studio can be truly staggering. It's not uncommon for the top-level professional studios of this nature to consist of $200,000 or more of hardware! But these days you can really do a lot with a minimum of equipment. You still should take a good look at both the overall and detailed structure of the MIDI project studio so you can see how everything works together.

The basic components of the MIDI project studio are as follows:

The computer and its associated peripherals

MIDI software

The MIDI interface

The MIDI controller keyboard or other MIDI controller

MIDI sound modules

A stereo audio mixer

An audio monitoring system

MIDI cables

Audio cables

Let's build a block diagram of the MIDI project studio, adding one component at a time. Each of these components is studied in great detail in Chapter 11, so consider this a primer for that chapter.

> **Warning:** With increased features come increased memory demands! It has been interesting to watch software programs run slower and slower with each upgrade. The increased features and graphics are real memory hogs, needing more processor time to run their advanced features. For this reason, I don't necessarily run the latest version of a sequencer program. Sometimes the increased features are unnecessary frills that really don't contribute to the MIDI recording process. I go for the version that does everything I need the fastest and most reliably. Call me dull, I guess.

The Personal Computer of Your Choice

Figure 10.4 shows the first building block of the MIDI project studio, the personal computer. You may want to recheck the computer specifications I recommended towards the end of the Introduction. Bear in mind that an enormous number of MIDI projects have been done with less powerful hardware than I recommend, so use what you have and see if it works. For example, you may be able to use less RAM (which means, of course, that you probably will work more slowly). I recommend medium-size hard drives, but you can get by with hard drives as small as 20MB. And a CD-ROM drive will turn this book into an interactive experience.

MIDI Software Applications[7]

The first piece of MIDI software you must own is a MIDI sequencer (Figure 10.5).

MIDI sequencing software actually serves as the modern-day equivalent of a tape recorder and can provide literally hundreds of tracks you can use for recording tempo- and meter-synchronized MIDI music passages. I call the process of recording and arranging MIDI music passages a MIDI recording

[7] *Because this book focuses on computer-based music applications, it doesn't discuss stand-alone sequencers or sequencers that are built into keyboard instruments. Some of these sequencers provide a really nice low-cost way to get into MIDI if you don't own a computer, but sequencers of this nature are definitely harder to work with and more limited than computer software sequencers.*

session. You used a simple MIDI sequencer in Chapters 6 and 7 when you had your first MIDI recording session using sound cards. In your MIDI project studio, you'll require much more sophisticated software than you used for those sessions.

The more professional software has many user-definable functions, such as adding and deleting tracks and displays at will, editing track and note information (much as you'd use a word processor to edit words and paragraphs), slaving the composition to external tape machines when you want to add live instruments, specialized track viewing, notation printing, and more. These advanced sequencers also enable you to use more than the 16 original MIDI channels provided by basic sequencers.[8]

I find that the biggest difference between full-blown professional MIDI sequencers and entry-level ones lies in the display and editing functions. The improved functions in the professional sequencers enable musicians to work faster and more creatively when they're in a MIDI recording session. Some musicians actually use different sequencers for different kinds of recording projects. Some sequencers work faster for album recording sessions, some are better for film and video work, and others incorporate tracks for recording live instruments in CD-quality digital sound files, as you'll see in Chapter 14.

Over 200MB of sequencer demos, examples, and exercises are on the enclosed CD-ROM. Many major manufacturers have been kind enough to provide their software at no charge, so these demos are among the best in existence. Bear in mind that these demo versions don't have all the functions the full versions do. Some of the demos won't let you save; some will shut down after a few minutes. But this is a great opportunity for you try several

sequencing programs and then select the one(s) you want to purchase.

Other nonsequencer software packages exist that can make your MIDI project studio run more efficiently (Figure 10.6). Some of these include patch editing and librarian software to manage all the sound files generated by your MIDI synthesizers, automation software for audio mixers that provides computer-assisted mixing of all the sounds generated by your MIDI modules and synths, and digital waveform editors like Digidesign Sound Designer II.

The MIDI Interface

Figure 10.7 shows an example of a MIDI interface. You might want to go back to Chapter 5 for a review of the basic principles of MIDI interfaces. Remember that the interface you select will be determined in part by the computer platform you use. There are major differences between interfaces for the PC and those for the Mac.

PC users should refer to Chapter 6 to review how to select and install a MIDI interface on a PC.

Mac users should refer to Chapter 8 to review how to select and install a MIDI interface on a Mac.

[8]*When used in conjunction with a multiport MIDI interface. Keep reading, you'll get to this subject in just a minute.*

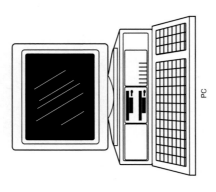

PC

Figure 10.4. *The MIDI project studio is based around the personal computer of your choice.*

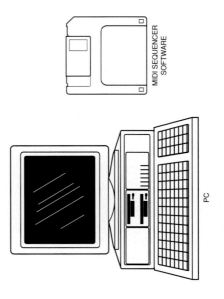

MIDI SEQUENCER SOFTWARE

PC

Figure 10.5. *The MIDI sequencing software is the "conductor" of your MIDI project studio. It provides the user interface that allows the computer to control many MIDI device functions.*

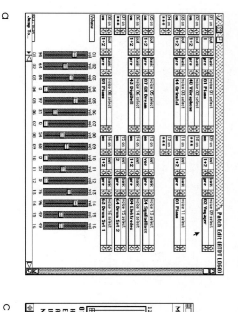
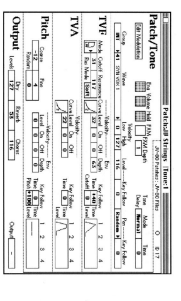

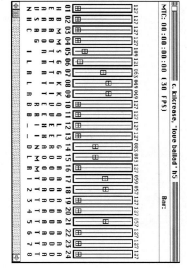
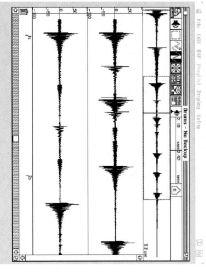
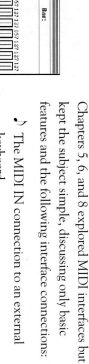

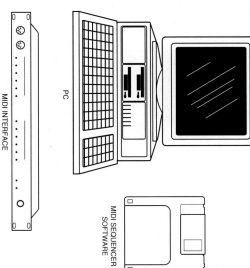

Figure 10.6. Other software that supports music composition and production: (a) Unisyn and (b) Galaxy librarians, (c) Megamix mixer automation, and (d) Sound Designer II.

Figure 10.7. The MIDI interface allows the computer to exchange MIDI event data with the other devices in the MIDI project studio.

Chapters 5, 6, and 8 explored MIDI interfaces but kept the subject simple, discussing only basic features and the following interface connections:

- The MIDI IN connection to an external keyboard
- The MIDI OUT connection to an external keyboard
- Connection of the interface to the computer

That was because those segments focussed on the consumer-oriented use of sound cards. A MIDI interface for the project studio should provide many more features, such as the following:

♪ The ability to serve as a multiport interface. This will enable you to expand your MIDI system to as many as 256 (or more) output channels.[9] You might never use 256 channels of MIDI, but you certainly will use more than the basic 16 channels provided by a single port interface.

♪ The ability to read and write SMPTE time code[10] at all frame rates.[11] You will use this feature any time you synchronize your sequencing software with audio or video tape machines.

♪ At least two MIDI inputs and as many MIDI outputs as possible. The inputs are important because they enable you to merge MIDI data you're recording from your keyboard or other controller with MIDI time-code (MTC) timing information from an external MIDI device, such as another sequencer or drum machine. This enables you to record your MIDI performance while your sequencer runs in sync with the other external MIDI device. Very important![12]

A MIDI Keyboard or Other MIDI Controller

Figure 10.8 adds a MIDI keyboard or other MIDI controller. MIDI controllers of various types are introduced in Chapter 5. Far and away the most

popular type of MIDI controller is the MIDI keyboard, and that's why you used that particular controller in your studies in Chapters 5, 6, and 8. I suggest you review Chapter 5 at this time.

Remember, a MIDI controller is the source of the MIDI data that is recorded by the MIDI sequencing software. This MIDI data is made up of MIDI *events*, and it provides the commands that make music happen for the computer musician. These MIDI events are what are recorded and played back by the MIDI sequencer. You should also remember that some MIDI controllers generate sound, and others don't. MIDI controllers are discussed in great detail in Chapter 11.

MIDI Sound Modules

In many cases, the computer musician uses the MIDI controller to generate the sounds as well as the MIDI event data.[13] But sometimes the sounds the musician wants to use are not the ones generated by the keyboard he or she is using. In that case, the musician adds a MIDI *sound module* (Figure 10.9). Many musicians use several modules

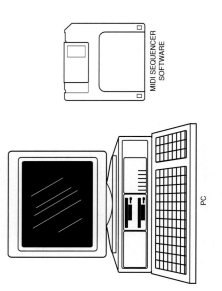

MIDI SEQUENCER SOFTWARE

PC

MIDI INTERFACE

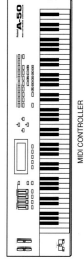

MIDI CONTROLLER (KEYBOARD)

Figure 10.8. *The MIDI controller is the original source of the MIDI event data that commands your MIDI system to perform special MIDI functions and to generate sound.*

---

[9]*When used in conjunction with MIDI software that accesses this feature.*

[10]*SMPTE time code is explained in Chapter 1 and the Glossary.*

[11]*This is really a topic for another book. You can think of moving pictures (film and video) as a series of fast-moving still photos. National and international standards committees have selected the speeds at which these photos are recorded and reproduced, assigning specific frame rates for specific uses. Frame rates are measured in fps (the number of moving picture frames per second). Here are some of the standard frame rates and their uses:*

30fps—Music and audio projects and audio/visual slide shows.
29.97fps—The most common frame rate you will see. Color and black-and-white TV and video. (Nondrop- and drop-frame modes exist for the above frame rates and are used for special applications.)
25fps—PAL European video and TV standard.
24fps—Film productions.

[12]*Just thought I would mention it again. Very important!*

[13]*Most MIDI keyboard controllers do have on-board sound-generation capability.*

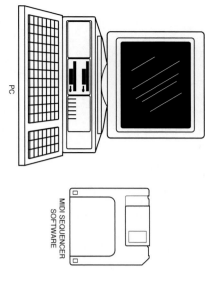

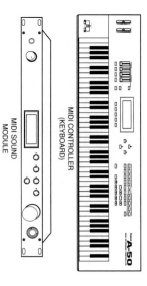

MIDI INTERFACE

PC

MIDI SEQUENCER SOFTWARE

MIDI CONTROLLER (KEYBOARD)

MIDI SOUND MODULE

Figure 10.9. *MIDI sound modules receive MIDI event data and then generate the instrument sounds you hear.*

to get exactly the sounds they want for their projects. For example, a drum machine is actually a specialized type of sound module that can be used with or without its own onboard sequencer. MIDI sound modules are available at a wide number of price points and offer a very diverse number of features, and they are discussed in greater detail in Chapter 11.

A Stereo Audio Mixer

An audio mixer (Figure 10.10) combines the sounds generated in the project studio into a stereo mix. You can then record and/or listen to this mix using standard stereo audio hardware. You can also use the mixer to control special effects such as reverb, echo, chorusing, and EQ changes that may be added to the MIDI-generated or live acoustic sounds.

An Audio Monitoring System

But you still haven't made any sound! To actually make sound, you must amplify the audio signal provided by the mixer to create an electronic signal strong enough to drive the monitor speakers and physically move the speaker components. Gee, I'm sure glad this is a lot easier to accomplish than it sounds.

There are two methods you can use to set up your audio monitoring system. Figure 10.11 illustrates the first method, which uses a separate stereo power amp and two monitor speakers. An easy way to install this system is to use your home stereo system components. Your home stereo system usually consists of either a preamplifier and a separate stereo power amplifier that powers two speakers, or a powered stereo receiver that powers two speakers. Connect the stereo outputs from the audio mixer to the auxiliary inputs on these units.

Warning: Keep in mind that some of the sounds generated by your MIDI system can create huge peaks in volume (this measure of volume is called *level*). These peaks can cause distortion and may even damage home stereo components, so be careful!

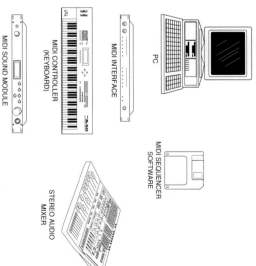

PC

MIDI INTERFACE

MIDI SEQUENCER SOFTWARE

MIDI CONTROLLER (KEYBOARD)

MIDI SOUND MODULE

STEREO AUDIO MIXER

Figure 10.10. *Synthesizers and sound modules can generate dozens of sounds in your project studio. An audio mixer enables you to combine these multiple sounds into an easily recordable and listenable format: stereo audio.*

Hmmm. Considering the warning just given, you might want to think about going another route and adding an audio monitoring system designed for project studio applications. You still use a stereo power amplifier to drive a pair of monitor speakers, but the components are more rugged and deliver performance more suited to the demanding needs of the project studio. These components can be purchased from a music store or pro audio retail store. Installing a system of this nature is the way I would elect to go. It's also the choice of most serious project studio musicians, producers, and engineers.

A good way to monitor your audio is by using a pair of powered monitor speakers. This method is very popular. Figure 10.12 shows how a pair of powered monitor speakers can replace the stereo power amplifier and two speakers in the block diagram.

These powered monitors have an amplifier built into each one, and they are easy to use because they require the fewest number of wiring connections. You simply connect the stereo outputs of the audio mixer to the inputs on the powered monitors, turn them on, and jam! You'll find the sound quality of some of these units to be very poor and the sound quality of others to be outstanding. Some of them sound so good that they're used for monitoring audio from video tape machines in professional video production operations.

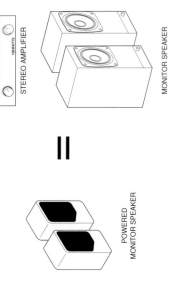

STEREO AMPLIFIER

MONITOR SPEAKER

=

POWERED
MONITOR SPEAKER

Figure 10.12. *A pair of powered monitor speakers can simplify your audio monitoring system*

Hooking It All Up

All of this neat hardwre and software does you no good unless it's connected…probably a good idea! This section is being applauded by music store MIDI specialists and manufacturers. They hope you will follow these directions carefully so that their equipment works as it was designed to do. Take your time; you won't regret it.

MIDI Cables and MIDI Connections

Figure 10.13 shows the components in your project studio being connected to create a MIDI system. Start by connecting the MIDI equipment using special MIDI cables. MIDI connections were introduced in Chapter 5; here you'll actually connect the MIDI components.

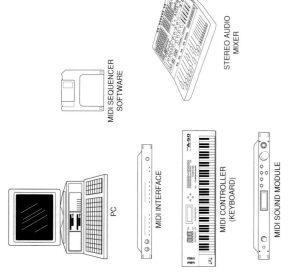

PC

MIDI INTERFACE

MIDI CONTROLLER
(KEYBOARD)

MIDI SOUND MODULE

MIDI SEQUENCER
SOFTWARE

STEREO AUDIO
MIXER

STEREO AMPLIFIER

MONITOR SPEAKER

Figure 10.11. *An amplifier and speakers do the final job of converting the little electrons running around in your project studio into sound waves, which you can hear.*

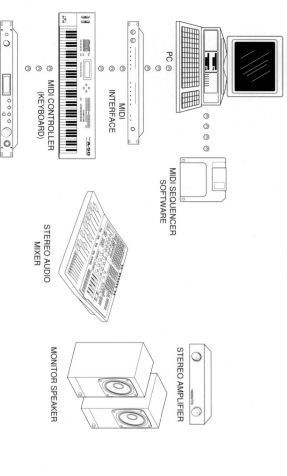

MIDI SOUND MODULE

MIDI CONTROLLER (KEYBOARD)

MIDI INTERFACE

PC

MIDI SEQUENCER SOFTWARE

STEREO AUDIO MIXER

MONITOR SPEAKER

STEREO AMPLIFIER

Figure 10.13. *MIDI cables are indicated by the "MIDI icon" lines. These connect to the five-pin jacks on MIDI devices.*

MIDI cables are special three-conductor cables that terminate with a male 5-pin DIN connector on each end. MIDI cables look much like microphone cables, except for the DIN connector.[14] Most people call this connector a *MIDI plug*.[15] These cables are available at your local music store in lengths of one to fifty feet. The computer musician uses MIDI cables to connect the various MIDI components in his MIDI project studio.

The 5-pin MIDI plug fits perfectly into the 5-hole female DIN receptacles on the back panels of the MIDI components. These female receptacles are called *MIDI jacks*.

Warning: *Do not force MIDI plugs and jacks together!* When I say these connectors fit perfectly, "perfectly" is a relative term. The MIDI plug is circular in shape, but the pin arrangement is not symmetrical.

---

[14] *In the early days of MIDI, we wondered why manufacturers didn't use standard mic cables for MIDI connections. We'd all resented the fact that we had to purchase these special DIN MIDI cables. Now MIDI musicians hardly think about it. It is interesting to me, though, that the more recently standardized transfer of sound file data between digital components such as digital workstations and DATs uses standard 3-pin mic cables for the AES/EBU connections. No editorial comment—just a fact you should know.*

As shown in Figure 10.14, the MIDI plug features a tab that must be aligned with a slot on the MIDI jack. Only when the tab and slot are perfectly in line can you connect the two.

This next part is a little crazy, so hang in there with me. There are three kinds of these female MIDI jacks; they all look the same, each serves a *completely* different function, and not all MIDI hardware features all three kinds of MIDI jacks. The three kinds of jacks are named MIDI OUT, MIDI IN, and MIDI THRU.

This next part is very important. Figures 10.15 and 10.16 illustrate how MIDI OUT, MIDI IN, and MIDI THRU jacks are connected.

In Figure 10.15, the MIDI OUT jack sends out MIDI event data from a device that generates it, such as a keyboard controller or a MIDI interface. A MIDI component *must* have a MIDI OUT jack to be able to send any MIDI event information. A MIDI OUT jack is always connected to a MIDI IN jack.

In Figure 10.16, the MIDI IN jack receives MIDI event data. A MIDI component *must* have a MIDI IN jack to be able to receive any MIDI event data. MIDI IN jacks are found on controllers that generate sounds, MIDI sound modules, MIDI interfaces, and other MIDI components you want

[15] *Superior grades of MIDI cables also use special low-capacitance, data-certified wire for the three conductors. Not all MIDI cables are created equal, so don't buy the cheapest ones you can find.*

Table 10.1. The steps for connecting MIDI hardware.

Step#	Component	Connection	Next Component	Connection
1	Controller	MIDI OUT	Interface	MIDI IN
2	Interface	MIDI OUT	Controller	MIDI IN[16]
3	Controller	MIDI THRU	Sound Module	MIDI IN

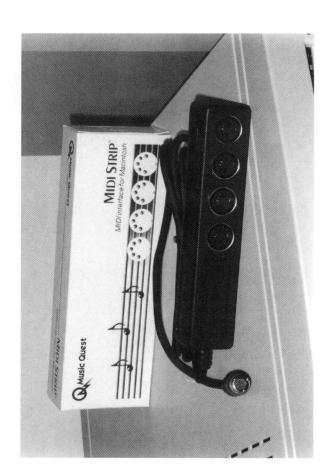

Figure 10.14. *A MIDI plug (left) and a MIDI jack (right). MIDI connectors are five-pin DIN connectors.*

[16]*The MIDI keyboard controller featured in this example also generates sound. This is the most common way MIDI systems are designed.*

MIDI OUT

Figure 10.15. *MIDI event data is transmitted through MIDI OUT jacks.*

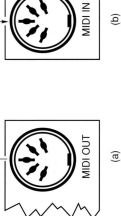

(a)   (b)

MIDI OUT   MIDI IN

Figure 10.16. *MIDI event data is transmitted through MIDI OUT jacks (a). MIDI event data is received through MIDI IN jacks (b).*

component's MIDI IN jack. This MIDI event data is sent to the MIDI IN on another MIDI component in your MIDI system. This enables you to daisy-chain MIDI components in your project studio. This is important if your MIDI interface has only one MIDI OUT. Without a MIDI THRU, you couldn't get the MIDI event data to all your MIDI components. Remember, a MIDI THRU jack is *always* connected to a MIDI IN jack on another MIDI component.

The connection of your MIDI hardware is somewhat dependent on what hardware you're connecting, but here are the steps based on the components in the block diagram.

to send MIDI information to. A MIDI IN jack is connected to a MIDI OUT or MIDI THRU jack on another MIDI component.

In Figure 10.17, the MIDI THRU jack *echoes* or *passes through* any MIDI event data received by a

When you look at it this way, you can make all the components "talk" to each other pretty easily. Chapter 11 explains how all those little electrons that make up the MIDI event data move through the MIDI system.

Audio Cables

To connect the audio connections in a project studio, a computer musician uses audio *patch cables*. Figure 10.18 shows where patch cables are used.

Audio patch cables usually terminate with a male connector on each end.[17] These are also called *plugs*. There are many different types of these male plugs. Figure 10.19 shows some commonly used male audio plugs.

These male plugs fit perfectly into female audio jacks on the back panels of the MIDI and audio components. Note how the male plugs in Figure 10.19 fit the corresponding female jacks in Figure 10.20.

Audio components in your project studio feature audio output jacks and audio input jacks. MIDI components feature audio output jacks only.[18] An audio output jack is *always* connected to an audio input jack on another component in your project

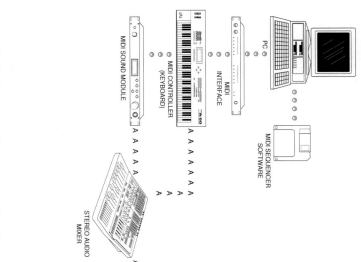

Figure 10.17. MIDI event data is sent from a MIDI OUT (a) on one device, such as a controller; to the MIDI IN (b) on another device, such as a sound module. The MIDI THRU (c) retransmits the MIDI event data to the MIDI IN jack (d) on another MIDI receiving device, such as another sound module or perhaps a drum machine.

(a)   MIDI OUT
(b)   MIDI IN
(c)   MIDI THRU
(d)   MIDI IN

PC

MIDI INTERFACE

MIDI SEQUENCER SOFTWARE

MIDI SOUND MODULE

MIDI CONTROLLER (KEYBOARD)

STEREO AUDIO MIXER

MONITOR SPEAKER

STEREO AMPLIFIER

Figure 10.18. *The audio patch cables connect the audio inputs and outputs in your MIDI project studio. These are represented by rows of the letter A, which stands for "audio."*

Figure 10.19. *Common male audio plugs.*

Figure 10.20. *Common female audio plugs.*

[17]*Readers who are experienced in the world of audio have to cut me a break here. I am trying to keep this basic for now.*

[18]*Except for some very exotic and specialized cases.*

studio, and an audio input jack is *always* connected to an audio output jack. You could think of it as shown in Figure 10.21.

Two different kinds of wire are used in audio cables: shielded and unshielded. Shielded cables are designed to reject external interference that might cause hums and buzzes in your audio monitoring system. Shielded cables must be used for all connections, except the connections from the stereo amplifier to the monitor speakers. These connections should use unshielded cables, which avoid power loss and heat build-up caused by capacitance.

How you connect the audio ins and outs of your components is greatly dependent on what hardware you're connecting. Here are the steps, again based on the components in the block diagram.

AUDIO OUTPUT JACK	AUDIO INPUT JACK
AUDIO OUTPUT JACK	AUDIO OUTPUT JACK
AUDIO INPUT JACK	AUDIO INPUT JACK

Figure 10.21. *The right plug in the right jack leads to great satisfaction; the wrong plug in the wrong jack can make for very bad times.*

Warning: If you break these simple rules, you may very well find yourself contributing your hard-earned cash to the repair department of your favorite music or audio store.

Cable Lengths and Audio Quality

Here is one of the most important of all rules for connecting any audio components in any application: Keeping all cable lengths as short as possible maximizes audio quality while minimizing potential audio problems.

Now, you *can* plug the power cords into the AC power outlets, but any MIDI or audio professional would recommend that you plug everything into a good surge protector or power line conditioner. Making this small investment now could save you hundreds of dollars in repair bills the next time the power company decides to turn your electricity off and on again. Or during the next thunderstorm. Or when your air conditioner turns off, or your sister's hair dryer. Trust me, I learned the hard way.

Moving On

Since you just can't wait to make MIDI noise…er…uh…music, let's get right into Chapter 11.

Table 10.2. Making proper connections in the MIDI project studio.

Step Number	Component	Audio Connection	Component	Audio Connection
1	MIDI Controller	Audio OUT[19]	Audio Mixer	Line IN
2	MIDI Sound Module	Audio OUT	Audio Mixer	Line IN
3	Audio Mixer	Master OUT	Stereo Amplifier	Line IN
4	Stereo Amplifier	Speaker Outputs	Monitor Speaker	Input

[19]*Please understand that most modern MIDI and audio components have two OUTs per unit—in other words, stereo outputs. These are often labeled LEFT OUT and RIGHT OUT, OUT L and OUT R, or OUT A and OUT B. Also, a component may feature stereo inputs. These might be labeled LEFT IN and RIGHT IN, IN L and IN R, or IN A and IN B.*

11

Wow, Is MIDI Black Magic? Or, How Does It All Work?

For this chapter you will need the following:

♪ The information you learned in the previous chapters (no hardware is necessary)

I love my job!

Sometimes it all seems like magic. A bit like the alchemist in the king's court who worked at turning lead into gold, the computer musician uses this collection of wire, plastic, and metal to convert the power of moving electrons into the power of the musical sound wave. This chapter explores how these devices do their job of helping you turn a musical idea into a musical sound wave.

This chapter runs very much parallel to Chapter 10, "MIDI In-Out-Thru: The MIDI Project Studio," and it more fully explains each of the elements introduced to you in building the block diagram of the MIDI project studio.

The MIDI Controller Generates MIDI Event Data

Many types of MIDI controllers are used in MIDI project studios. So far, this book has primarily discussed the keyboard controller, but the following is a fairly complete list of the types available:

Keyboard controllers

Percussion and drum pad controllers

Wind instrument controllers (brass and woodwind)

Guitar controllers

Orchestral string instrument controllers (violin, viola, cello, bass)

As you can see, a controller instrument is available for nearly any acoustic instrument you play. Figure 11.1 shows one interesting controller.[1]

The controller serves as the primary user interface to the MIDI system. The function of the controller is to generate MIDI data that other MIDI-compatible devices can receive, record, process, and redistribute to other MIDI-compatible devices that can receive and process MIDI data.

Officially, these MIDI data are called *MIDI events*.

Viewing MIDI Event Data in an Event Window

The MIDI event window in Figure 11.2 (from a flute track recorded in Cakewalk Professional for Windows) lists MIDI events that have been recorded. Column 6 lists the names for the MIDI events. Note refers to a Note On event; Control refers to a MIDI controller event. The controller events listed in this window represent Breath Control, MIDI controller 2, listed just to the right of the Control abbreviation.

I find the MIDI event window to be one of the most useful features of any sequencing software because it is the window that displays *every* MIDI event that is recorded during a MIDI recording session. I often base my opinion of a sequencer on the ease of working with the individual MIDI events in this window. One important feature enables you to filter the events you are viewing, so you view only the one or two types of event you need to work with at any one moment. You should also be able to click-and-drag edit these events, and you must be able to insert and delete events at any measure and beat you want. Chapters 12 and 13 study this in detail.

Table 11.1 gives a list of MIDI events that are commonly used by the computer musician.

Table 11.1. The most commonly used MIDI events and what they do in a MIDI system.

MIDI Event	Function
Note On	Tells a synthesizer to "turn on" or Start generating a specific note
Note Off	Tells a synthesizer to "turn off" or Stop generating a specific note
Velocity	Tells a synthesizer how hard a note is played or struck (or released), which can affect the loudness or other character of the synthesizer sound

[1] *In the Chapter 5 interview with drummer/percussionist Kenny Aronoff, you learned ways drummers can benefit from using drum and percussion-pad controllers to record their MIDI performances into sequencing software. I have often used a Yamaha WX-7 wind controller to create very interesting synthesizer sounds, even when I am not emulating an acoustic woodwind sound.*

MIDI Event	Function
Program Change	Tells a synthesizer which patch or instrument to use when generating sound
Pitch Bend	Tells a synthesizer to smoothly and continuously raise or lower the pitch of a note

I highly recommend that any controller you use should be able to generate *at least* the events listed in Table 11.1. Beware! Not all controllers on the market do. And the more serious you are about MIDI recording, the more you will want your controller to generate the events listed in Table 11.2.

MIDI Controller Events

The MIDI events in Table 11.2 are called control-ler events.[2] These are MIDI events that can be used to control special functions called Parameters on your synthesizers, depending on how the synthesizer receiving this event is configured. Controller events are represented by values of 0-127,[3] with the larger number creating more of the desired effect.

MIDI controller events are assigned Controller Numbers in MIDI Spec 1.0.

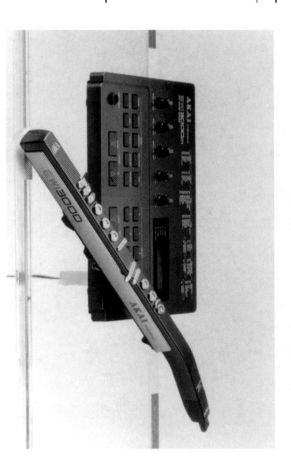

Figure 11.1. The Akai EWI3000 wind controller enables acoustic wind instrument players to enter the world of MIDI and computer-assisted music. Photo provided by AKAI Professional.

[2] I hope you do not confuse the use of this term with the term MIDI controller, which has been used to describe controller instruments. The MIDI industry uses this word to describe both the controller instrument generating MIDI event data and certain types of MIDI event data. Read carefully.

[3] Some instruments and software use values of 1-128.

The computer musician changes how a receiving synthesizer responds to these controllers by assigning the Controller Number to a certain parameter on the synthesizer. For example:

1. I want controller #2, Breath Control, on an Akai EWI3000 wind control instrument to control the volume of a flute patch on a Kurzweil K2000 synthesizer. That way, when I blow harder into the EWI, the flute will sound louder. Kind of like a real flute, huh?

2. I assign the "volume" parameter on my K2000 synthesizer to respond to MIDI events sent from controller #2 on an Akai EWI Wind controller instrument.

3. When I blow softly into the EWI, the value of controller #2 will be about 45. Figure 11.2 shows what this MIDI event looks like at the start of measure 1 of the MIDI event window from Cakewalk. This is the controller event at measure 1:1:004.

4. When I blow harder, as in measure 2, breath control might increase to 90; if I blow very hard, as in measure 3, the value might go to 127, which is the highest level permitted by MIDI. Controller values above 127 cannot be transmitted, recorded, or received by MIDI.

5. The K2000 receives this breath control information and increases or decreases the volume of the flute sound in response to the increasing or decreasing breath control values.

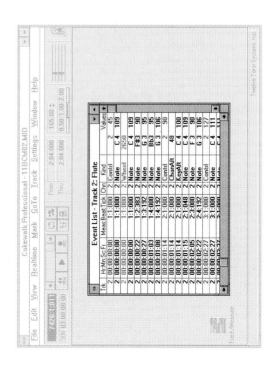

Figure 11.2. *A MIDI event window from Cakewalk Professional.*

Table 11.2. Commonly used MIDI controller events, with Controller Numbers and their standard functions.

MIDI Event	Controller	Function Number
Mod(ulation) Wheel	1	Usually used to add vibrato to a sound
Breath Control	2	Usually used to add performance control to synthesized acoustic wind instrument sounds
Data Entry	6	Depends completely on how the synthesizer is configured
Volume	7	Controls the volume level of an instrument
Panning	10	Moves sound to and from the left and right outputs of a stereo synthesizer
After Touch	None	Can control volume, brightness, envelopes, vibrato, and so on
Sustain Pedal	64	Turns the sustain pedal on-off, as on an acoustic piano damper pedal

Many other controller numbers can be defined by the user. This enables you to use your sequencer to record controller events which control real-time changes such as brightness, panning, volume, reverb decay time, number of echo repeats on a digital delay unit, and many, many other potentially exciting parameters. These capabilities have become so vast that many sequencers provide a user-definable "mixer" window, where the user can assign controllers to control the synthesizer sounds while MIDI recording takes place, or MIDI controller information can be recorded and edited on separate tracks later. Recording engineers and musicians call this later recording "recording another pass."

All of these controller events can be edited in a properly designed sequencer event window. Chapters 12 and 13 teach you how to use this capability.

> **Note:** These types of controller events are often called *continuous controllers* and can require large amounts of memory. They can even clog up the MIDI stream, causing lock-ups, stuck notes, and other problems. Still, they are very helpful if used properly.

Generating MIDI Events with a Controller

Figure 11.3 shows the top-view drawing of a Roland A-50 keyboard controller. Take a minute to study the layout of the controller wheels and sliders.

Some MIDI events are generated simply by playing the controller instrument. The most common example uses a keyboard controller. You generate a Note On event when you strike a key. You generate a Note Off event when you release the key. The velocity of the key attack and the key release are automatically generated when you perform these actions. Another example. A properly configured wind controller would automatically generate breath control. That is one of the main ideas in using a wind controller.

Other control events are generated only when you perform some special action on your controller instrument. No pitch bend events will be generated until you move the pitch bend wheel on your controller up or down. And MIDI controller #7, volume, doesn't change until you move a slider or wheel on your controller to start the event generation.

String, guitar, wind, and even some percussion controllers provide wheels, sliders, and buttons used for generating MIDI controller data. This creative control of the sound synthesizer is one reason so many acoustic instrument performers are using a MIDI version of their instrument today.

MIDI Timing Clocks: Staying in Sync

Just as a symphony has a conductor who keeps all the players performing in perfect time, a sequencer has a "conductor," too.[4] We call this conductor the sync *clock*. When you run a sequencer, the timing of all of the MIDI events is controlled by this sync clock, and all of the timing information is generated within the software. This information is generated on *internal sync* or *internal clock*. The rate (speed) of this internal clock is controlled by the tempo you select when setting up the sequencing software. Chapters 2 and 3 taught how to do this.

Some computer musicians run basic MIDI setups where they use only a single sequencer, and maybe a sound synthesizer or two. They always use internal clock, but many become interested in simultaneously running an additional MIDI sequencer or perhaps an external drum machine. A major problem immediately arises:

> ♪ Each MIDI sequencer or drum machine has its *own* internal clock running at its *own* rate (speed). These multiple clock rates will not match perfectly.

> ♪ No matter how quick your reflexes are, it is *impossible* to put more than one unit in play at exactly the same fraction of a second.

[4]*This discussion about sequencer clocks and timing holds true for sequencers built into keyboards, external stand-alone sequencers, and drum machines, as well. These devices all follow the same timing clock rules.*

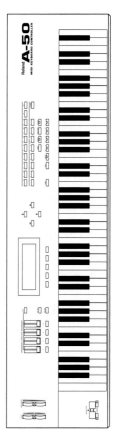

Figure 11.3. *The Roland A-50 provides many features common to good keyboard controllers. Note the pitch bend and modulation wheels in the upper-left corner, and the set of four controller sliders to the left of the LCD display. The user can program these four sliders to generate controller events such as those listed in Table 11.2.*

The result is similar to the performance you see in a three-legged race at a picnic. The two racers don't start exactly together and aren't able to go at the same speed, and thus the whole situation becomes humorous very fast. But if we are trying to make music, our idea of fun is a more efficient system that enables us to concentrate on composing—not on making the hardware work.

The inventors of MIDI designed a very effective solution to this timing problem. A MIDI Beat Clock (MIDI Clock) built into the MIDI data stream provides sync reference between multiple MIDI devices. Here is how it works:

Step 1. You determine which sequencer or drum machine will serve as the Master for your MIDI system. Sequencer or drum machine software enables you to select Internal Clock (or Sync) or External Clock

(or Sync) in a menu or window.[5] Be sure that you select Internal Clock or Internal Sync. This Master generates MIDI Clock and a MIDI Start command whenever it is put into Play or Record.[6]

Step 2. This MIDI clock is sent to the MIDI OUT port on a MIDI interface[7] and then distributed throughout the MIDI system.

Step 3. Other sequencers and drum machines in your MIDI system serve as Slaves. Be sure that you select External Clock, MIDI Clock, or External Sync for these units. This enables the Slave devices to follow the MIDI Clock generated by the Master.

Step 4. When the Master is put into Play or Record, the Slaves receive the MIDI Start command and follow the Master in perfect sync.

Figure 11.4 illustrates how this setup is configured. Study this figure and then reread Steps 1, 2, 3, and 4 until you thoroughly understand this subject. This has been an area of great confusion to many computer musicians, and I think this little procedure straightens the problem out clearly.

Most of the software we use for the tutorials in this book allow Internal or External Sync. Table 11.3 shows where you select these options:

[5] *Sorry. I can tell you where to select these options in all of the software included with this book, but you'll need to check your owner's manuals to find out how your specific setup works.*

[6] *In some cases you may need to access a Send Sync (Clock) window and set up your Master to send MIDI Clock.*

[7] *This assumes you are using the computer sequencer as Master.*

Synchronizing Multiple MIDI Devices

Figure 11.4. *The Master-Slave setup for using MIDI Clock to synchronize multiple sequencers and drum machines. Illustration by Mark Evans, Bowen Music Productions.*

Table 11.3. Selecting the sync options for software used in *Becoming a Computer Musician.*

Software Title	To Be Found
WinSong	Under the Controls menu
DeluxeMusic	Internal Sync Only (designed to be used as a Master)
Midisoft Studio	In Preferences under the Setup menu
Musicshop	External Sync under the Setups menu
Cakewalk	In Clock under the Settings menu
Vision	In Receive Sync mode under the Options menu

More about MIDI Interfaces

Chapters 6 and 8 studied MIDI interfaces briefly and explained them in enough detail that you could get started with most MIDI recording sessions. Additional capabilities provided by some MIDI interfaces are useful to a computer musician working with more complex projects.

> **Note:** If you didn't read the sections under the heading "The MIDI Interface" in Chapters 6 (PC) and 8 (Mac), you must read them now. You need to know information from those sections to understand the following discussion.

SMPTE and MIDI Time Code

Some projects require the computer sequencer to run in sync with live instrument and voice tracks that have been recorded onto tape machines. Or

perhaps you are syncing the computer to video or film. In these situations SMPTE time code[8] is recorded on and played back from a track on a video or audio tape machine. These are situations where the MIDI interface is called to perform the synchronization work. Many moderately priced ($200 and up) MIDI interfaces now feature built-in SMPTE time code generator/readers and will convert SMPTE to the MIDI time code or MIDI Beat Clock required for syncing MIDI software to tape machines. This procedure is described in great detail in Chapter 14 in the section titled "Using SMPTE and MIDI Time Code for Sync."

Expanded Multiport Capabilities

Sometimes 32 channels of MIDI is just not enough. Well, it usually is, but if you had *dozens* of MIDI channels you could have an interesting arrangement; almost every synthesizer receiving MIDI in your studio would have its own dedicated set of 16 MIDI channels. One multiport interface is Mark of the Unicorn's MIDI Express (Figure 11.5).

Setting up a properly functioning multiport system requires good planning and careful design. I recommend scheduling an appointment with a knowledgeable sales person or MIDI consultant before making your purchase. You will very likely need help configuring your system, and having a local contact could be useful.

[8] *SMPTE time code is introduced in Chapter 1.*

Figure 11.5. *This illustration of the rear panel of a MIDI Express PC multiport interface shows the multiple MIDI IN and MIDI OUT ports. Each MIDI input could be connected to a different controller. You could then select which controller you would use for a specific MIDI recording session, or even play multiple controllers at once. The six outputs allow 6×16-96 channels of MIDI. Also note the SMPTE time code IN and OUT jacks.*

MIDI Synthesizers

There may be one in the sound card inside your computer.

You might have one built into your keyboard controller.

One might be inside the sound module sitting beside your computer.

You might have a number of them mounted in 19-inch racks.

When you use your phone card, one says, "Thank You."

They are sound *synthesizers.*[9]

Many of you will recall the maze of wires once used by synthesizer players to create their elaborate sounds. The synthesizers in those early days were *modular;* they actually consisted of pieces of hardware called *modules.* These modules were linked together with patch cables, and they interacted to create the sounds designed by the synthesist.

We got away from all that spaghetti when synthesizers became chip- and software-based instead of hardware-based. Now, software built into the

synthesizer can be used to program[10] all the functions once requiring modules and patch cables.[11]

Some features of contemporary synthesizers are the following:

1. Varying numbers of on-board sounds, programs, or patches. This can be any number from four to a couple of hundred. 64 and 128 are typical numbers.

2. Varying polyphony.[12] *Polyphony* is the number of notes the sound synthesizer can play at any one instant. A 32-voice synthesizer can play many more notes at one time than an 8-voice synthesizer.

3. Varying MIDI reception capabilities. Some MIDI synthesizers support General MIDI[13], but others do not address that specific MIDI configuration. A few synthesizers permit the

use of only one MIDI channel and one sound or Timbre at a time. Multitimbral synthesizers receive MIDI event data on more than one MIDI channel, enabling you to use up to 16 different sounds at a time.

4. Some synthesizers generate only a single, certain kind of sound. An FM synthesizer may generate only FM synthesized sounds, some synthesizers might generate only analog sounds, and some wave table synthesizers might contain no analog sounds at all.

5. Varying degrees of patch editing and programmability. Some GM synths allow practically no editing, while other GM synths let you completely reprogram or customize the factory sounds.

6. And as mentioned at the start of the chapter, synthesizers come in a wide variety of hardware configurations.

Requirements of a Synthesizer for the MIDI Project Studio

Even if you are using a very basic computer-assisted music set-up, you must have some kind of sound synthesizer. Otherwise, you won't have any sound at all. And for a synthesizer to be useful, it must have certain features:

---

[9]*Earlier chapters determined that for the purposes of this book, MIDI devices that generate sound are called synthesizers.*

[10]*Many manufacturers use the word* patch, *but some use the word* program. *The two terms are usually interchangeable.*

[11]*Those guys at Sequential are again credited with the first popular programmable synthesizer, the Prophet 5.*

[12]*The concept of polyphony is introduced in Chapter 4.*

[13]*General MIDI (GM) is explained in Chapter 5. Midisoft Studio for Windows and Musicshop GM sequencer configurations are implemented in the tutorials in Chapters 6, 7, 8, and 9.*

A MIDI IN port. This is so the synthesizer can receive MIDI event data.

At least one audio output. A stereo output with two jacks would be better. Everyone prefers stereo sound.

A multitimbral synthesizer. Few musicians are happy generating only one sound at a time anymore.

A MIDI THRU jack is important if you plan to add more than one synthesizer to your MIDI system. MIDI THRU enables the daisy-chaining of MIDI devices. These connections are explained in Chapter 10.

Types of Synthesizers

The number of technologies used to synthesize sound changes too often to keep comprehensive track of at any one point in time. We can, however, discuss the more popular or more useful synthesis methods—those synthesizers that interface with your computer gracefully through the use of MIDI. These can be organized into some broad categories:[14]

Analog Synthesis
FM Synthesis
Wavetable Synthesis
L/A Synthesis
Sampling Synthesis

Analog Synthesis

It's a little like playing with a leather basketball. Sure, a synthetic basketball is easier to find for sale, works well in a greater number of playing environments, is less expensive, and is easier to maintain than a leather ball. But when you are on a real hardwood court, no synthetic ball has the textural feel or flexibility in handling that leather offers. If you want a synthesized (and I really mean synthesized, as in created from scratch) sound, analog synthesizers often still cannot be beat. That is why most serious computer musicians have at least one analog synth around.[15]

The basic building block of analog synthesis is the VCO, or Voltage Controlled Oscillator. Increasing the number of VCOs in use results in the generation of richer sounds.

FM Synthesis

FM synthesis actually had its roots with Dr. John Chowning at Stanford University back in the late '60s. Yamaha catapulted FM synthesis into the limelight with production of the DX-7 synthesizer, considered to be the most commercially successful synthesizer in history. FM synthesis does a great job of generating bright, chimey sounds and sounds with a gritty edge, but it falls a good bit short on simulating acoustic instruments or in generating nice, soft ethereal "New Agey" pads.

An inexpensive form of FM synthesis is commonly used in sound card synthesizers. The terms OPL or FM on the outside of the box tell you that FM synthesis is used on the card. This level of FM synthesis is fine for game, educational, and hobby applications, but don't expect the acoustic instruments to sound realistic.

The basic building block of the FM synth is the digitally controlled Operator. The more Operators that are in use, the richer the synthesized sound can be.

Wavetable Synthesis

This is the happening synthesizer these days. The majority of the popular synths on the market use wavetable collections of factory-recorded and -processed digital samples as the building blocks for sound synthesis. Because this form of synthesis begins with a digital recording (sample) of an acoustic instrument, wavetable synthesis can produce startling acoustic instrument sounds.

Samples of analog and FM instruments are often included in the wavetable, which means that a wavetable synthesizer is your best choice for a do-it-all, all-round multipurpose instrument. For example, E-mu Systems takes great pride in the performance of its Vintage Keys wavetable sound

---

[14]Okay, Okay. You guys who are pros have to give me a break here. You know it is actually impossible to cover every kind of synthesis in a 400-page book. Synthesist Larry Fast could write a 400-page book about Moog synths alone! I'm just trying to help the reader get started, and the synthesis designs I discuss here the ones the reader is most likely to use. Okay? Thanks. By the way, there is a really nice article about physical modeling synthesis in the February 1994 issue of Keyboard magazine.

[15]I keep a Roland MKS-80 Super Jupiter around for mine. This unit cost me about $3000(!) and features a very unglamorous 8-note polyphony with a maximum of one or two timbres at a time—but when you want the bottoms of the seats in a big theater to shake, it is a tough animal to beat.

Watch for this high-quality form of synthesis to appear soon on Media Vision PC soundcards.

module, which specializes exclusively in recreating classic, old analog sounds. A scan through the menu is like a tour through an electronic music wax museum. ARP, Moog, Sequential, OBX, Jupiter....

The basic building block of wavetable synthesis is the digitized sound file. These sound files are simply combined in layers, and various filter and envelope functions are applied to create complex, interesting sounds.

L/A Synthesis

L/A Synthesis played a huge part in ushering in the New Age music genre, as it was the featured form of synthesis on the Roland D-50 L/A synthesizer. Many products in the Roland line still are based on this successful kind of synthesizer, and in fact other types of synthesizers often try to emulate the D-50 sounds.

A wavetable provides the building blocks for L/A synthesis. This wavetable features digitized sound files, as in other wavetable synthesis, but here the waveforms are broken into little segments such as attacks, sustain segments, and decays. This enables the user to create interesting combinations such as a flute attack with an analog synth middle and a brass release...all of which can then be saved as one "new" waveform. Very powerful creative opportunities here.

Sampling Synthesis

Properly used, digital sampling produces the most accurate electronic versions of natural acoustic instruments and sound effects. Information provided in Chapter 4 explained the process, requirements, and pros and cons of using various digital sampling techniques. The focus here is on musical applications.

Sampling synthesis is actually wavetable synthesis, but with a huge difference—the user invents the wavetable! In other words, the user "samples" or digitally records the actual sounds of his or her choice, stores them in RAM memory (which is built into the synthesizer), and then processes them to create exactly the sound needed for a specific use. For example, you might want to sample the sound of a trash can lid being hit by a rock, such as drummer Kenny Aronoff alludes to in his Chapter 5 interview. This sample is then programmed to respond to specific Note On and Note Off commands from a MIDI controller, and to other MIDI control data as well. The sound of the sample can now be played back with various pitches, and a musical phrase using that sample can be created. One pitch is turned into many. This is the technique used to build many popular wavetable drum kits. Only one tom-tom might be sampled, but then it is assigned to several keys so as to create the sound of several toms with different pitches. This prevents having to sample lots of different toms at different pitches, which saves production time and memory in the sampler. Data for these edited sounds can then be saved to floppy disks or to hard drives and can be transferred to other samplers or recalled for additional editing at any time in the future.

Some keyboard synthesizers have sampling capabilities built right in. Some samplers are MIDI sound modules that fit into the 19-inch racks described earlier in this chapter. Figure 11.6a shows the Kurzweil K2000S, which is a professional-level MIDI controller, wavetable synthesizer, and sampler—all in one package. Figure 11.6b shows the Akai S3000 sampler module, which provides powerful digital sampling in a compact MIDI sound module that can be mounted in a 19-inch rack.

Many levels of technical specifications and features are available in samplers. Your choice depends on your needs, your taste, and your budget. Be sure to keep two things in mind when selecting a sampling synthesizer:

1. How much RAM memory is built in, and how expandable is it? In Chapter 4, you learned that a stereo CD-quality sample requires 10MB of RAM per minute. Even a five-second cymbal roll will require almost 1MB of memory. So you can see how a sampler should have at least 4MB-8MB of memory if you plan to do much high-quality sampling.

2. How do you save? You can save a lot of samples to floppies, and there are even some really good reasons to do so (backup... backup), but if you are going to be a sampling fool you ought to save to a hard drive. Some samplers have a hard drive built in and some provide a SCSI connector, which enables you to use a drive made by a third party. The manufacturer of your sampler will provide a list of drives that are compatible

with your unit. Listen to them—they want your sampler to work well for you.

Adding a MIDI Sound Module

Okay, so now you have a fast computer online with a nice new dual port interface, a keyboard controller with built-in synthesizer featuring 8MB of wavetable sounds, a nifty 8-channel mixer, an amp, and a pair of speakers that part your hair. Ready, set, go.

Tic-toc-tic-toc....

Four weeks later you think to yourself, "Okay, I've been through all 8MB of the wavetable sounds, and I've even edited some of those to get them closer to what I need. But why didn't they include a decent piano in this 8MB!?!"

Synthesizer manufacturers face a constant juggling act in trying to design synthesizers with a good balance of the following:

- The number of user operable features
- Good audio specs—that is, low noise, wide bandwidth
- The amount of available ROM for wavetable storage
- The amount of RAM for waveform sounds in use
- The number of keys (believe it or not)
- Chassis construction and durability
- Sound-editing flexibility
- Cost to manufacture
- Selling price to the customer

Every synthesizer that comes to market has a slightly imperfect balance of these elements. It is impossible to get every feature you want on a synthesizer at exactly the price you want to pay. So in the end, you select the best base package that will service 90 percent or so of your day-to-day computer music needs.

But about that piano sound that you were looking for earlier: You have a solution. Add a MIDI sound module.

A MIDI sound module is a synthesizer in a box, with no controller built in. Figure 11.7 shows the Kurzweil MicroPiano MIDI sound module. An external MIDI sound module such as a Kurzweil MicroPiano can fill in the gaps in your synthesizer sound palette by supplying sounds your synthesizer generates poorly or not at all. Adding an external sound module also increases the polyphony of your MIDI system, which prevents voice stealing.[16]

Figure 11.6 *Keyboard synthesizers may have a digital sampler section built in, as in the case of the Kurzweil 2000S (a). In some cases you might want your sampler to be a MIDI module or "rack mount" version, such as the Akai S3000 (b).*

a

b

MIDI sound modules are popular for use in educational and hobby applications because of the following:

- You can use the computer, interface, software, and a sound module to create music very inexpensively.

- This setup doesn't require much space.

- Most low-cost keyboard synthesizers provide a very poor acoustic piano sound. The piano is the most important instrument for these particular applications, and you can add a sound module with very good piano sounds relatively inexpensively.

- Adding external sound modules enables a hobbyist to build a MIDI project studio bit by bit, instead of shelling out a big chunk of cash all at one time.

---

[16]Voice stealing occurs when more Note-on events exist than are provided for by the polyphony of a synthesizer. Notes begin to drop out or not play, leaving "holes" in the music.

synthesizer patches and configurations in a type of MIDI data called Systems Exclusive or Sys Ex. Sys Ex data can be recorded by any MIDI sequencer and stored with a sequence to floppy or hard disks.

To reload your synth sounds, you enable your synth to receive a Sys Ex file and then play back the sequencer track containing the MIDI data that you saved. This method of storing your sound data does not help you edit, however. The sound still must be programmed on the synthesizer panel, sometimes working through layer after layer of multitasking buttons. Mark of the Unicorn and Opcode have written software to help you design and manage your sound library in a tidy, efficient manner. Figure 11.8 shows a screen from Unisyn.

Figure 11.7. *Not only does the MicroPiano provide those famous Kurzweil Grand Piano sounds, but it also features string, organ, and electric piano sounds, as well as digital reverb and chorus. Photo by Kurzweil Music Systems.*

MIDI enables you to control multiple synthesizers from one controller and/or one computer. There is no longer a need for a keyboard to be built into every synthesizer. You will find many sound modules present in any professional MIDI studio environment. Here are some reasons:

A collection of sound modules enables the musician to have exactly the sounds she/he wants or needs for music production.

A module version of a synthesizer usually costs a little less than a keyboard version. Using fewer keyboards saves space.

A professional can add and delete modules from the MIDI system so as to keep pace with obsoletion and new developments in the electronic music industry.

Some musicians mount their synthesizers in standard 19-inch portable racks. This enables them to easily move their

synthesizers from studio to studio or from home to studio. Often an audio mixer is mounted right in the racks, which enables the musician to leave all MIDI and audio cables connected. Try this with 20 keyboard instruments!

And sound modules are available featuring all of the types of synthesis discussed earlier in this chapter. Analog, FM, wavetable, L/A...you make the choice!

Managing Synthesizer Sounds and Setups: Sys Ex

As synthesizers have become more and more complicated, programming and archiving all of these different kinds of sounds can be very difficult. The forefathers of MIDI took care of this problem upfront, also. Many synthesizers enable you to do a Sys Ex *dump*, which saves your

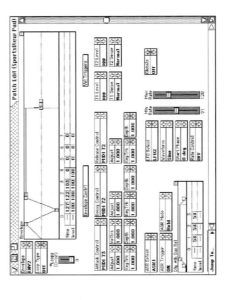

Figure 11.8. *Patch editor/librarians such as Unisyn (Mark of the Unicorn) and Galaxy Plus (Opcode) provide a handy user interface that enables you to program and catalogue your synth sounds. A screen from Unisyn is shown here.*

These editor/librarians enable you to load templates that emulate the controls found on the front panels of a number of synthesizer models, and often show several layers of controls simultaneously. You can then program your sound with this software, using A-B comparisons to see how the last change affected it, and then save your custom patches to floppy or hard disk. Much cheaper than using those little RAM and ROM cards or cartridges.

The Audio Monitoring System

A quick review of Chapter 10 will remind you that all this MIDI stuff is great, but if you don't use some kind of audio monitoring system, you still will not hear any sound. The essential elements for any audio monitoring system are the following:

Amplification
A Speaker System

Note: Manufacturers persist in having no standard system for labeling the inputs and outputs on their stereo audio hardware. After years of watching my guitar students wrestle with this problem, I came up with this little chart that might help you get the right plugs in the right jacks. The vertical rows list different names for exactly the same connector function. Thus, "Left Out" on one device is the same output connection as "Out A" on another device, and "In L" is the same input as "Input 1" on another stereo audio device:

Names for Device Outputs	Names for Device Inputs
Left Out and Right Out	Left In and Right In
Out L and Out R	In L and In R
Out A and Out B	In A and In B
Output 1 and Output 2	Input 1 and In-put 2

The most basic monitoring system uses a set of headphones plugged into the headphone jack located in the back of a sound card or other synthesizer. The sound card or synth provides an internal amplifier, and the headphones are the speaker system. This is not only the most basic system, but often is the best one to use. Headphone monitoring enables you to perform without disturbing others in your environment and without them disturbing you. I highly recommend that you purchase a really good set of headphones, even if you plan to install a more elaborate monitoring system.

Some sound cards provide a speaker-level output (see Chapter 4), which usually drives an inexpensive pair of unpowered "multimedia" speakers. I find that the performance of these speakers might be suitable for playing back a CD-ROM encyclopedia or computer game, but very few of these speaker systems can handle more than very basic music projects. Another basic (yet very good) way

Warning: Do not...do not...do not...plug the speaker level output from a sound card into the input jacks on a pair of powered monitors. This will almost always cause severe distortion and possibly will damage the speakers as well.

to monitor your computer music productions is by using a pair of powered monitor speakers. Figure 11.9 shows a pair of Audio Technica MMS 557 multimedia speakers.

I like these. The MMS 557 speakers feature a solid-sounding, two-way, bass reflex design powered by 20 watts of very clean power. The well-built enclosures have a durable platinum finish (à la Macintosh) and angled stands that tilt the sound projection toward the listener. They might not have the thunder that studio monitors can deliver, but I use a pair of these with a Mac, a Kurzweil 2000, and a MIDI Strip for demonstrations and have found them to work very well. Fostex and JBL also make some nice powered speaker systems, although at a slightly higher price.

Adding an Audio Mixer

If you have more than two audio outputs (stereo) from your synthesizers, you will have to add a stereo audio mixer to the system. After you have used a mixer a bit, you'll wonder how you ever did without one. There are certain features I think you should have on any mixer you purchase. You should be able to find a semipro-level mixer for

$400 and up. The better the quality and the features, the higher the price. Some good names to know in the small mixer business are Mackie, Fostex, Peavey, Yamaha, Tascom, and ART. I have selected the Samson 2242 mixer in Figure 11.10 as a good example of a mixer that has features useful to a small-to-midsized MIDI project studio.

A) The Input Module (from top to bottom):

1. *Input Trim or Gain control*—Enables the user to adjust the level of the signal coming into the mixer so as to prevent clipping distortion while maximizing the signal-to-noise ratio.

2. *"EQ" or Equalizer section*—Called "highs and lows" by some musicians, these controls are the high-tech equivalent of super-tone controls. Simple mixers might have one or two "bands" of EQ; a better mixer will have three or four. Some EQ sections have selectable band centers and are called *quasiparametric or sweepable.* This kind of EQ gives you maximum control over the tonal character of your instruments.

3. *Auxiliary Sends*—Enable you to send the sound of an instrument on this particular channel to an outboard effects device such as a reverb unit. The more "aux" sends you have, the more control you have over sending sounds from different channels to different independent effects devices.

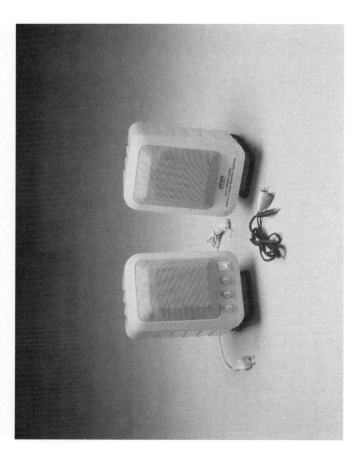

Figure 11.9. A pair of powered monitors, such as the MMS 557 speakers by Audio Technica ($149.95), makes a nice, easy solution for monitoring computer music productions that have been mixed in stereo. The MMS 557 is also magnetically shielded, which prevents interference with your computer and video monitors. Photo supplied by Audio Technica US, Incorporated.

4. *Pan*—Called *Balance* on the 2242 mixer. To put it perhaps a bit too simply, the pan control enables you to position the sound on this channel in the left or right speakers.

5. *Assignment Switches*—A mixer is called a *something-by-something* mixer, such as an 8-by-2 mixer or a 24-by-4 mixer. The first part of the phrase refers to how many input channels are on the mixer; the second part refers to how many Submix or "Sub" outputs are available. Thus, an 8-by-2 mixer has 8 inputs and 2 outputs. A two-output mixer is a stereo mixer. A 24-by-4 mixer features 24 input channels and 4 submix outputs. A mixer with 4 or more subs is useful for multitrack recording.[17]

6. *PFL*—Pre-Fade Listen or Solo. Pushing this button lets you hear only the instrument plugged into this mixer channel. Releasing this button lets you hear your entire mix again.

7. *Fader*—Controls the volume of this channel.

[17]See Chapter 14 for more information about recording live and acoustic instruments.

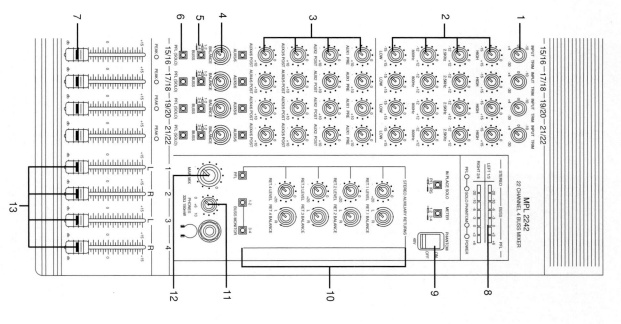

Figure 11.10. The Samson 2242 mixer is an example of a mixer with many features the computer musician will find essential or useful—in the studio, in the home, or rack-mounted for live performance. Illustration courtesy of Samson Technologies Corporation.

B) The Master Module or Section:

8. *Meters*—Meters help visually monitor the volume levels of the outputs.

9. *Phantom Power*—Provides power to remote-power equipped condenser microphones, which eliminates microphone batteries.

10. *Auxiliary or Effect Return Section*—Also called Aux returns. Controls the level of outboard effects returning to the mixer and routes these effects to the stereo mix. Works in conjunction with the Aux Send. A pan control is often present here, which enables you to keep the two returns from stereo effects "split" into left-right stereo.

11. *Headphone Level*—A must-have! This controls the volume level to the headphones recommended earlier in this chapter. You'll use this feature often.

12. *Master, Main, or Stereo Mix Controls*—Sometimes a pair of faders, sometimes a knob. On the 2242 mixer this is a knob. On basic mixers, this sends the stereo mix to a cassette recorder or DAT (called a *mixdown machine*) for stereo mixdown, or to an amplifier and speakers when not recording a mixdown.[18]

13. *Subgroups or Submixes*—Subgroups are useful for multitrack recording. They serve as master volume faders for groups of input

channels sent to them by the assignment switches (see List a, number 5). The outputs from these subgroups are then sent to four corresponding channels on a tape or disk-based recorder. You can split or "Y" the outputs from these four subgroups to use the subs to control the level sent to eight tracks on a recording device.

It would be a big challenge to list all of the companies that have good-quality, small mixers available for the MIDI project studio. Shop around, and take this book with you if it will help. Use the preceding section to show the sales people what features you want in *your* mixer.

Recording the Mixed Sound

If you want to remix your music every time you want to hear it, then you do not need a mixdown machine with which to record the mix. This would mean that you have entirely too much time on your hands; call me for a work assignment.

The most popular recording machines used for mixdown are the following:

- Cassette recorders. Good for recording mixes of hobby- and educational-level projects, or

---

[18] *Here's a great trick. Connect the Master outputs from your mixer to the inputs on your mixdown deck (cassette recorder or DAT machine). Then connect the outputs of the mixdown machine to your powered speakers or to the amp driving your monitor speakers. When you want to monitor your work, switch the mixdown machine into input or source monitoring. This allows the sound from your mixer to pass through the cassette or DAT machine to the monitoring system, even if you are not recording. That way you can leave your cassette deck or DAT connected in-line, always ready to record a mix.*

for recording rough versions that a client can take for approval or additional rehearsal.

♪ Two-track, reel-to-reel recorders. One of the industry-standard professional mixdown formats for many years, and even today.

♪ DAT, or Digital Audio Tape. The newest number one standard for semipro and professional mixdown. Although DAT has never caught on as a consumer format, use of the DAT format is standard in professional studios and is almost required by most paying clients. The DAT recording format allows program numbers, or PNOs, to be recorded on a "hidden" subcode data track. These PNOs enable the cataloging and fast location of different mix versions, as well as being useful for locating sound effects and narrative sound bites in radio and video production. DAT has become a widely accepted format for supplying master mixes to CD mastering labs, where the material is prepared for CD duplication. Figure 11.11 shows the very popular Panasonic SV-3700 DAT recorder.

Amplifying the Mixed Sound

Now that the sound is in a stereo or two-channel mixed form, you are ready to move some air. Yes, I said move some air. Until you turn all of this electrical energy into a sound wave, it will be inaudible. It is kind of cool to watch the computer sequencer count off measures, to see the software

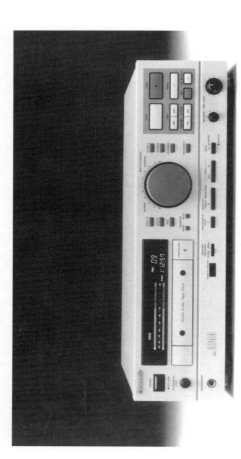

Figure 11.11. *The Panasonic SV-3700 DAT recorder/player is commonly used for stereo mixdown recordings.*

faders jump up and down, and to watch the meters bounce on the cassette recorder, but the real fun is in hearing your musical masterpieces.

Again, I remind you of the convenience and cost effectiveness of using powered speakers. But if you want top-notch sound quality sound and/or serious volume level, I must recommend that you use a stereo amplifier and a pair of good studio monitors. You can even use your home stereo amp and speakers if you are careful with your volume level. The music created by a MIDI project studio is often not in the compressed form that recordings released by record companies are in. This means you might have transient peaks or spikes in your mixes that could be too tough for home speaker systems to handle. True studio monitors are designed to take a thumping that consumer hi-fi speakers may not be able to handle. And studio monitors meet certain frequency response requirements that might provide a more accurate picture of what your mixed music will sound like on other people's stereo systems.

On With the Show

Whew! What a chapter (for you and me both!). But now I think we are ready to divide up the class and move forward. How many of you want to learn how to use professional-level sequencing software on your computer?

 PC users may advance to Chapter 12, "Professional MIDI Recording with the PC."

 Mac users may advance to Chapter 13, "Professional MIDI Recording with the Mac."

PROFESSIONAL MIDI RECORDING WITH THE PC

12

For this chapter you will need the following:

♪ 386SX, 25 MHz or higher PC running DOS 5.0 and Windows 3.1 or higher

♪ 4MB of RAM (8MB is faster)

♪ A hard drive, a computer keyboard and a mouse or a trackball

♪ A CD-ROM drive (necessary for using the software provided on the enclosed *MusicPower* CD-ROM)

You must have a MIDI interface for the PC and two MIDI cables; this interface may be built onto a sound card.

You must have *one* of the following setups to generate MIDI event data and sound:

♪ A MIDI controller *and* a multitimbral MIDI sound module

♪ A multitimbral MIDI-equipped keyboard synthesizer

♪ A MIDI controller and MIDI-capable sound card (preferably one that is General MIDI-compatible)

Note: This chapter assumes that you have completed the tutorials in Chapters 6 and 7, where you learned how to use the Midisoft Studio for Windows sequencing software from Twelve Tone Systems. Make sure you understand the information in those chapters before you start on this new material.

About the "Fox-59 SportsView" Exercise

In January of 1994, Bowen Music was commissioned by the Fox TV network affiliate WXIN-59 to create an original music package for their *Nightcast News* program. The idea was to create a thirty-second (:30) theme, a sixty-second (:60) version of the theme, a couple of variations of the :30 and :60 themes, and several little five- to eight-second transitions called *bumpers*. These bumpers are short pieces of the theme that you hear when the program cuts to and from the commercials. We also composed a version suitable for the Sunday night *SportsView* show. That show features interviews with sports celebrities, usually describing their big play of the day, and so on. The client edited all of the video together first, then brought the completed segments to us. Our work is thus called a *post-score*, because the work is done after the video is complete. This is the way I prefer to work, as it enables me to compose effective music phrases and cues that enhance the action and graphic animations on the screen. The "SportsView Theme" is a high-energy pop-rock piece with lots of tracks of MIDI recordings. In the final version (featured on the CD-ROM), you will hear several tracks of guitar in addition to a couple of dozen channels of synthesizers and drum samples. Let's use the "SportsView Theme" for the Cakewalk Professional for Windows 2.0 tutorial.

Software Development Editor Wayne Blankenbecker suggested showing you the completed *SportsView* video opening. I thought that would be great. You'll find it in the file named SPORTS.AVI. To play this video file, open the Computer Musician Tutorials group in Program Manager, then double-click the SportsView Video icon.

You will not do any MIDI recording here, since you learned how to record, quantize, and perform basic editing functions in Chapter 7 with Studio for Windows. This chapter focuses on the powerful editing features available in truly professional sequencing software.

Setting Up the Synthesizer

To make this tutorial as simple as possible, I have again elected to use the GM configuration for MIDI channel and patch assignments. Make sure your synthesizer is set up in a GM configuration, just like in Chapter 6. If you are not using a GM-compatible synthesizer, you will have to refer to the owner's manual for your synthesizer and set the Receive mode to Multi or Multitimbral. Then assign the MIDI Receive channels and patches as shown in Table 12.1.

If you are using a non-GM synthesizer, you will also want to load the demo versions with the "NoGM" suffixes. These have no program changes.

Table 12.1. MIDI Receive channels and patches.

MIDI Channel Number	Sound Type	GM Program or Key
1	Off	(none)
2	Strings Ensemble 1	48
3	Off	
4	Off	
5	Percussive Organ	17
6	Synth Pad 3	90
7	Off	
8	Synth Lead 7	86
9	Slap Bass 1	36
10	Toms	43, 45, 47
	Open and Closed Hi-Hat	46, 44
	Kick Drum, Snare	36, 38
	Cymbals	49, 55
11	Off	
12	Off	
13	Off	
14	Off	
15	Off	
16	Off	

Loading a Demo of "SportsView Theme"

As mentioned in Chapters 2 and 7, a good way to get started with any software is to load a completed

work and experiment with it.[1] Boot Cakewalk 2.0 as you learned in Chapter 6. Select Open under the File menu. Double-click the file SVIEWGM.MID.[2] You will see the screen shown in Figure 12.1.

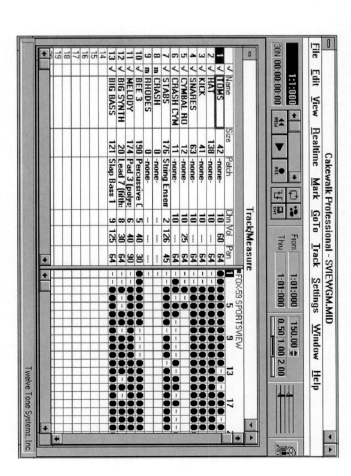

Figure 12.1. A section of the "SportsView Theme" post-score.

[1] Professional-level software like Cakewalk is almost infinitely flexible (sorry!). There is actually a bit of setup involved the first time or two that you use it. I have arranged this version of the "SportsView Theme" to run easily on 16 MIDI channels, even though I used a couple of dozen channels when I actually produced the score. You can use any standard single- or dual-port interface. I also based this chapter on the use of a single multitimbral synthesizer in a GM configuration.

[2] Load the SVIEW.MID version if your synthesizer is not GM-configurable.

For PC Users

Note: Your screens will look slightly different from those shown in this chapter. Cakewalk enables you to move the controls so as to configure the most user-friendly setup for your needs.

For this chapter, I have moved together the controls you will use so that you can see them at a glance. The Help menu will tell you how to set up your screens like the ones shown—or just use the scroll bar to see controls as needed.

There are two major windows on the screen: the Control Bar window and the Track/Measure View. I have labeled the functions you will use the most. Twelve Tone Systems has designed online help into Cakewalk 2.0. You will find it under the Help menu. I recommend taking a couple of minutes to familiarize yourself with the various areas and icons on the screen. To return to this screen, select Track/Measure under the Windows menu.

Learning the Control Bar

I can't discuss every Cakewalk feature in this amount of space, but let's learn about Control Bar functions you will use in this chapter (Figure 12.2).

1. *The Transport Controls.* You know what to do with these. After all, you're a real computer musician now!

2. *The Counter.* This displays bars and beats but also provides a second counter that displays SMPTE time code. Since the "SportsView Theme" was a post-score, we

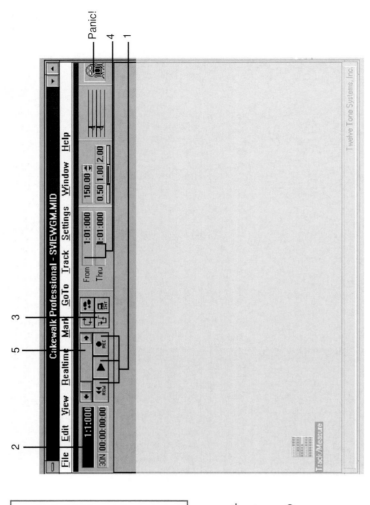

Figure 12.2. *The Control Bar window in Cakewalk, by Twelve Tone Systems.*

used this SMPTE readout for reference. The numbers you see displayed when the "SportsView Theme" is in play are the same numbers that were striped on the video master brought to us by Fox-59 producers. More about the use of SMPTE and video in Chapter 14.

3. *The Record Mode button.* This enables the Punch Recording function, and selects whether new recorded information will overwrite or blend with information already existing on the track.

4. *The From marker and Thru marker.* These enable you to set two user-defined location points in the composition, which determine the start and end points for looping, punch recording, and for editing. Referring to these two markers is very important when performing precise editing.

5. *The Scroll bar.* You can click the scroll arrows to move forward or backward one beat at a time, or you can drag the Scroll bar "thumb" to move quickly to any location in the sequence.

Oh, yeah. Don't forget the Panic button for all notes off. That's the little guy all the way to the right of the Control bar.

Exploring the Track/Measure View

The Track/Measure View is where you do much of your editing. It enables you to perform editing functions on entire tracks and groups of tracks. Figure 12.3 shows the Track/Measure View for the "SportsView Theme."

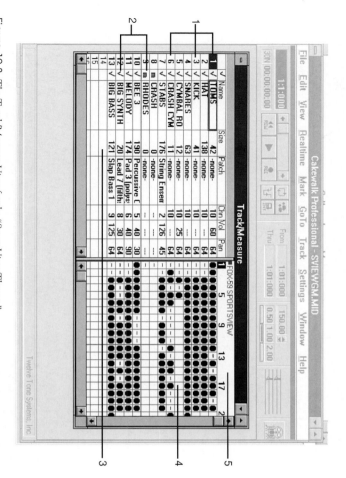

Figure 12.3. *The Track/Measure View for the "SportsView Theme."*

Features used from the Track/Measure View include the following:

1. *Track Selection Numbers.* Clicking these numbers will select a track for editing. If you click-and-drag down the row of numbers, you can select multiple tracks.

2. *The Track Function boxes are selected in the second column. Track Functions is explored in detail later in this chapter.*

3. *The Track Pane display enables you to (left to right) name a track, view the length of a track, select what synthesizer instrument and MIDI channel are assigned to a track, and to enter comments such as instrument volumes, effects settings, or sound descriptions.*

4. *The Measure Pane uses dots to show what measures have recorded MIDI event data. You can highlight entire blocks of measures and tracks and copy and paste them when editing.*

5. *The Bar-Beat Ruler.* You won't find this term in the help or owner's manual. I actually borrow this term from Opcode Vision software. The Ruler cursor (the little black square) shows you where you are in the score.

When you have a basic idea of how the screen is laid out, click the Play button in the Transport Controls window and you will hear the "SportsView Theme." Click Play again to stop. (There is no Stop button.)

The Track Functions Area

Note the Track Function boxes in the Track/Measure View. You will see three symbols: a single red square, the letter "m," and check marks. These stand for the following highly useful functions:

The red square is what Cakewalk calls the Highlight Tool. A Highlight Tool around the box enables recording for a track.

The letter "m" stands for "mute." An "m" in the box silences the selected track. You can mute as many tracks as you want.

The check mark symbol indicates play-enabling. A check mark in the box activates the sound of the selected track.

By using combinations of Mute and Play, you can find mistakes or listen to isolated tracks to see if there are ways to improve performance details. Put the "SportsView Theme" into play a few times. Double-click the check mark to mute a track. Mute the first six tracks. Notice that all of the drum and percussion sounds are gone. That is because the GM percussion bank is on MIDI Channel 10, and you have just muted all of the tracks on Channel 10. Double-click the Mute buttons to play-enable them again. Now mute the last track. It is named "Big Bass." Now mute the tracks randomly and note the effect. Be sure all the mute buttons are clicked off when you are finished.

Another important function is track solo. Click the check mark. Notice that a Highlight Tool appears around it. Then select Solo under the Tracks menu. This isolates the sound of the selected track by muting all other tracks. Only one track can be in solo mode at a time. Solo the track "Big Bass" and play the "SportsView Theme." Notice that all the other sounds disappear, leaving the bass track isolated. This will enable you to hear whether the bass performance is satisfactory. The solo function is commonly used to check tracks for "tightness" and accuracy before complet-

ing the MIDI recording session. If the performances sound "loose" or sloppy, many computer musicians will use the quantize function as you did in the Midisoft Studio tutorial. You can undo solo by selecting Un-Solo under the Tracks menu. The Track Functions are very helpful when you are polishing up your work.

Editing the "SportsView Theme" with Cakewalk 2.0

Every MIDI recording project we work on at Bowen Music Productions makes extensive use of software editing features, and I believe that the greatest difference between semi-pro and professional software lies in the editing and synchronization capabilities. The software should enable you to edit the same MIDI events in a number of ways: as single MIDI events or in large chunks or blocks—even so large as to include every track and every measure. Some computer musicians even record on one sequencer and then edit on another, so as to maximize the results of the recording and editing process.

Editing MIDI Event Data in the Piano Roll View

Click the check mark in the Track Function box for Track 1, named "Toms." The Highlight Tool will appear there. Click the New submenu under the View screen. Now select Piano Roll under this submenu. The Piano Roll View (Figure 12.4) will appear.

One of the features that Cakewalk users rave about is this really nice full-color display. If you look closely you can see the lines and dots that are the Note Blocks. You may need to use the scroll bars to find these. The little Note Blocks you see are actually visual representations of the MIDI note-on note-off event data recorded on the tracks. The length of the Note Block is the length of the note duration. The piano keyboard running down the left side of the window is a reference for which note the Note Block represents. A nice Time/Pitch Locator display in the upper left-hand corner of the Piano Roll window shows the position of the mouse in terms of measures and beats and note pitch at all times. Click the first Note Block. You will hear the tom sound triggered by the MIDI event the Note Block represents. You will also see the note name and octave in the Time/Pitch Locator display, complete with a measure and beat location. Click several Note Blocks and you will hear the notes and instruments triggered by the MIDI note-on events recorded on this track.

This kind of MIDI event display is called piano roll viewing. Cakewalk enables you to use the Zoom Buttons to enlarge or reduce the size of these Note Blocks. Remember that we are working in the first track, named "Toms." Find the first Note Block in the Toms track (near measure 2, beat 3). Place the cursor squarely on the center of the Note Block. Click it and hold the mouse button. The cursor turns into a crosshair with a pair of arrows and you will hear the tom sound triggered by this note-on event.

Select Tool

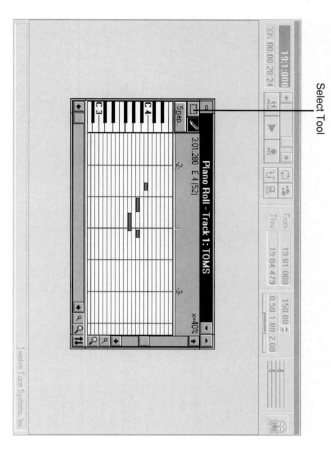

Piano Roll - Track 1: TOMS

Twelve Tone Systems, Inc.

Figure 12.4. *The Piano Roll View enables you to edit MIDI events in a graphical format.*

Maybe a different tom sound would be better. Hold down the mouse button and carefully drag the Note Block vertically up and down the display. Remember the original location of the Note Block so you can return it to the same location. As you drag the Note Block you will hear all of the sounds generated by the synthesizer that is on the MIDI channel this track is assigned to. Stop dragging the Note Block so that it is placed on the note D4. This selects another tom sound.

Drag the other Note Blocks around and select new sounds for them, as well. When finished, put the "SportsView Theme" into play. The sounds used for the toms are now different. If you have really

messed things up, just reload the file and start over. Or better yet, edit your way back out of trouble using the same method. That's the spirit!

You can edit all of the notes in the sequence in this manner, and can even slide errant events forward or backward in time. Close the Piano Roll View for this track. Open the Piano Roll View for Track 6, named "Crash Cymbals." (Refer to the beginning of this section if you need help doing this.) Use the scroll bar at the bottom of the window and go to measure 21 in the Piano Roll View display. You will see a Note Block on Track 6 that seems to be all alone. That is a stray crash cymbal. If you play the "SportsView Theme" you

will hear this as a mistake. Click this Note Block, hold down the mouse button, and drag the Note Block so that it begins on measure 20, beat 4. Now the "SportsView Theme" will sound correct. You can drag events around like this for reasons other than problem-solving, too. Sometimes you can drag a snare part "ahead" or "behind" a bit to create a slightly more "pushed" or "laid back" feel. Craig Sharmat mentions this in his interview in Chapter 1.

Open the Piano Roll View for Track 1 (Toms) again. Use the scroll bar at the bottom of the window to scroll to measure 2. Look at the first four Note Blocks. These are the toms you hear as pickup notes at the beginning of the "SportsView Theme." I don't like them anymore. Click the Select Tool. It is the dotted square in the upper left-hand corner of the window. Hold down the mouse button and drag across the four Note Blocks; they will highlight. Select Cut under the Edit menu. A dialog box confirms the Start Point and End Point of the edit. Click OK. The toms vanish. Play the "SportsView Theme." Hmmmm...I changed my mind. Select Undo Cut under the Edit menu. Many less-professional sequencers do not feature an Undo command. Nice to have creative options like this, huh?

Editing MIDI Event Data in the Event List Window

The Cakewalk Event List window is one of my favorite editing tools. Like the Piano Roll View, the Event List window (shown in Figure 12.5) enables you to edit MIDI event data. The Event

For PC Users

List can display *every* MIDI event in selected tracks in a text format.

Return to the Track/Measure Views window by selecting Track/Measure under the Windows menu. Click the Track Selection Number for Track 13, to the left of the track named "Big Bass." It will darken. Make sure that no other track numbers are darkened. Now click the Track Function box next to the track number. The Highlight Tool will appear there. This enables recording on the track and activates the MIDI THRU to the bass patch. Select Event List from the New submenu found under the View menu. You will now see the screen as shown in Figure 12.5. This is a list of all of the notes and MIDI controller events for the "Big Bass" track. The events shown on the Event List are named in Figure 12.5.

Locate the first note in the Event List, the note D3 at measure 3, beat 1.[3] Double-click "D3." This means that the first event is note-on for the note D in octave 3. Play the notes on your controller and the highlighted "D3" will become the notes you are playing. Now click the number 123, under the word Values. The Highlight Tool will appear there. This is the key-on velocity for the first note, D3. Click the number, hold down the mouse button, and drag. The value will change. Move the mouse forward and backward and it will change again. This is a very fast way to change notes and velocity.

Note: Note the SMPTE time code addresses listed in the first column. Sometimes you want a certain musical sound to hit perfectly on a film or video cue. You can "jog" the videotape machine and read the SMPTE time code address of the visual cue directly from a little window on your video monitor. Then you can edit the MIDI events in the Event List so they match the SMPTE addresses of the visual cues, and whammo—they fall perfectly in sync. More about syncing (synchronizing) to picture in Chapter 14.

Click again on the first note, D3. The Highlight Tool will appear there. Gently position the arrow cursor directly over the highlighted note and move the mouse around very slowly. Clicking and dragging the mouse will increase or decrease the pitch of the highlighted note. This editing procedure works for any event shown on the Event List.

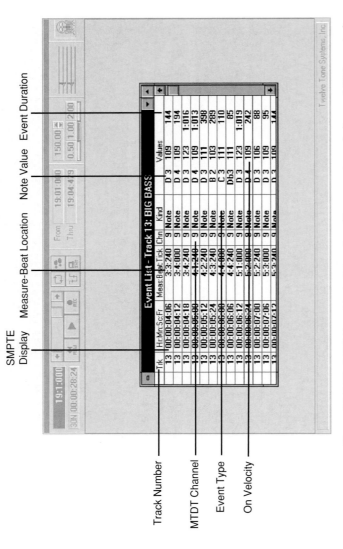

Figure 12.5. *The MIDI Event List in Cakewalk enables you to view and edit every MIDI event in the MIDI recording by name.*

[3]Note the "Ticks" column. All sequencing software divides a beat into some number of "ticks." The number of ticks per beat is called the "note resolution." Just as using higher resolution when digitizing sound makes for a more accurate representation of the sound, using a higher note resolution here enables a more accurate and less quantized recording of the performance. Most professional sequencers will allow a note resolution of 480 ticks per beat; some allow even higher resolution. I always use 480-tick resolution, which makes an eighth note 240 ticks, a sixteenth note 120 ticks, and so on.

Adding an Octave to a Track

Here's a neat trick that I use often. Sometimes it is effective to double a recorded part in octaves. You *could* replay the part an octave higher and record it on another track, but the magic of MIDI lets you do this another way:

1. Click the Track Selection Number in front of Track 7 (the track called "Stabs"). The box is highlighted. Again move the Highlight Tool to the Track Function box for Track 7. Select Piano Roll under the View menu. Move the Piano Roll View window off to the side a bit.

2. Select Copy Track under the Edit menu. A dialog box will appear. Enter the number 1:01:000 in the "From" box and 30:01:000 in the "Thru" box. This selects the start and end points of your edit. Click OK.

3. Keep Track 7 highlighted. Select Transpose Track under the Edit menu. A Transpose dialog box will appear. Enter the number 12 (for 12 half-steps) in the "Amount" box. Set the "From" and "Thru" boxes up as you did in Step 2. Click OK. Play back the "SportsView Theme." You will hear that Track 7 has been transposed up one octave. Solo the track to hear the change more clearly and alternate between Undo Transpose and Redo Transpose under the Edit menu. You can watch the changes in the Piano Roll View window. It's kind of like fireworks! Finally, leave the track transposed up one octave.

4. In Step 2 you copied the original Track 7. That copy is waiting in the PC edit buffer. Make sure that Track 7 is still highlighted, then select Paste under the Edit menu. A Paste dialog box appears. Set the "To Time" box to 1:01:000. You now have the following three options:

♪ *Blend Old and New Material.* This function is often called Merge by other software.

♪ *Replace Old Material with New.* This is the default paste mode for most software.

♪ *Slide Over Existing Material to Make Room.* This is called Insert or Splice by other software.

The default setting is "Blend...." Click OK. If you look closely at the Note Blocks in the Piano Roll View for Track 7, you can see that an extra set of notes has been added to the track. Now the part will play in octaves. Play the sequence and use the solo function to hear your work clearly.

Setting Location Markers

Professional-level software usually has a feature that enables you to set markers. Markers are used to set "in" and "out" points for punch recording and editing, and for marking sections of a song. You should be able to set the locations of the markers "on the fly" or with sequencer playback stopped. Find the From marker and Thru marker in Figure 12.2, then find them on your computer screen.

Let's set a From marker at measure 13, beat 1:

1. Put the sequence in play. When the Counter reaches measure 13, press F9 on your computer keyboard. The captured number will appear in the From marker window. Stop the sequence. Press F7 and the counter will move to the number that you captured. You probably got close to measure 13, beat 1, but most likely didn't capture it exactly. It still might be close enough for your needs.

2. If you want the marker at an exact location, click the marker number you would like to change. A dialog box will appear. Enter corrected numbers so the Counter reads exactly 13-1-000. You can do this from your computer keyboard or by using the incrementing/decrementing arrows furnished by the dialog box. Click Enter, and the edited number appears in the marker display.

Store the ending or Thru marker in the same way, but capture it using F10, and locate it using F8.[4] Try it.

Punch Recording

Tape recording engineers have long ago perfected the art of punching in and out of record mode on

[4]*Pro-level software such as Cakewalk enables you to program an unlimited number of other markers which function in much the same way as the From and Thru markers. The advantage in using markers is that you can view a complete list of markers in a Markers pop-up window, the markers appear in all list windows (where they may be edited), and a marker can have a text name, such as Verse, Chorus, and so on.*

tape machines. This enables the musician to keep all of a recorded track except perhaps a small segment that needs to be replaced. High-quality MIDI recorders like Cakewalk enable you to punch in and out of record also.

Load the "SportsView Theme" sequence again. Find the Record Mode and Loop Controls on the right side of the Control Bar window. Refer to Figure 12.2 if you have any difficulty. Using three features will enable you to determine the start and end points for punch-in recording:

The From marker. This display sets the punch record "In" point (that is, the point where recording will begin).

The Thru marker. This display sets the punch record "Out" point (the point where recording will stop). I have selected the From and Thru markers for this example.

The Record Mode button. This button, with both the down and up arrows, enables the Punch-Record Mode.

Here is how to punch record:

1. Determine which track you want to record on. Record-enable it by clicking on the Track Functions box. The Highlight Tool will appear. Record-enable Track 10 (the "Bee 3 Organ" track) for this example.

2. Determine the From marker and Thru marker locations that define the area where you want to record. There is an unrecorded section on Track 10 between measures 9 and 11 where you will punch-in record.[5] This will provide a good example. Enter the numbers 9:01:000 into the From marker display. Next, enter the numbers 11:01:000 into the Thru marker display.

3. Click the Record Mode button to open the Record Mode dialog box. Select Auto Punch. Verify that the numbers for the Punch-in Time and Punch-out Time are correct, then click OK.

4. Click the Record button in the Transport Controls display. You will hear a count-off. When the Counter reaches measure 9, Track 10 automatically starts recording MIDI event data generated by your controller device. So play some stuff. If nothing else, just play a chord with the notes D-F-A (this is a D minor chord). Playing eighth notes with the chord will be even better. The best scenario is for you to make up your own part. Recording will stop at measure 11.

Play back your recorded performance. You can keep re-recording this section as often as you want. Each new "take" will erase the previous one. You can "capture" new From markers and Thru markers on the fly by pressing F9 and F10 while the sequence is in play. The locations of these captured points may then be edited just as you edited the captured markers in the preceding section of this chapter.

[5]*This is the beauty of Cakewalk. You can actually see the best locations to punch in and out of record—or to edit—in the Piano Roll View.*

Incredible Multimedia Applications

We have talked about adding MIDI playback to multimedia presentation, but how about turning the scenario around? Cakewalk has been designed to serve as a complete multimedia control center: You can control CD-ROM drives, animation software, record, load and play back .WAV sound files (with the appropriate sound cards), and even control Microsoft Video for Windows—all from commands in the sequence Event Editor. Very cool.

Warning: Remember that configuring systems this complex can be a real hassle. But if you have the time to integrate your multimedia system in the way Cakewalk enables, you'll have a blast.

Digging Deeper into Cakewalk 2.0

Here is an overview of even more goodies. Select Info under the File menu. Cakewalk furnishes this really neat information form that is saved with your MIDI files. All software manufacturers should provide one just like this. Highly recommended. And the "Big Time" display at the bottom of the View menu is great if you are trying to see the monitor through 3 layers of glass from 20 feet away. Beats the heck out of having the engineer mouth the bar-beat count to you.

Tech Editor Steve Cooper tipped me off to CAL, Cakewalk Application Language, which enables a computer musician to create customized editing commands. Cakewalk includes some samples of ideas you might want to try after you really know how to use the sequencer.

Click New under the View menu. Then select Staff under the New submenu and you will see a score. While the notation may not be as flexible as a true notation package, it works very well for many applications.

Cakewalk 2.0 sports "view" functions (I just can't leave the puns alone) and editing functions that have made it one of the most-owned and best-liked MIDI recording packages available for the PC. The software retails for $349. And again, the Twelve Tone Systems staff is easily accessible and eager to answer your questions at 800-234-1171.

Additional Music Software on *MusicPower*

Master Tracks Pro 4 is hugely popular in the educational community because of its easy-to-use, nearly bulletproof design. Passport Designs was one of the very first software designers to success-fully incorporate the graphical method of editing, and it now manufactures a large number of good software titles. *MusicPower* also includes a demo version of Encore, which is one of the most popular high-quality music notation programs available. Encore, too, is from Passport Designs.

I received an excellent demo program from MiBAC (507-645-5851) that I must mention here. The program is called Music Lessons ($119). Music Lessons does a great job of teaching basic music principles such as note names, circle of fifths, scale theory, intervals, ear training—all in an interactive format that even grades the student and prints out a progress report. Work (don't just play) with the demo, and you will be greatly rewarded.

Where Do We Go from Here?

Electronics and synthesizers are great fun and great professional tools. But we will never totally eliminate the need to record live acoustic instruments and vocals. Chapter 14 teaches you the latest techniques for recording those sounds. You will explore analog tape recording, digital worksta-tions, film and video applications, and modular digital tape recording systems such as ADAT.

PC users should advance to Chapter 14.

PROFESSIONAL MIDI

RECORDING WITH

THE MAC

13

For this chapter you will need the following:

- A Macintosh Plus or greater running System 7.0 or higher
- A hard drive and 4 or more megabytes of RAM
- A CD-ROM drive (necessary for use of the software provided on the *MusicPower* CD-ROM)
- A MIDI interface for the Mac and two MIDI cables

You must also have *one* of the following setups to generate MIDI event data and sound:

A MIDI controller *and* a multitimbral MIDI sound module

A MIDI keyboard controller with a built-in synthesizer

A MIDI controller and a sound card with a synthesizer

Note: This chapter assumes that you have completed the tutorial in Chapters 8 and 9, which taught you how to use the Opcode sequencing software Musicshop. Make sure you understand the information in those chapters before you start on this new material.

About the "Fox-59 SportsView" Exercise

In January of 1994, my studio was commissioned by the Fox TV network affiliate WXIN-59 to create an original music package for their *Nightcast News* program. The idea was to create a thirty-second (:30) theme, a sixty-second (:60) version of the theme, a couple of variations on the :30 and :60 themes, and a bunch of little five- to eight-second transitions called *bumpers* (short pieces of the theme that you hear when the program cuts to and from commercials). We also composed a version suitable for the Sunday night *SportsView* show that features interviews with sports celebrities, usually describing their "big play" of the day. The client edited all of the video together first, then brought in the completed segments. Our work is thus called a *post-score*; we are doing our work after the video is complete. This is the way I prefer to work; it enables me to compose effective music phrases and cues that enhance the action and graphic animations on the screen. The "SportsView Theme" is a high energy pop-rock piece with lots of tracks of MIDI recordings. In the final version featured on *MusicPower*, you will hear several guitar tracks in addition to a couple of dozen channels of synthesizers and drum samples. Let's use the "SportsView Theme" for our Vision 2.0 tutorial.

 Software Development Editor Wayne Blankenbeckler suggested that we show you the completed *SportsView* video opening, which sounded great to me. Open the

Video Clips folder and double-click the SportsView Video icon.

You will also find three CD audio versions of the "SportsView Theme" on *MusicPower*. Play back CD tracks 6, 7, and 8 to hear them.

I have selected Vision 2.0 by Opcode Systems for this tutorial. The staff at Opcode was kind enough to prepare a demo version especially for this book, for which I am truly flattered and grateful.[1] Vision is one of the most popular sequencers available; you might recall Kenny Aronoff mentioning Vision in his Chapter 5 interview.

You will not do any MIDI recording here; you learned how to record, quantize, and perform basic editing functions in Chapter 9 when you learned to use Musicshop. This chapter focuses on the powerful editing features available in truly professional sequencing software.

Setting Up the Synthesizer

To make this tutorial as simple as possible, I have again elected to use the GM configuration for MIDI channel and patch assignments. Make sure your synthesizer is set up in a GM configuration, just like you did in Chapter 8. If you are not using a GM-compatible synthesizer, you will have to refer to the owner's manual for your synthesizer.

[1]This demo version is fully functional, but it will not print or save and will shut down after about 40 minutes.

and set the Receive Mode to Multi or Multitimbral. Then, assign the MIDI Receive channels and patches as shown in Table 13.1.

If using a non-GM synth, you will also want to load the Demo versions with the *NoGM* suffixes. These have no program changes.

Installing the Vision 2.0 Demo

The demo version of *Vision* must be installed to your hard drive before you can use it. Open the *MusicPower* folder named Vision Demo 1 of 2 and double-click the Install Vision icon. When the install program starts, click the Install button and follow the instructions.

Installing OMS

This particular demo version of *Vision* requires that you run OMS, which is Opcode Music System. OMS is a Mac system extension that provides a MIDI system management "center," allowing communications between OMS-compatible software and hardware. OMS software is included free with all Opcode products, and the OMS standard is widely subscribed to by manufacturers of music industry products. OMS is installed in the following way:

1. Open the OMS folder. It is in the Vision 2.0 Folder on the CD-ROM *MusicPower*.

2. Double-click the OMS Installer icon. A Welcome dialog box appears. Click OK. An installation dialog box appears.

3. Click Switch Disk until the name of your hard drive appears. Then you can click Install.

4. After the Installation procedure runs, you are prompted to restart your Mac.

Table 13.1. MIDI Receive channels and patches.

MIDI Channel Number	Sound Type	GM Program or Key Number
1	Off	
2	Strings Ensemble 1	48
3	Off	
4	Off	
5	Percussive Organ	17
6	Synth Pad 3	90
7	Off	
8	Synth Lead 7	86
9	Slap Bass 1	36
10	Toms	43, 45, 47
	Open and Closed Hi-Hat	46, 44
	Kick Drum, Snare	36, 38
	Cymbals	49, 55
11	Off	
12	Off	
13	Off	
14	Off	
15	Off	
16	Off	

Loading a Demo of "SportsView"

In Chapters 3 and 9, you learned that a good way to get started with any software is by loading a completed work and experimenting with it.[2] Launch Vision 2.0, as you learned in Chapter 8. Select Open under the File menu. Select the MusicPower CD-ROM drive and open the SportsView folder. Double-click the file SportsView-GM[3]; you will see the screen shown in Figure 3.1. You may see a dialog box that asks if you want Vision to remap MIDI channel assignments to match your setup. If so, click Remap.

There are two major windows on the screen: the Control Bar window and the Tracks window. I have labeled the functions we will use the most. Opcode has designed "pop-up help" into Vision 2.0. Hold down Command-Option-Shift and click the icons on the screen. A Help dialog box appears, telling you about the area you selected. I recommend taking a couple of minutes to familiarize yourself with the various areas and icons on the screen.

Learning the Control Bar

We cannot discuss every Vision feature in this amount of space, but let's learn about Control Bar functions used in this chapter (Figure 13.2).

1. *Record Mode.* This button enables you to select whether recording erases (Replace) MIDI events already recorded on the Track or merges (Overdub) the new MIDI event data with it. All work done in this exercise uses the Replace mode.

2. *The Transport Controls.* These work very much like the controls on a tape recorder, providing play, record, rewind, and other functions.

3. *Counter.* Displays bars and beats but also provides a second counter that displays SMPTE time code. Because "SportsView" was a post-score, this SMPTE readout was

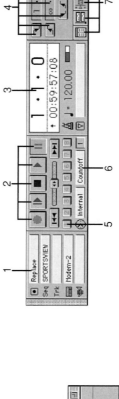

Figure 13.2. *The Control Bar window from Vision by Opcode.*

[2]*Professional-level software like Vision is almost infinitely flexible (sorry!). There is actually a bit of setup involved the first time or two that you use it. I have arranged this version of "SportsView" to run easily on 16 MIDI channels, although I used a couple of dozen channels when I actually produced the score. You can use any standard single- or dual-port interface, although Vision allows incredible capabilities when using a multiport interface. I also based this chapter on the use of a single multitimbral synth in a GM configuration.*

[3]*Load the SportsView-NoGM file if your synthesizer is not GM-configurable.*

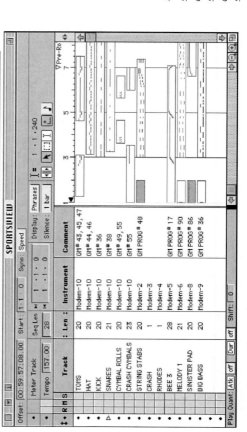

Figure 13.1. *A section of the post-score from "SportsView."*

used for reference. The numbers you see displayed when "SportsView" is in play are the same numbers that were striped on the video master brought to us by Fox-59 producers. More about the use of SMPTE and video in Chapter 14.

4. *Punch Record* and *Loop*. These controls enable you to determine the In points and Out points for punch recording and looping.

5. *Locators*. Enable you to set eight user-defined location points in the composition. Clicking a Locator automatically sends the sequence to the corresponding Counter location.

6. *Countoff*. Enables you to set the number of measures of click before recording. Click the number 0 in the little box. Place the cursor over the box and it becomes a small arrow. Gently move the mouse, and the arrow points up and down. If you click the mouse button with the little arrow pointing up, the number will increase. The opposite is also true. Fun, huh? Fast, too! And since we are talking about professional (earns us dollars...earns us dollars...) software, fast operation is important. We do not use the Countoff in this chapter, but I thought you should know about it for your own MIDI recording.

7. This section of five Window buttons opens your choice of the *Sequences*, *Tracks*, *Event List*, *Graphic* (piano roll), or *Notation*[4] windows.

Exploring the Tracks Window

The Tracks window is where you do much of your editing. It enables you to perform editing functions on entire Tracks and groups of Tracks. Figure 13.3 shows the Tracks window from "SportsView."

Features used from the Tracks window include the following:

1. *Selection Dots*. Clicking these Dots selects a Track for editing. If you click-and-drag down the row of dots, you can select multiple Tracks. Use Shift+click to skip some of the Tracks.

2. *Track Functions*. Track Functions are covered in detail later in this chapter.

3. *Track Columns* enable you to (left to right) name a Track, view the length of a Track, select what synthesizer instrument and MIDI channel are assigned to a Track, and enter comments such as instrument patch numbers, effects settings, or sound descriptions.

4. *Track Overview*. This really nice, full-color display is one of the features Vision users rave about. If you look closely you can see tiny lines and dots in the Track Blocks. Those are actually visual representations of the MIDI event data recorded on the Tracks. This kind of MIDI event display is called *piano roll viewing*. Vision enables you to view the Track Blocks in a couple of different Display Modes. You will find these options under the Phrases window. I have

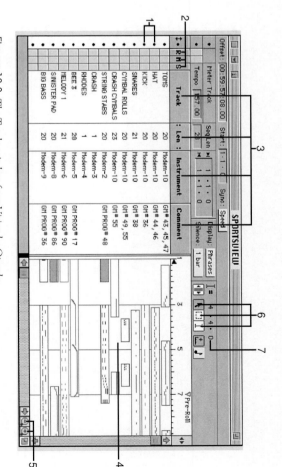

Figure 13.3. *The Tracks window from Vision by Opcode.*

---

[4] *Vision 2.0 provides Notation viewing that enables you to enter and edit notes by clicking and dragging with your mouse and using other editing tools. This is not really notation software, but Vision 2.0 will print a score or a lead sheet.*

selected the Phrases option, which divides my MIDI event data into discrete musical phrases.

5. *Zoom Buttons*. These enable you to enlarge or reduce the size of the events that are on display.

6. *Selection Tools*. You have used tools like these in the other tutorials. Here, they are used to define regions for editing. Use the pop-up Help function if you need help now.

7. *Cursor Display* shows you *exactly* where the cursor currently is located in the score. Checking the Cursor Display is very important when performing precise editing.

When you have a basic idea of how the screen is laid out, click the Play button in the Transport Controls window and you will hear "SportsView." Vision 2.0 provides two kinds of Play. The Play button with the vertical bar on the left side (second transport button from the left) returns the composition to the beginning before playback begins. The other Play button (second from the right) starts playback at the point where the vertical line cursor (the Bar-Beat indicator) is positioned on the Bar-Beat ruler. Note that the Bar-Beat cursor flashes all the time.

The Track Functions Area

Note the Track Functions section in the Tracks window. You will see the letters R-M-S. These stand for very useful functions:

R: Record enables a track.

M: Mutes a track. Clicking this button silences the selected track. You can mute as many tracks as you want.

S: Solo isolates the sound of the selected track by Muting all other Tracks. More than one track can be in Solo mode at a time.

The Track Mode functions are very helpful when you are polishing up your work. By using combinations of Mute and Solo, you can find mistakes or listen to isolated Tracks so as to see if there is a way to improve performance details. Put "SportsView" into play a few times. Mute the first six tracks. Notice that all of the drum and percussion sounds are gone. That is because the GM percussion bank is on MIDI channel 10, and you have just muted out all of the Tracks on Channel 10. Undo the Mute buttons. Now mute the last track; it is named "Big Bass." Now mute the tracks randomly and note the effect. Be sure all the Mute buttons are clicked off when you are finished.

Click the S or Solo button on the "Big Bass" track. Play "SportsView," and notice that all the other sounds disappear, leaving the bass track isolated. This enables you to hear if the bass performance is satisfactory. While the bass track is in play, also Solo the first six tracks. This isolates the sounds of the bass and drums. It is common to check this combination of tracks for "tightness" and accuracy

before completing the MIDI recording session. If the performances sound "loose" or sloppy, many computer musicians will use the Quantize function as was done in the Musicshop tutorial.

Editing "SportsView" with Vision 2.0

Every MIDI recording project we work on at Bowen Music Productions makes extensive use of software editing features, and I believe that the greatest difference between semi-pro and professional software lies in the editing and synchronization capabilities. The software should enable you to edit the same MIDI events in a number of ways...as single MIDI events or in large chunks or blocks...even so large as to include every track and every measure. Some computer musicians even record on one sequencer and then edit on another, so as to maximize the recording and editing process.[5]

Editing MIDI Event Data in Track Overview

Find the Track Overview display in the Track window. Notice how the blocks of MIDI event data are located to the right of the track they represent. The blocks are color coded so that tracks sharing the same MIDI channel share the same color. The first track is named Toms. Click

[5]*Vision and Performer, by Mark of the Unicorn, are my favorite sequencers when it comes to editing. Other professionals also like to use Passport Pro 5, Cubase, and Metro.*

the first block to the right of the Toms track. The block will highlight. These are the toms you see here as pickup notes at the beginning of "SportsView." I don't like them anymore. Select Clear Selection under the Edit menu. The toms vanish. Play "SportsView". Hmmmm…changed my mind. Select Undo Clear under the Edit menu.

Maybe a different tom sound would be better. Double-click the Toms block again. The window enlarges, looking like Figure 13.4.

This is the Graphic editing window. Each of the little rectangles and dots you see is a Note event. And the length of the rectangle is the length of the note duration. The strip running down the left side of the window is the reference for which note the rectangle represents. Click the first rectangle. You will hear the Toms sound triggered by the MIDI event the rectangle represents. You will also see the note name and octave in the Cursor Display in the top center of the window. Click

several rectangles and you will hear the notes and instruments triggered by the MIDI note-on events recorded on this track.

Place the cursor squarely on the center of the rectangle. It will turn into a cross-hair with a pair of arrows. Hold down the mouse button and carefully drag the rectangle vertically up and down the display. Note that the original rectangle stays solid and that the rectangle you are dragging is an "alias." This is so you can remember the original location of the rectangle. As you drag the rect-angle you will hear all of the sounds generated by the synthesizer on the MIDI channel this track is assigned to. Stop dragging the rectangle so that it is placed on the note D2. This selects another Toms sound.

Drag the other rectangles around and select new sounds for them, as well. When finished, put "SportsView" into play. The sounds used for the pick-up notes on the toms are now different. If you

have really messed things up, just reload the file and start over. Or better yet, edit your way back out of trouble using the same method. That's the spirit!

You can edit all of the notes in the sequence in this manner and can even slide errant events forward or backward in time. Close the Graphic window. Find Track 6, named Crash Cymbals. Use the scroll bar at the bottom of the window and go to measure 21 in the Track Overview display. You will see a block on Track 6 that seems rather all alone. That is a stray crash cymbal. If you play "SportsView" you will hear this as a mistake. Click this Block, hold down the mouse button, and drag the block so that it begins on measure 20, beat 4. Now "SportsView" will sound correct. You can drag events around like this for reasons other than problem solving. Sometimes we can drag a snare part "ahead" or "behind" a bit to create a slightly more "pushed" or "laid back" feel. Craig Sharmat mentions this in his Chapter 1 interview.

Editing MIDI Event Data in The List Window

The Vision List window is called the MIDI event list by many manufacturers. Just as the Track Overview and Graphic windows enable you to edit MIDI event data, so does the List window, shown in Figure 13.5. The List window displays every MIDI event in the selected track in a text format.

Click the Record button for Track 13, titled Big Bass. Then, click the Selection Dot to the left of the track name. The Track highlights. Click the

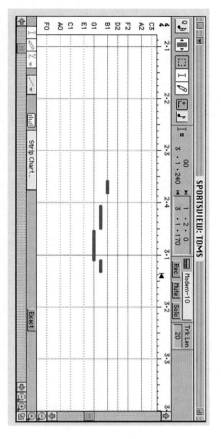

Figure 13.4. The Graphic window enables you to edit MIDI events in a graphic format.

third Window button in the Control Bar, the button with the A2 icon. You should now see the screen shown in Figure 13.5. This is a list of all of the notes and MIDI controller information for the Big Bass track. Clicking the Selection dots in this window will play each of the MIDI events in the List. Click the very first Selection dot. This is the first note of the Bass track. The events shown on the list are named in Figure 13.5.

Locate the first note in the event List, the Note D2 at measure 3, beat 1.[6] Click the letters D2; these mean the first event is note-on for the note D in octave 2. Play the notes on your controller, and the highlighted D2 becomes the notes you are playing. Now click the number 123, the one with

the down arrow beside it. This is the key-on velocity for the first note, D2. Play any note on your controller softly and the value will change. Play it harder and it will change again. This is a fast way to change notes and velocity.

Click the first note, D2, again. Gently position the arrow cursor directly over the highlighted note and move the mouse around very slowly. The cursor will become an up or down arrow. A single click of the mouse will increase or decrease the value of the highlighted event incrementally. Holding down the mouse button will scroll through new values for the event. This editing procedure works for any event shown on the event List.

Note: The SMPTE time code addresses are listed in the second boxed column. Sometimes you will want a certain musical sound to hit perfectly on a film or video cue. You can "jog" the video tape machine and read the SMPTE time code address of the visual cue directly from a little window on your video monitor. Then you can edit the MIDI events in the event List window so they match the SMPTE addresses of the visual cues, and whamo—they sync up perfectly. More about syncing to picture in Chapter 14.

Adding an Octave to a Track

Here's a neat trick that I use often. Sometimes it is effective to double a recorded part in octaves. You *could* replay the part an octave higher and record it on another track, but the magic of MIDI lets you do this another way:

1. Click the Select dot in front of Track 7, called String Stabs.

2. Select Copy Track under the Edit menu.

3. Keep Track 7 highlighted. Select Transpose Track under the Do menu. A Transpose box appears. Make sure that the Key Transpose button is selected and click the word "Up" or "Down" until it is on "Up," making sure that the box says "plus 1 octave." Click the Transpose button and play back

---

[6]*All sequencing software divides a beat into some number of "ticks." The number of ticks per beat is called the note resolution. Just as using higher resolution when digitizing sound makes for a more accurate representation of the sound, using a higher note resolution here allows a more accurate and less quantized recording of the performance. Most professional sequencers will allow a note resolution of 480 ticks per beat; some allow even higher resolution. I always use 480-tick resolution, which makes an eighth note 240 ticks, a sixteenth note 120 ticks, and so on.*

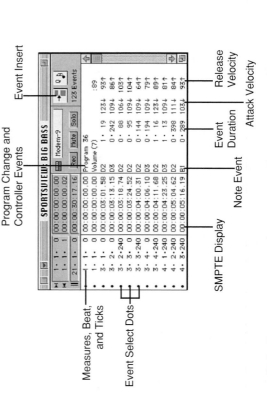

Figure 13.5. *The MIDI event List window in Vision enables you to view and edit every MIDI event in the MIDI recording by name.*

"SportsView." You will hear that Track 7 has been transposed up one octave. Solo the Track to hear the change more clearly and alternately select Undo Transpose and Redo Transpose under the Edit menu. Finally, leave the track Transposed up one octave.

4. Step 2 copied the original Track 7. That copy is waiting in the Mac edit buffer. Make sure that Track 7 is still highlighted, then select Merge into Track under the Edit menu. If you look closely at the blocks in the Overview display for Track 7, you can see that an extra set of notes has been added to the Track. Now the part will play in octaves. Try it, using the Solo function to hear your work clearly.

Setting Locate Points

Professional-level software usually has a feature that enables you to set Locate markers. You should be able to set the locations of the markers "on the fly" or with sequencer playback stopped. Find the row of eight Locator buttons in Figure 13.2. Then find them on your computer screen.

When you click a Locator, the measure, beat, and tick number shown on the Counter are captured and automatically stored as a locate point. The following steps show how to set a locate point at measure 13, beat 1:

1. Put the sequence in play. Position the cursor over Locator 1. When the counter reaches measure 13, click Locator 1; it will highlight.

Stop the sequence. Click Locator 1 again, and the counter will move to the number that you captured. You probably got close to measure 13, beat 1, but most likely you didn't capture it exactly. It still might be close enough for your needs.

2. If you want it exact, click the Counter number you would like to change. Enter corrected numbers so the Counter reads 13-1-000. You can do this from your computer keyboard or by using the incrementing/decrementing arrows furnished by the cursor and clicking (as done in the List window).

3. Hold down Command+Shift and click Locator 1 again. It will unhighlight. Click it again to store the exact location of 15-1-000.

Vision enables you to store eight Locators per sequence.[7] Try it.

Punch Recording

Tape recording engineers long ago perfected the art of punching in and out of record mode on tape machines. This enables the musician to keep all of a recorded track, except perhaps a small segment that needs to be replaced. Better-quality MIDI recorders like Vision also enable you to punch in and out of record.

Select Open under the File menu. Double-click the file SportsView Punch-GM to load it. Find the Punch Record and Loop Controls in the right side of the Control Bar window. (Use Figure 13.2 if you have any difficulty.) Using three buttons enables you to determine the start and end points for Punch-in recording:

The In Point button. This button, with the curved down arrow, sets the punch record In Point—the point where recording will begin.

The Out Point button. This button, with the curved up arrow, sets the punch record Out Point—the point where recording will stop. I have selected the punch In Point and punch Out Point for this example.

The Punch Record toggle button. This button, with both the curved down and up arrows, enables Punch-Record mode.

To punch record:

1. Determine which track you want to record on and record enable it in the Track Functions box by clicking "R." Record enabled Track 10, the Bee 3 organ track, for this example.

2. Determine the In Point and Out Point that define the area where you want to record.

[7] In addition to the eight Locators, Vision enables you to program an unlimited number of other markers that function in much the same way as the Locators. The advantage of using Markers is that you can view a complete list of markers in a Markers pop-up window; the markers appear in all List windows, where they may be edited. A marker can have a text name, such as Verse, Chorus, and so on.

For this example, there is an unrecorded section on Track 10 between measures 9 and 11 where YOU will punch in record.[8] This will make a good example. *Click each number to the right of the In Point button.* Enter the numbers 9-1-0. Next, click each number to the right of the Out Point button. Enter the numbers 11-1-0.

3. Click the Punch Record toggle button. This activates the punch record mode.

4. Click Locator 1. This advances the counter to measure 7, so that you do not have to wait for the first 7 measures to pass before going into Record.

5. Click the Record button in the Transport Controls display. When the Counter reaches measure 9, Track 10 automatically starts recording MIDI event data, generated by your controller device. So play some stuff. If nothing else, just play a chord with the notes D-F-A (this is a Dm chord). Playing eighth notes with the chord is even better. The best scenario is for you to make up your own part. Recording stops at measure 11.

Play back your recorded performance. You can keep re-recording this section as often as you want; each new take erases the previous one. You can "capture" new In Points and Out Points on the fly by clicking the respective In Point buttons while the sequence is in play. The locations of these captured points may then be edited just as you edited the captured Locators in the previous section.

Importing Multiple Sequences into Vision

Most inexpensive sequencer software enables you to have only one sequence loaded at a time. When I am arranging multiple versions of a theme, I need to be able to copy and paste tracks from a finished master sequence into new sequence templates, so as to create the other versions I need in a time- and labor-effective manner. This helps me keep my costs down, my profit margin higher, and it enables me to complete projects faster than my competitors.

Vision provides a perfect solution to this need. Open the file SportsView-GM. Select Sequences under the Windows menu. You will see a screen resembling Figure 13.6.

SportsView-GM		
Sequence	Key	Comments
SPORTSVIEW	A	GM
ALT SPORTSVIEW	B	
NIGHT CAST :30	C	
RETURN BUMP 1	D	
RETURN BUMP 2	E	
ID :10	F	
DELAY OPEN	G	
WEEKEND DELAY	H	
WEEKEND OPEN	I	

Figure 13.6. *The Sequences window enables you to add, delete or create duplicates of sequences in Vision, which enables you to save collections of sequences in a single Vision file. This saves you from having to archive and load each sequence independently, and it enables very fast editing between sequences.*

The Sequences window lists any sequences currently loaded. Only "Fox-59 SportsView" is loaded in the furnished software, so it is the only sequence you see. Click the selection dot to the left of the sequence title. Now find the little triangular pop-up menu button in the drag strip in the top of the window. Click it and select Duplicate. A new sequence named "Fox-59 Sport #2" has appeared. Double-click the selection dot to the left of this title, and the Tracks window for the new sequence fills the screen. Play the sequence. It is an exact copy of the original.

Now, let's edit this into a shorter version such as would be used when returning from a commercial.

1. Vision enables you to quantize the cursor, which helps make perfectly clean edits. For this example, set the Cursor Quantize to whole notes. Select the Cursor Quantize button just to the right of the Selection tools. It is the box with the ruler and the "+" in it.

To the right of the Cursor Quantize button is a button with a music note on it. Click this and hold down the mouse button; a menu of note values pops up. Select a whole note. Now, any edits you make will occur at the beginnings of measures.

2. Select the I-Beam tool in the Selection Tools display. Check Figure 13.3 if you need help.

3. Place the I-Beam tool directly over measure 5, beat 1 (5-1) on the Bar-Beat ruler. The Bar-Beat ruler displays all of the measures

---

[8]*This is the beauty of Vision. You can actually see the best locations to punch in and out of record (or to edit) in the Track Overview and Graphic windows.*

and beats in the sequence. Hold down the mouse button and drag the I-Beam tool all the way to measure 17, beat 1. Release the button and all of the Tracks are highlighted, from measure 5 through measure 17.

> **Warning:** Perform this edit selection very carefully! The I-Beam tool must be exactly on beat 1 of the measures to perform this particular edit successfully. Other edits enable or even require you to place the I-Beam tool on eighth or even sixteenth notes, but you are working with complete measures in this example.
>
> This is why you were asked to quantize the cursor to whole notes in Step 1. Other edits require you to quantize the cursor to the smallest note value you plan to edit.

4. Select Delete Selected Time under the Edit menu; the 12 measures between measures 5 and 17 will vanish. Play the edited sequence. You now have one of the bumpers I arranged for Fox-59.

The track is a little rough at the edit point. I might now go back in and punch record the measure right before the edit point to make the measure between phrases a bit more musical and polished. I often find that the hi-hat, kick, and snare Tracks need this treatment. Or I might change an instrument assignment or two to give this version a different sound. Try muting a track or two; that can be an effective way to create new instrumentation for this edited sequence.

Digging Deeper into Vision 2.0

Vision 2.0 sports "view" functions (I just can't leave the puns alone) and editing functions that have made it one of the most owned and best-liked MIDI recording packages available. Truly a professional tool, the software retails for $495 and comes bundled with Opcode's Galaxy universal librarian, which is discussed in Chapter 11. Galaxy enables you to store all of your synthesizer patch data, organize your patches into custom groupings, and perform searches for patches simply by entering a keyword such as *flute*. Galaxy and Vision work together to create a system where only rarely will you have to write down the names and numbers of your synth patches. In May 1994 Opcode announced the release of Overture, its professional music notation program ($495). I have not worked with Overture as of press time, but it has been designed to integrate completely with Vision 2.0 and Galaxy—while being fast and easy to use. And again, the Opcode staff is easily accessible and eager to answer your questions.

Additional Music Software on *MusicPower*

Two excellent demo software programs from MiBAC (507-645-5851) must be mentioned here. The first is called Music Lessons ($119), which does a great job of teaching basic music principles such as note names, circle of 5ths, scale theory, intervals, and ear training—all in an interactive format that even grades the student and prints out a progress report.

The second is named MiBAC Jazz ($125), which is an intelligent "auto-accompaniment" program—but that description really sells the product short. When I loaded up the Jazz demos, I was amazed. You can tell that Jazz was designed and recorded by real jazz musicians who want computer-assisted music to sound like real music—not like computer games. Work (don't just play) with the demo, and you will be greatly rewarded.

Where Do We Go from Here?

Electronics and synthesizers are great fun and great professional tools. But we will never totally eliminate the need to record live acoustic instruments and vocals. Chapter 14 teaches you the latest techniques for recording those sounds, exploring analog tape recording, digital workstations, film and video applications, and modular digital tape recording systems such as ADAT.

 Mac users should advance to Chapter 14.

14

Adding Live
Instrument and
Voice Sounds
to MIDI

For this chapter, you will need the information you learned in the previous chapters (no hardware is necessary).

When to Use Acoustic or "Live" Sounds

MIDI has certainly become established as one of the primary tools for creation and production of music and sound design. And professional level synthesizers and samplers have now been around long enough to have proven themselves as reliable and useful with regard to generating high-quality sounds triggered by MIDI event data. But the computer musician will eventually find that using electronics exclusively will be very limiting in a number of situations.

Electronic synths and samplers might provide digital sounds that *sound* exactly like their live instrument counterparts when played alone or as single notes. The problem is that all live instruments have certain unique tonal characteristics caused by the very manner in which they generate their own sound. These characteristics can vary greatly from note to note even on the same instrument, and a performer uses them to create a personal musical signature. I call these *performance characteristics*. The way you control the bend of a guitar string...how a sax is not in tune with itself from note to note...the sound of air as it moves through a wind instrument...the uneven way the sound between strokes on a snare drum decays when playing a seven-stroke roll...the difference in the sound of harmonica when you draw instead of blow...these are examples of performance characteristics of live instruments. When a "perfect" sax sample is played back from a MIDI-controlled keyboard sampler, it lacks *many* of these performance characteristics; the simulation can sound stiff and unrealistic. That is a major reason a live sax player will blow the socks off of a MIDI-generated sax line every time.

Table 14.1. A partial list of instruments that often do not work well when used in sampled form.

Instrument	Solo Usefulness	Ensemble Usefulness
Saxophone, Alto	Poor	Maybe
Saxophone, Tenor	Poor	Maybe
Oboe	Poor	Good
Bassoon	Poor	Poor
Tuba	Poor	Poor
Trombone	Poor	Good
Trumpet	Poor	Good
Violin	Carefully	Good
Harmonica	Poor	Maybe
Banjo	Poor	Maybe
16-Note Tambourine	Poor	Poor
Snare Rolls	Poor	Maybe
Timpani Rolls	Poor	Maybe
Cymbal Rolls	Carefully	Carefully
Electric Guitars	Poor	Poor
Acoustic Guitars	Poor	Poor
Nylon String Guitar	Poor	Maybe

Some Instruments Sound Unrealistic in Electronic Format

There are some instrument sounds that undoubtedly *do* sound better in live acoustic form, and a purist would argue that a live sound will always beat a sample. Table 14.1 is a list of some instruments I have often found to work poorly when used in digital sampled form, even as high-quality digital samples. This is because the performance characteristics of these instruments are very difficult to recreate using MIDI controllers. Note that the list shows some instruments as okay to use in ensemble form but not solo form, and vice versa. The author acknowledges that this table may set him up for a firing squad, but every job has its occupational hazards.

This is the *ultimate* subjective topic for musicians. The bottom line: If the sound works for *you*, it's great!

I have found that a certain K2000 snare sample works great for my Tuesday project, a TV spot—and sounds terrible for a documentary soundtrack on Friday. A friend of mine uses a tenor sax sample for final music mixes that I wouldn't dream of using, even for a demo. And many producers actually like to use distorted guitar samples that don't sound at all like a real guitar but that make for a great musical sound effect. Ev'ry-buddy-dance-now!

It is all up to you in the end. I do feel that most acoustic instruments work better when recorded

live—if time, budget, and availability of talent is not an issue (tell me when this is!).

And the acceptable standards are different for each composer-producer-musician who uses these sounds. You get to make the choice. That's what is neat about becoming a computer musician.

And Don't Forget about Vocals!

Vocal sounds generated by synthesizers are great for ethereal pads, oohs and ahs, and for all sorts of great special effects such as those used very creatively in rap and alternative music styles. But we still have to sing lyrics and build stacks of group vocals. And film, video, and radio work will always require the recording of dialog and narrative voice tracks. So the use of MIDI technology has not and will not eliminate the process of recording live sounds. So how do you get the MIDI tracks and the live tracks to work together?

Synchronized Sound Recording

If you record several tracks into a MIDI sequence, then record vocals and guitars on a tape machine, you must have some way of "linking" the sequencer and the tape machine together. Chapter 11 called this *synchronization*, or *syncing*, and explained how to synchronize two MIDI devices. Any time you are recording and playing back with more than one recording device, whether MIDI-

or tape-based, all of the devices must be synchronized. If our recording devices are not synchronized, the tracks on the two devices will be completely out of time (out of sync) with each other, and the resulting sound will be useless. This would be like a music version of a bad foreign movie where the lips don't move in sync with the dialog—except worse! You know how bad it is to play with another musician who can't keep the beat.

One of the devices is designated as a *master*. Other devices to be synchronized are then designated as *slaves*. You can have many slaves in a synchronized MIDI project studio, but only one device is designated as a master. The master supplies the timing information that controls all of the slaves in the system.

Three methods are used for keeping recording devices in sync:

MIDI beat clock. Used for syncing two MIDI devices.

Frequency Shift Key (FSK) clock. Used for syncing MIDI devices to tape recorders.

SMPTE-MIDI time code (MTC). A better way of syncing MIDI devices to tape recorders.

The Chapter 11 section, "MIDI Synchronization," taught you how to sync two MIDI devices using MIDI beat clock. Refer to that section now if you need a quick refresher.

Using FSK Clock for Sync

FSK requires you to record an *FSK sync tone* onto a track of tape. The FSK sync tone is recorded *after* you have determined the final tempo for the music piece and usually after you have recorded your MIDI sequences. The tape machine is put into record, the MIDI sequencer is put into play, and the MIDI sequencer generates MIDI beat clock at a rate determined by the sequence tempo. An FSK interface converts this MIDI beat clock into the FSK sync tone which is recorded onto the tape. The clock rate of the recorded FSK sync tone is variable depending on the rate of the MIDI sequence.

The recorded FSK sync tone is played back into the FSK interface, which counts the frequency shifts in the tone and reconverts this count back into MIDI beat clocks. These beat clocks are then sent from a MIDI port to a slaved MIDI device, which runs in sync with instruments recorded on the tape recorder.

FSK is one of the oldest MIDI-to-tape synchronization tools and has the horrible problem of not having any actual real-time basis for location. This means that you cannot stop and restart anywhere you want in the middle of a recording, but rather that you have to start at the very beginning of the music piece for every "take." If you don't, the MIDI device[1] slaved to the FSK clock does not

have any idea which measure it is supposed to be playing.

Ta-da! Smart FSK is an updated FSK format that includes Song Position Pointer, which provides location updates for the slave devices. Smart FSK sync enables you to stop and start recording and play back anywhere you want in your recording. For this to work properly, your MIDI devices must be designed to follow Song Position Pointer. If they are not, they will still get lost in time.

Using SMPTE and MIDI Time Code for Sync

Using SMPTE and MIDI time code as a timing reference for synchronization is far superior to using an FSK clock. With FSK (even Smart FSK), the tempo and length of a composition are set in stone at the time you record the FSK tone onto tape. Any change in the tempo or number of measures in the MIDI sequence will require the recording of a new FSK tone. If you already have instruments recorded on the tape machine...well, uh...bummer. You are just out of luck. You get to record them all over again. But hey, maybe you need the practice anyway. I sure do.

Sometimes I don't have time to re-record three passes of sax, two passes of 12-string guitar, one pass of oboe, and four vocal tracks—and all the other musicians left two hours ago. The needs of

the professional computer musician drove the recording industry to incorporate the use of SMPTE time code for synchronization of all recorded material, tape- *and* MIDI-based.

Chapter 1 introduced you to SMPTE time code. Chapter 11 mentioned it again in the section titled "SMPTE and MIDI Time Code." I repeat that explanation here because it is so important. I guess you could call this a review!

SMPTE actually stands for Society of Motion Picture and Television Engineers. This is an organization that determines all the standard protocols for data communications in the television and motion picture industry. Time code was actually invented by NASA as a tool for analyzing launch and flight data and was adopted by SMPTE in the early '70s as a standard tool for film, video, and sound synchronizing and editing.

You can think of moving pictures (film and video) as a series of very fast, moving still photos. National and international standards committees such as SMPTE have selected the speeds at which these photos are recorded and reproduced, assigning specific frame rates for specific uses. Frames rates are measured in fps (the number of frames per second of moving picture). Here are some of the standard frame rates and their uses:

30fps	Music and audio projects and audio-visual slide shows[2]
29.97fps	The most common frame rate you will see; color and black-and-white video and TV

---

[1] Usually a drum machine or a sequencer.

[2] Tech editor Larry Fast is a T.V. history buff. He explained to me that the 30fps rate originally specified for black-and-white television was quietly eliminated in 1953. The frame rate for black-and-white is incorrectly listed as 30 in most publications. I thank Larry for this clarification.

Non-drop and drop-frame modes exist for the preceding frame rates and are used for special applications.

| 25fps | PAL European video and TV standard |
| 24fps | Film productions |

SMPTE time code is created by a time code generator[3], which is capable of generating all or some of the preceding frame rates. This generated time code is recorded on one track of an audio or video tape machine. SMPTE time code is recorded on tape at a *constant* rate, which is not at all dependent on the sequence tempo or length. Thus, SMPTE time code can be recorded at any time before the recording process. The recording industry calls this *striping tape*.[4]

SMPTE time code measures time in hours, minutes, seconds, and frames. Sections of the recording can be located by the "SMPTE addresses" specified by these SMPTE time code numbers.

Figure 14.1 shows the readout from a Fostex 4010 time code generator-reader.

The recorded SMPTE time code stripe is played back from the tape machine and is sent into a SMPTE-to-MIDI converter. This converter then

does one of two things; it generates MIDI beat clock, or it generates MIDI time code.

In the old days, the converters would only generate MIDI beat clock and Song Position Pointer. The tempo of the composition had to be programmed into the converter in beats-per-minute, beat-by-beat, one bar at a time. Computer musicians called this a *tempo map*. The converter then generated MIDI beat clock based on the tempo(s) programmed into the converter tempo map. This MIDI beat clock then controlled the tempo of the sequencers and drum machines.

Sequencing software began to appear that enabled you to construct the tempo maps in the sequencer software rather than in the converter. This was much easier because you didn't have to program beat-by-beat anymore—and the tempo map saved to disk as an integrated part of the sequence!

The invention of MIDI time code (MTC) provided the next step in the syncing scenario.[5] SMPTE-to-MIDI converters are now designed to generate MTC that includes SMPTE-based address information *as well as* MIDI beat clock.[6] Software designers now write professional-level sequencer software to list MIDI events not only in terms of measure and beat, but also in terms of where these events happen relative to the SMPTE

time code stripe recorded on the tape machine. Figure 14.2 shows a MIDI event list from Digital Performer. Notice how the MIDI events are listed by measure and beat as well as by SMPTE address. This is especially useful when working with film or video projects; a MIDI event can easily be lined up with a SMPTE address location on a video tape master.

Warning: 29.97fps is not necessarily drop frame!!! Most video post houses actually operate on 29.97 non-drop, except for some special applications such as closed captioning. If the video was mastered using 29.97 non-drop time code, don't try to take a completed post score into the edit bay for a layback with all of your work completed using drop-frame time code. You will not stay in sync. Yet manufacturers persist in shipping interfaces with time code generators that do not actually generate 29.97 non-drop code. Watch carefully for this feature if you plan to do serious postscoring work.

Figure 14.1. The SMPTE time code readout from a Fostex 4010 time code generator-reader. Note the division of hours-minutes-seconds-frames.

[3]The SMPTE time code generator may be a stand-alone piece or may be built into a MIDI interface, or even into a video or audio tape machine. For example, the MIDI Express interface by Mark of the Unicorn and the Fostex RD-8 ADAT format digital recorder both have time code generator-readers on board.

[4]When the Bowen Music staff is preparing for production of a music project, I will often prepare MIDI sequences in my home. One of our engineers will record the SMPTE stripe at our downtown studio at a time when sessions are not booked. I then take a disk with my MIDI files to the downtown studio and sync my MIDI sequencer tracks to the pre-striped time-code on the tape machine there.

[5]Another of the brilliant guys at Sequential, Chris Meyer, is generally credited as being the father of this great idea.

[6]Remember that MIDI beat clock enables you to base timing reference only on measures and beats.

Syncing Up all of this Sync Information

Table 14.2 shows some commonly used recording devices and which method to use for synchronizing their tracks.

The Recording Hardware

I can divide the tools used for recording into three categories:

♪ MIDI recording, also called virtual tracking[9]

♪ Tape-based recording

♪ Direct-to-disk, or random access, recording

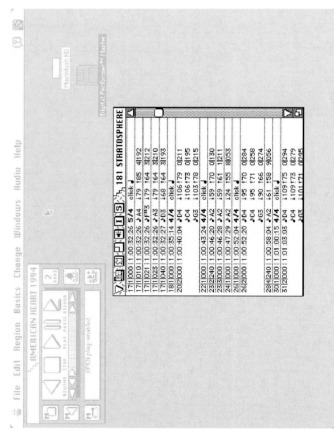

Figure 14.2. *Sequencing software designed to support MIDI time code enables the computer musician to view MIDI events by measures and beats or by SMPTE address.*

This syncing issue forces you to design a game plan for your MIDI project studio. Your MIDI interface must support Smart FSK if you plan to sync using FSK. Your MIDI interface and sequencing software must support MTC if you plan to sync using MTC.[7] MTC-compatible software and interfaces may cost a bit more up front, but if you plan to do any serious sync recording, MTC really is the way to go.

Table 14.2. Synchronizing various recording devices.

Master Device	Clock from Master	Slave Device	Need Converter?	Need Slave Syncs To
Sequencer	MIDI beat clock or MTC	Drum machine	No	MIDI Beat Clock or MTC[8]
Drum machine	MIDI beat clock or MTC	Sequencer	No	MIDI Beat Clock or MTC
Sequencer	MIDI beat clock or MTC	Sequencer	No	MIDI Beat Clock or MTC
Tape recorder	FSK	Any of the above	Yes	MIDI Beat Clock
Tape recorder	SMPTE time code	Any of the above	Yes	MTC or MIDI Beat Clock

[7]*Several companies, such as Opcode and J.L. Cooper, do make SMPTE-to-MTC converters costing $100-$200, which you can add inline to your old FSK or MIDI beat clock-equipped interfaces.*

[8]*You might want to refer to Chapter 11, which explains this kind of MIDI-to-MIDI synchronization.*

[9]*Computer musicians have invented the term virtual tracks to refer to the tapeless sounds generated by MIDI software and hardware.*

I have thoroughly discussed MIDI recording, so now I will explore the other two categories. The study of tape-based recording can be divided into two topics:

- Analog tape recording
- Digital tape recording

Syncing MIDI with Analog Tape

A number of available MIDI interfaces read SMPTE time code and convert it to MIDI time code (MTC). These interfaces enable you to synchronize MIDI sequences with sounds recorded on tape machines. This SMPTE-MTC synchronization is essential to the modern interfacing of tape machines and computers. Remember, this is a far superior method to using FSK clock. I feel so strongly about this that I will base the remaining syncing discussions in this book on the use of SMPTE and MTC. Figure 14.3 reviews how it all works.

Synchronizing MIDI with Audio Tape Machines

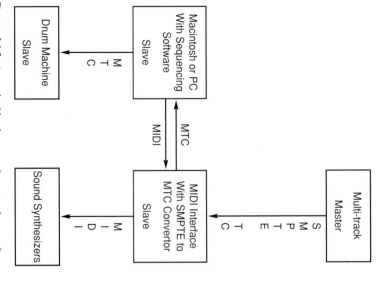

Figure 14.3. *A standard hardware configuration for recording live tracks in sync with virtual tracks. Illustration by Mark Evans, Bowen Music Productions.*

In a tape-based system, you usually use a tape machine with 8, 16, or 24 tracks, although you can synchronize a MIDI sequencer to a machine as basic as a 4-track cassette recorder, such as a Tascam Portastudio or a Fostex 380S (Figure 14.4).

Striping Tape with SMPTE Time Code

To prepare for a SMPTE time code synchronized recording session, follow this procedure:

Figure 14.4. *The Fostex 380S is a 4-track cassette recorder that can be used on the hobby or educational level for recording live acoustic instruments and vocals in sync with a computer-based MIDI sequencer. Several manufacturers build recorders similar to the 380S.*

1. Forward wind and rewind the reel of tape completely to get any sticky spots or tiny kinks out of the polyester tape backing. This step prevents tape drop-outs, the worst enemy of the synchronized recording session.

2. Record enable your highest numbered tape track. The recording industry has agreed to the standard that time code should be striped on the highest numbered track of tape. Run the time code generator a bit to check for a proper record level.

> **Note:** There is no technical standard for proper time code record level. We receive tapes with levels as high as +3dB (!) and as low as -10dB (?). Levels in the +3 range and higher may have a tendency to "bleed" across audio tracks, and levels in the -10 range and lower will be very susceptible to drop-out and unreliable sync. The level recommended at Bowen Music Productions is -5dB.
>
> And never *dub* time code. Always use a time code generator to generate a *new* SMPTE stripe or to *regenerate* existing (called Source) time code from another audio or video tape machine. Some people call this *jam syncing*. The jam sync mode of a time code generator allows the generator to continue striping at the proper frame rate and level if a bug or dropout appears in the source time code being regenerated.

3. Turn any noise reduction off on the channel where you are recording the SMPTE stripe.

4. Set your time code generator up to start at 01:00:00:00, with a frame rate of 30 frames per second (fps).[10] Many MIDI interfaces now feature SMPTE time code generators that enable you to use a desktop accessory or other utility to set up this start address and frame rate. More about this back in the section "More about MIDI Interfaces," found in Chapter 11.

5. Put the tape recorder into record-play, then start the time code generator. The time code will appear on the VU or LED meter for the striped track.

6. If this is not a sound for video project, stripe the entire reel of tape. *Do not stripe the tape in discontinuous sections.* You create the segment for each composition by using the Sequence Start or Offset function built into your sequencer software.

7. Rewind the tape and prepare for playback.

Setting Up the Interface for Sync to Tape

The time code from the tape machine is fed to your SMPTE-to-MIDI converter, or to your MIDI interface if the MIDI interface has a converter built in. You must set up the interface software for syncing. This procedure varies depending on the particular interface you have online, but the control panels for this setup usually look something similar to the one for the J.L. Cooper Sync-Link (Figure 14.5).

You can assure timing accuracy in your work by always selecting the same frame rate as you used when striping tape with SMPTE time code. If these frame rates do not match, you will be headed for a major hassle; your tape and MIDI tracks may shift noticeably in and out of time with each other.

Setting Up the Sequencing Software for Sync to Tape

Your sequencer software provides a window where you determine the type of sync clock you want the sequencer to follow. In Cakewalk this is the Clock window under the Settings menu. Vision uses a sub menu called Receive Sync Mode, found under the Options menu. Figure 14.6 shows the sync options for Cakewalk Professional.

If you select SMPTE or MTC, professional-level software will also enable you to determine which SMPTE/MTC frame rate the MIDI events are referencing to. Figure 14.7 shows how Vision lets you make this selection.

Now You Are Ready to Go

This is really a magical thing we have happening here. When you have properly configured your software and hardware to run in sync, all you have to do is be sure that your sequencer is set up to receive external sync, put your sequencer in to play, and start the tape machine. All of your virtual tracks will leap into action, and that little 8-track tape machine over in the corner will suddenly control dozens of tracks of MIDI.

[10] *If this session were for post-scoring video or film, you would "regenerate" or "jam sync" new time code based on the SMPTE stripe on the video tape master you would be working with. This would guarantee that the time code numbers and frame rates striped on the audio tape recorder (ATR) would be exactly the same as those supplied by the video tape master. Important!*

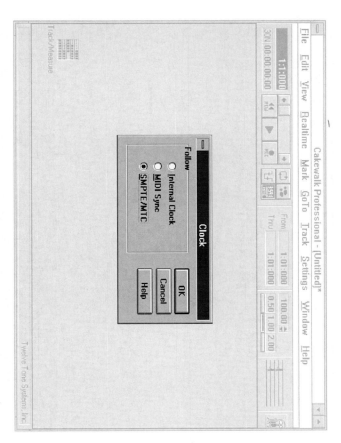

Figure 14.5. The J.L. Cooper Sync-Link features a SMPTE Controls window. PC and Mac MIDI interfaces with built-in SMPTE-to-MTC converters have a Setup window like this, where you select options that determine how the interface converts SMPTE time code to MIDI time code. This window also provides the settings for a built-in SMPTE time code generator, which is used for striping time code on a tape recorder track.

Figure 14.6. You select the type of clock a sequencer will follow in windows and menus such as these provided by Cakewalk.

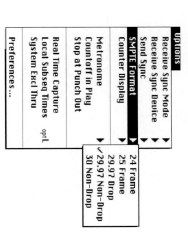

Figure 14.7. Opcode Vision's SMPTE Format menu enables you to select the frame rate for SMPTE/MTC sync.

Warning: I know I already said this in the text, but it is important. You can assure timing accuracy in your work by always selecting the same frame rate that you used when striping tape with SMPTE time code. If these frame rates do not match, you will be headed for a major hassle; your tape and MIDI tracks may shift noticeably in and out of time with each other.

Syncing MIDI with Digital Tape

As consumers became spoiled by listening to CD-quality sound, the recording industry found the need to incorporate expensive digital recording technology in the early stages of a recording project. Until 1991, digital tape recording was the exclusive domain of very high-end major studio operations. Machines by manufacturers such as Mitsubishi and Sony featured 32-track digital recording using special digital-quality, reel-to-reel tape for storage of the digital data. Many successful albums have been recorded on these expensive machines (in many cases costing more than $100,000), and they certainly have elevated the sonic standards of the recording industry. But then....

High-Tech Helps Shape Classical Music Recording

An Interview with Victor Muenzer of Classic Digital, Inc.

The author caught up with Victor Muenzer in between recording sessions, editing sessions, conferences…wow, is this guy on the go! Victor and the staff of Classic Digital, located in the Chicago suburb of Evanston, are highly respected in the demanding field of recording and producing classical music. Since 1985, Classic Digital has edited and mastered nearly

1,000 compact disk recording projects, many using its two Sonic System digital workstations. Victor graciously took the time to discuss applications for workstation technology, as applied to the classical music genre. The following comments are excerpted from that discussion.

"We record to DAT and then we load that (recording) into a digital work station. Then we edit and manipulate the source material in

whatever way we need to come up with the best product possible. Years ago, we were the first facility in the Midwest with any capacity to edit digitally. We were using the Sony DAE1100 system, which some of your readers will be familiar with. This system was a tape-based system, and it worked much the same way as a video-editing system worked and, of course, back in 1984 and 1985, we were all kind of thrilled with it. We were glad that we could at least edit digital material without going into the analog domain…putting it on analog tape and cutting it with a razor blade. We first looked at the Sonic System because the System answers two big problems for us. One is to put all our source material onto large hard disks and then access all of that source material immediately—without having to pull through loads of 3/4-inch videotape, which is what the old DAE1100 series used. And then, secondly, the sonic system makes edits that are just far and away superior to what the Sony DAE1100 could do. The edit cross-fades are longer and can be made to work better because they are not just linear cross-fades. The cross-fades can be based on cosine, root cosine, or various other mathematical curves, which means that the energy of the signal through the edit can be balanced. We can truly make seamless edits. For the first time, with the Sonic System, it really becomes possible to edit in the middle of notes, not just on attacks or between notes, but actually in the middle of notes. And, ultimately, this gives us a lot of flexibility in the sorts of editing that we can do."

"Usually, the standard procedure is that we might do two complete takes of a work and then examine problem areas…where the performance really hasn't quite been up to what we would want. Then we will do what we call patches or inserts, where we will record just that specific piece of music. Later, it is the job of a producer, who usually is me, to sift through all this source material and decide what is best. The beauty of hard-disk editing is we can decide what we think is best, and put it all together. As you know, in editing things don't always go together the way you think they might. With the Sonic System you can change your mind. And you don't destroy any tape, basically, it is nondestructive editing. You just don't run the risk of ruining original source material."

"Recently, we did a record with Itzhak Perlman, and he was quite involved in the approval process, because he knows the technology, he likes to work with it, he understands it. So, he was able to be quite specific about what he wanted. For instance, his project was very unique in that we actually did it 4-channel and we did it as a 4-channel edit on the Sonic digital work station. Two of the channels contain the orchestra tracks, the left and right stereo source material. The other two tracks

contain his violin alone. We edited in 4 channels so that at all times, even as we made edits, we had 4 channels of source material. That allowed us to change his sound. He wanted this passage up 2 1/2 dB, or this passage down 3 dB, or that sort of thing. We literally mixed it after we edited, and we had complete creative flexibility in making that record."

"We do a lot more live recording now, where records are actually made during performances. We might record 3 or 4 whole concerts or a record from that source material. Some of the editing then gets very complex because we are not just dealing with musical issues. We are dealing with removing coughs and unwanted noises. So, the new work station technology has been very useful because it has allowed us to do this sort of detailed editing…to remove most noises and coughs. We still can't remove them all, but we can certainly make a record that is still live but has the same approximate level of quality as a studio recording. In addition to that, live recording situations tend to be a little bit more difficult acoustically, and the digital work station technology has allowed us to do more manipulation with the sound after the fact. Often, we record in digital 24-track, then we mix down. Even after we have edited the

source material on the Sonic, we might do some significant digital signal processing, using various reverb and/or signal processing programs in the [Lexicon] 480L and EQ in the Sonic."

For the first time…it really becomes possible to edit in the middle of notes, not just on attacks or between notes, but actually in the middle of notes.

"In general, I would say that the digital work-station technology has been a real boon to us. The one danger in the whole process is that, because we can do so much with the digital work station, we tend to, in fact, go ahead and pursue all of these various creative possibilities. That is great in one sense, but we always have to be sure that we are still leaving the integrity of the music there—especially for people in our business, where we are really here to represent an artist and an organization. When we make a record with the Chicago Symphony Orchestra, we are there to recreate their image to the public and to make sure that we are presenting what they are all about musically. So, it is very important that we not get carried away too much with the technology, because it is very powerful now and we could, in fact, make changes that might degrade that image to the public. So, we are very careful and very cautious, and work always to make positive creative changes, not negative ones."

The ADAT Digital Tape Format

In January of 1991, Alesis Studio Electronics announced the development of an 8-track, CD-quality recording machine that used S-VHS tape as the storage medium for the digital audio data. The machine, pictured in Figure 14.8a, was called ADAT.

The retail price of the machine was under $4000! As you might imagine, this revolutionized the industry, as the following quotes of the time demonstrate:

"I can't think of any reason not to have an ADAT." Roger Nichols, *EQ* magazine, October 1992.

"Every musician in the world is going to own one of these things; count on it." Michael Molenda and Neal Brighton, *Electronic Musician*, October 1992.

"I'm not sure whether this is a review of a product or a phenomenon." George Petersen, *Mix* magazine, 1992.

According to Alan Wald of Alesis, as of January 20, 1994 "there are already over 20,000 ADATs in use all over the world." In the autumn of 1992, the remarkable ADAT Group was formed. The ADAT Group is composed of a diverse group of manufacturers who work together to ensure that new products support and enhance the use of the ADAT recording system. At press time, more than 35 manufacturers were participating in the ADAT Group, and several new ADAT-compatible

Figure 14.8. *The revolutionary Alesis ADAT 8-track digital recorder (a) and the ADAT-compatible Fostex RD-8 (b). The ADAT format enables recording up to about 40 minutes of 8-track digital recording when using a 120-minute, S-VHS tape. You can record up to 54 minutes if you use a 160-minute tape. Multiple machines synchronize with each other using a built-in sync connector, so you simply add more machines (up to a maximum of 16 machines or 128 tracks!) if you want more tracks. Photos courtesy of Alesis Studio Electronics and Fostex, Incorporated.*

products were being released. One of the most notable of these is the Fostex RD-8 (Figure 14.8b), another 8-track recording system that also uses the S-VHS tape format for digital data storage.

Fostex has designed many professional features into the RD-8 that are not included in the standard ADAT unit. Some of these include MTC

inputs and outputs; SMPTE generators, readers, and synchronizers; and MIDI machine control. But the really good news is that tapes recorded on either the Alesis ADAT or on the RD-8 are completely interchangeable, due to the standardization between the two manufacturers.

Syncing ADAT Format Digital Recorders

One of the neatest features about ADAT is that you do not have to use an audio track for SMPTE/MTC synchronization.

Earlier, this chapter discussed synchronizing MIDI equipment with live tracks recorded on an analog tape recorder. To accomplish this synchronization, you recorded a SMPTE time code stripe on one of the tracks. Too bad we had to use that track; it might have been useful for one more pass of lead vocals.

This is not necessary with the ADAT format. A data track featuring a very high resolution timing clock, called Alesis time code, is recorded when you format a blank ADAT tape. Converter boxes by Alesis, J. L. Cooper, MIDI Man, and other ADAT Group manufacturers can convert the Alesis time code into SMPTE time code or MTC. The Fostex RD-8 has this converter built in, so MTC is automatically sent from the MIDI OUT ports on the rear of the machine. Very smart!

The Tascam DA-88 Digital Tape Format

Tascam has always been a powerhouse player in the tape-recording business and has developed its own proprietary 8-track digital recording system, the DA-88 (Figure 14.9). The DA-88 is another modular digital multitrack recorder that features 8-track digital recording. It syncs to external SMPTE time code while generating MTC (when used with the optional SY-88 sync card).

The DA-88 stores digital audio data on Hi-8mm video tapes with about 100 minutes of 8-track recording time per tape. It is built like a tank and shuttles tape very fast—much faster than ADAT-format machines. And just like the ADAT-format machines, the DA-88 sounds very good.

The Tascam DA-88 tape format is not compatible with ADAT machines. One way to convert the timing data from the Tascam clock track is by using the optional SY-88 sync card, which provides SMPTE and MTC outputs. Other manufactures are now designing products that support and enhance the use of the DA-88.

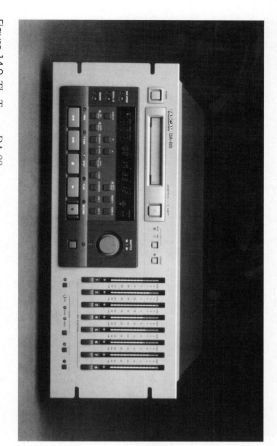

Figure 14.9. *The Tascam DA-88.*

Direct-to-Disk (or Random-Access) Recording

Direct-to-disk recording is gaining widespread popularity as a must-have technology for recording dialog, narration, sound effects, musical instruments, and singers on the professional level. This book focuses on the musical applications of this technology.[11]

Chapter 4 discussed digital audio and sound files. The applications for digital audio in that chapter were fairly simple, such as recording and playing back a sound effect or a sampled instrument sound. And Chapter 11 talked about more exotic uses for sampling—for example, sampling synthesizers and sampling sound modules. The concepts taught in those chapters are applicable in this section, because recent expanded development of digital audio sampling and processing technology,

combined with new advancements in computer software and hardware, enables you to record completely within a computer system. These computer-based recording systems are known as *workstations*. Figure 14.10 shows the popular Pro Tools workstation by Digidesign.

Direct-to-disk recording is also called random access recording and also nonlinear recording. The terms *nonlinear* and *random access* are explained beautifully by the graphics in Figure 14.11. Figure 14.11a shows the linear nature of tape recording, meaning that recorded sections are physically distant from each other, sometimes separated by many feet of tape. This separation requires shuttling (rewinding and forward winding) tape, which can be very time-consuming. In Figure 14.11b, you can see how the recorded sections are accessed almost instantaneously by the moving heads of the drive mechanism, which enables you to seamlessly output different "takes" in any order, and with no time spent shuttling tape!

The D-to-D recording process can be summarized as follows:

1. Sounds to be recorded are sent to an A-D converter, which converts an analog sound into a digital sound file.

2. The large, digitized audio sound files are then stored on large hard, removable, or magneto-optical (MO) drives.

[11] *Random Access Audio is a book by David Miles Huber and published by Sams. It provides an in-depth study of this fast-growing area of recording technology. Highly recommended.*

4. These edited playlists may be saved to hard and MO drives and recalled at a future time for additional editing or for revision.

5. When the drives are full they are *backed up*, or offloaded to a tape-based backup system.[12]

Jeff Boone at Alaska Software has prepared a demo of his company's Digitrax Software—just for this book! Digitrax is a Mac-based, direct-to-disk recording and editing system that allows up to six channels of audio when using a NuMedia card or an A/V Mac.

This is a special treat for readers and an opportunity to experiment with a nice piece of software. If you have any questions, you can find the phone number and address for Alaska Software in Appendix E.

3. The sound files can be uploaded into multitrack editing software, where you can perform complex editing operations such as cutting and pasting, programming automated mixes, or adding digital processing such as reverb, eq, and level normalization, to name a few options. These assembled multitrack productions are called *playlists*.

Figure 14.10. *The most popular professional workstation is the Pro Tools system, by Digidesign. Digidesign also manufactures a moderately priced 8-channel system they call the Session 8, for both the PC and Mac platforms.*

Figure 14.11. *These illustrations (provided by Akai Digital) show how audio is accessed on (a) tape-based recording systems, and (b) direct-to-disk recording systems.*

[12]*Many studios using a magneto-optical drive system simply remove the full disk and insert a blank one.*

Intro

Verse 1

Chorus 1

Verse 2

Lead Solo

On tape, the sections of music are physically located far from each other, separated by many feet of the tape itself. Since you have to move all that tape past the heads to get where you want to go, it's impossible to jump instantly from one section to another. It wastes time, and limits creativity!

a

Rotation (4500 RPM)

Lead Guitar Solo Take 1

Chorus 1

Verse 2

Verse 1

Chorus 2

Lead Guitar Solo Take 2

b

Advantages of Using Direct-to-Disk Recording

There are many advantages to using D-to-D recording:

1. The entire recording/editing/assembly process is nondestructive. The computer musician can record as many tracks and channels as his or her hardware/software configuration permits, then edit at will without deleting the original takes. This enables the musician to record multiple passes of each segment of the song and then edit good takes together to make a composite (or *comp*) track.

2. Because D-to-D recording/editing is nonlinear, requiring no tape shuttling, access to recorded information is very fast.

3. The audio is all CD-quality. No tape noise. Bouncing tracks cause no signal degradation.

4. The playlist becomes the track log. No messy paper to lose. The names of the different versions of the songs, song segments, tracks, mixes, and so on are saved to disk with the playlist files and can all be reloaded as one tidy, complete file. Management of materials and track logs in a bustling commercial studio with several engineers is a big, big issue.

Disadvantages of Using Direct-to-Disk Recording

There are also many disadvantages to using D-to-D recording:

---

1. Standardization and compatibility issues have not been fully resolved. The sound files and playlists you work with on one manufacturer's workstation may not load and play on one made by another company.

2. Certain kinds of edits and effects processing, such as digital noise reduction, normalization, and digital equalization, might require significant processing time and thus slow down the production process.

3. System crash and lockup is a common problem with workstations. Fragmentation of files saved on the hard drive is a serious workstation problem, resulting in slower access times and possibly even gaps in the audio. Fragmentation can be relieved somewhat by using third-party defragmentation utilities such as Public Utilities, Norton Disk Utilities, or Central Point Software Optimizer[13]—and this book

> **Note:** This is a good time for a clarification of the distinction between a *track* and a *channel*. Most workstation systems enable the user to configure a nearly unlimited number of tracks for editing. But the number of sounds that can be played back simultaneously by the system *is* limited and is referred to as the number of channels. Random access channels are analogous to voices provided by a MIDI synthesizer, which are described in the Chapter 11 section, "Polyphony."
>
> Bear in mind that the terms *track* and *channel*, when used regarding recording systems, are not to be confused with these terms when used to discuss MIDI.

---

4. Chapter 4 discussed sampling rate and memory requirements for sampling. Remember, the formula for required disk storage space is 10MB per minute of stereo audio per track; a hard drive can fill quickly. What do you do when your hard drive is filled up? You offload the data to some sort of data storage device. This is called *archiving*. Archiving is accomplished in several ways:

   ♪ The least expensive (but slowest) archiving uses a tape streamer to a data tape. Older archiving systems might have to offload in real time, one track at a time. This means eight full tracks with a length of twenty minutes would take 8×20 or 160 minutes to archive to a data DAT—and the same time to load! Fortunately, manufacturers have responded to the slow tape archiving problem by implementing double-speed archiving and background archiving, which runs in the background (get it?) while you are performing other tasks with your workstation.

has taught you to save often and to save your files under two different names, right?

---

[13]This information is borrowed from the *NuMedia* sound card reference manual supplied with the *NuMedia* card sent to me by Mike Kane of Spectral Innovations. This reference manual features a really nice tutorial concerning hard disk facts and sampling facts. I urge you to write and request a reprint:

Spectral Innovations, Incorporated
1885 Landy Avenue, Suite 208
San Jose CA 95131
Attn: Mike Kane

By using MO drives for the whole workstation process and simply removing the MO cartridge when it is full. This can work well for two-track files, but at the time this book went to press, professional consensus was that MO drives were not fast enough to handle the recording and playback of four or more tracks of audio. But MOs *are* being used very successfully as an archiving medium.

Removable cartridge drives. These, however, are *generally* too small (44MB, 88MB, 105MB, or 270MB) to hold a significant amount of high-resolution audio data.

WORM drives can "write-once, read-many" times. Sure, they hold 900 or more MB of data, but a WORM drive cannot be erased or rewritten. Don't even think about four-track recording or playback (too slow).

Using a DAT audio machine. Most manufacturers consider this to be a cost-effective but chancy way to archive audio data. The error correction employed by DAT decks causes your audio data to be downloaded and uploaded inaccurately. Believe me, there is no audio problem as severe as corrupted data. Warning…Warning…Danger…Danger!

5. Synchronization problems. Slaving a workstation to external sync sources is not for those who are faint of heart or frugal with cash. Digital recording devices can slave to external clocks, but slaving to SMPTE or MTC alone generally does not get the job done. This is because the recording and playback of digital audio is a very speed-dependent process. Tape machines (especially analog) are flawed by the "wow" and "flutter" of analog transport design. Even the rock-solid ADAT and DA-88 transports may not be reliable enough all the time for digital-to-digital transfers.

The internal digital workings of a workstation are controlled by a very sophisticated *word clock*, which keeps all of the digital *words*[14] lined up with the sampling rate of the D-A converter. If this alignment is lost, the effect is very similar to the result of two sets of gears that are lined up, but with different tooth sizes; the gears would gnash and grind and create a heck of a racket. When digital audio loses word sync, the sound is unearthly. In minor cases, you hear unwanted pops and clicks; in worse cases, the sound turns into chatter, buzzes, gronks, and stuff defying description. Word clock is the clock that any slaved digital audio device wants to see.[15] If slaving two digital devices, the master usually sends a word clock to the slave machine. If slaving

multiple digital audio devices, you should sync to a master word clock generator, which will send the generated word clock to each slave device.

6. Cost. The cost of basic workstation hardware and software is rapidly reaching hobbyist and semi-pro level affordability. But workstations still are pricey if you start adding truly professional features such as lots of channels, digital eq, high-quality digital reverb, sync to video, and a fast archiving system. And the price of a fast computer with lots of RAM (at least 8MB) with a serious-sized hard drive (*at least* 360MB) contributes greatly to the overall cost of a workstation.

You can see that a tape-based system such as an Alesis or Fostex ADAT, a Tascam DA-88, or even a high-quality analog recording system still has a solid place in the studio of the computer musician. Tape-based recording formats currently hold the upper hand in the price battle between disk- and tape-based recording formats. And reliability, compatibility, and ease of installation are areas where tape may win as well (for now, that is).

[14] *A digital word is a 16-bit chunk of data.*

[15] *In film and video work, the workstation still receives SMPTE time code, but in this case time code is used for helping audio devices locate to external SMPTE addresses, to control rewind, forward wind, play, and for visual time-based reference when editing.*

Stand-Alone, Direct-to-Disk Systems

Some manufacturers are responding to the call for more reliable, lower-cost workstations by using proprietary systems that do not require the central processing unit (CPU) of a computer to do the actual work. Workstations like the Akai DR4d (Figure 14.12a) and the Roland DM-80 (Figure 14.12b) use a low-powered computer[16] for the user interface, basically to enable you to *control* the recording and editing functions of the workstation. The stand-alone workstation does all of the number crunching and processing work that the CPU does in some computer-based workstations.

The Akai DR4d is a modular system; each DR4d unit provides 4 channels of D-to-D recording *and* an internal 200MB hard drive (four full tracks equals 36.5 minutes at 48kHz sampling). Up to seven external hard drives may be added to allow a theoretical maximum of 24 hours of recording time. The DR4d system is expanded by daisy-chaining additional DR4d units via the 7-pin DIN connectors shown on the front of the unit. Four units may be linked to create a 16-channel system. The base unit carries a list price of about $2500, which definitely puts the unit in the hands of a hobbyist or semipro. The Roland DM-80 is available in a 4-track version with one internal 100MB hard drive ($7295) or in an 8-track version with two internal 100MB hard drives

[16] I have actually seen these systems in operation with engineers using a Mac Plus or SE with 2.5MB RAM and a 20MB hard drive for the user interface!

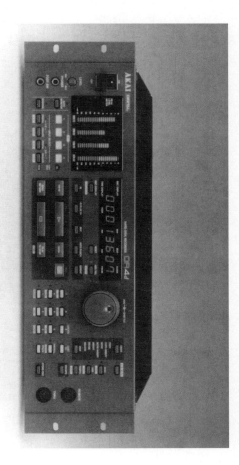

a

b

Figure 14.12. The Akai DR4d (a) and Roland DM-80 (b), two stand-alone workstations do not actually use a PC or a Mac CPU for processing but perform those tasks in their own proprietary processors. This enables the user to purchase an inexpensive computer that controls only the software functions of the workstation.

($10,750). Up to four units can be linked to permit 32-channel operation. This unit is especially popular for sound design and audio-for-video post-production.

Integrated Digital Audio/ Sequencer Packages

Workstation manufacturers have responded to the need for synchronized playback of MIDI files by implementing a basic, playback-only MIDI sequencer. Figure 14.13 shows a screen from OSC's Deck II Version 2.1 digital recording system.[17]

The MIDI sequencers integrated into most workstations offer very little or no editing capability; the tracks are generally merged into one Type 0 MIDI file, which means you had better have at least the final tempo of your MIDI tracks figured out before you import them and start digital sound recording. But interesting new software from Mark of the Unicorn, Opcode, and Cubase[18] integrates a full-featured sequencer with a D-to-D recording system. Figure 14.14 shows screens from two of these three software titles. Note the interview with Yes recording engineer Michael Jay elsewhere in this section, which explains how the CD Talk was recorded entirely using Digital Performer—the same software you can purchase and use at home.

Figure 14.13. The Deck II direct-to-disk recording system converts a Mac into a 4-channel workstation, complete with MIDI playback of standard MIDI Files. Note the MIDI sequencer window in the upper-right corner of the screen. The Pro Tools system by Digidesign provides this same MIDI import feature, as do workstations produced by a number of other manufacturers.

[17]Deck II has received very good marks from critics and reviewers associated with major magazines. The price of version 2.1 is only $399, and Deck II provides 6-channel recording and playback on a Mac 660av using no additional hardware and 6 channels on a Mac with a NuMedia sound card. Deck II also supports 8 channels on a 840av system using no additional hardware, and allows 8-channel record/playback using a single Digidesign Pro Tools card. Deck II also provides a live video window, seen in the lower-right corner of the screen featured in Figure 14.13. The "Box Packing" video shown in this example is borrowed from the Tutorial folder that is shipped with Passport Producer, a multimedia authoring program currently shipping as a bundle with the Spectral Innovations NuMedia card. Check Appendix F to find out how to contact these companies. They want to hear from you.

[18]I received a copy of Cubase just before press deadline. It looks very promising, but I couldn't get the product online in time to discuss it here. Cubase Audio is available for the Mac or the PC.

The Making of Talk by Yes

An Interview with Yes Recording Engineer Michael Jay

In the spring of 1994, Victory Music recording artists Yes released the album *Talk*, featuring band members Jon Anderson, Trevor Rabin, Chris Squire, Tony Kaye, and Alan White. *Talk* is considered the first major album release to be completely produced using a commercially available, integrated MIDI sequencer/disk recording software package—Digital Performer, by Mark of the Unicorn (MOTU). *Talk* was engineered by Michael Jay and Yes member Trevor Rabin. Michael had previously engineered the first television program to be mixed

digitally, the Neil Young concert special "Berlin." The author had the opportunity to interview Michael the week before the release of *Talk*, and the following comments are excerpted from that interview.

"I started work on the album in the summer of '92. Trevor and the band were impressed with this [Digital Performer] technology and were happy to be recording this way, happy that they could get the songs the way they wanted and, finally, really happy with the way it all came out sounding. I believe that it's the first major

album release to be done with an integrated sequencer/digital workstation. I think some albums have been done previously with units such as the Synclavier, but not with such a Mac-based home/consumer sequencer. Certainly MOTU had never seen the likes of this."

"We worked on the album with a kind of pioneering spirit, in that we committed to using a consumer sequencer, Digital Performer, while it was still limited to just four tracks of digital audio and before it had been used in these ways and to such a demanding level. We did this because Trevor Rabin and I were both long-time users and fans of MIDI Performer, and we decided that the advantages of having our audio tracks bound up within a familiar sequencer platform would outweigh the use of any other digital recorder, be it tape or disc. I quickly found that, in order to simply engineer the recording, I had unwittingly signed on to become a beta tester[19] for lots of new software."

"But the main reason we went with DP was not that it was just digital, but because, unlike a digital tape recorder, it was random-access. And, as Trevor actually put it, this factor allowed him and the band to creatively zoom in on what they felt was the ideal form of each song's sections, arrangements, and length. That means that even in the mix stage we could say, 'We like this section, it's working great, let's

[19] A beta tester is a person who tests the final versions of newly developed software before it hits the market.

add eight bars to it,' or, 'We like it to the exclusion of this other section; let's replace these four bars with that and lengthen this other one.' The band members could come in periodically and say, 'Well, we hear this idea now, let's try it.' It was just a really ideal way for them to continuously edit and perfect the songs. I think this was a bit of an experiment for the band members, in that [when recording previous albums] they would write and rehearse the material and then enter the studio to record, and here, it was often being written as it was recorded, and even as it was mixed."

"As for the equipment, we kind of progressed through the course of the project, starting out by linking two Mac CIs and getting our feet wet with the process and the bugs, actually recording and mixing a couple of the early songs with only these eight tracks and MIDI. Then we added the third Mac, a Quadra 700, and pretty quickly abandoned the tape recorder for good, added another Quadra, and completed about the last half or two-thirds of the album with just these 16 audio tracks of Digital Performer."

"The fact is that we needed at least 16 tracks per Mac, but this was before the 16-track engine existed. I accomplished this by linking the four Macs, each computer running Digital Performer with four tracks. The key was to run all four copies of our sequence 'slaved to external sync,' and then centrally link all the Macs with a common timing source, which in this case was a Time Line MicroLynx. It would

have been nice to sync everything with MIDI time code (MTC) only, which could have controlled the transports of all four Macs from one master Mac, enabling 'markers' and so on—we could have just hit 'play' on the main Mac sequencer and all the Macs would have rolled—but MTC does not have the fine timing signals needed for digital audio, which won't roll at all in that mode. The MicroLynx can derive several different time sources from the same generator, which allowed us to roll SMPTE time code to two MOTU MTP II MIDI interfaces, each of which controlled transport of two of the Macs, while simultaneously providing common word clock to all four Digidesign Pro Tools audio interface cards, keeping all audio files in sync with sample accuracy."

"This common word clock provided not only what we felt was an especially jitter-free external clock for the Pro Tools hardware, but also allowed us to record 'wild' to a single Mac without slaving to external sync. That meant not having to rely on Performer's early versions of Continuous Sync, whose time processing, I felt, degraded the audio fidelity. With this setup, I configured the MicroLynx to provide time code as if the code were a 'master' machine, slaving all the Macs. We could 'shuttle' the code around; in fact, if you fast forward or rewind, the code 'speeds up' exponentially like it was a tape transport!"

"The fact that we had our audio tracks at our fingertips in a sequencer also allowed us to

exploit special sonic effects. Trevor, especially, did some things, just cutting and pasting, experimenting to create new, sometimes unexpected soundbites. We got to play with a lot of aspects of the waveforms, bending some rules as far as phase, room ambiance, and some other intangibles that often give this album its sound and feel. We were limited as far as tracks, but the quality of the digital audio allowed us to bounce down such things as the vocal stacks, building up masses of tracks without sonic problems. There were several things that actually wound up being bounced several times [but] still sounded fine."

"In most ways, though, this record really recalls the organic feel of the early Yes albums, with strong melodies, Hammond organ, and lots and lots of vocals. So, though it is a sonic tour de force, I think it really gives Yes fans from all periods a lot to enjoy musically—a lot of great melodies, a lot of great singing."

"Digital Performer served as a wonderful digital multitrack that led us to keep experimenting and heading where the band wanted to go. For Trevor and me, so much of the experience of this period was this decision to put our eggs in this basket, to get MOTU and all this technology to go a little further than it had gone before. We often said that we'll be laughing when we look back ten years from now, when everyone can do this with some device on their wristwatch."

a

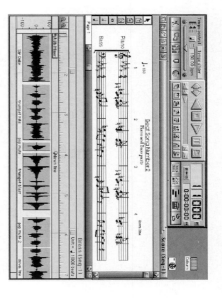

b

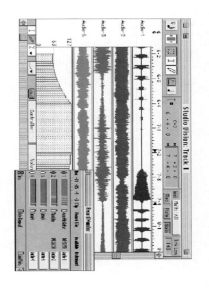

Figure 14.14. *Screens from (a) Digital Performer by Mark of the Unicorn, and (b) Studio Vision by Opcode Systems. Digital Performer and Studio Vision are currently available only for the Mac. These innovative software titles combine a full-featured MIDI sequencer with a direct-to-disk recording system. This software must be used with an av/e Mac or a digital audio sound card to provide up to four-channel D-to-D recording and playback.*

I have never seen or heard an industry name for this new generation of products, so I call them Digital Audio Sequencers (DAS). A DAS enables you to retain all of the MIDI track separation and editing features of a full-featured MIDI sequencer, while gaining the benefits of a digital audio workstation. Even though syncing to external SMPTE and MTC remains a problem, just as on any digital audio device, DAS MIDI systems are fast gaining popularity. Manufacturers are working very well *together* to ensure that this recording tool continues to improve, which means the DAS will be around for a long time.

The Big Wrap-Up

Well, that kind of wraps up the nuts and the bolts, the wires and the cables, the disks and the drives. You now understand better how to take all of those little electrons running around in your computer music systems and use them to help you create music.

The music industry never sits still for long. Chapter 15 tells you about some of the potential future applications for computer-assisted music, and it explores how computer music technology crosses over into the exciting worlds of video, multimedia, and interactive television.

All readers may proceed to the final chapter, Chapter 15.

15 Future Computer-Assisted Music Applications: Interactive Multimedia Explored

This chapter could also be called "The Future of the Computer Musician." Computer musicians are certainly not static creatures. They're constantly evolving, learning, and growing. Statistics prove that students who are highly active in school music programs exhibit more academic motivation than their classmates who aren't. The serious music student is generally an achiever who wants to be exposed to new learning opportunities. As the computer musician experiments, learns, and grows, he or she is exposed to communications and arts media in addition to the medium of music.

Various Media Available to the Computer Musician

As a computer musician, you're surrounded by audio, video, software, and hardware technologies in an environment that can enhance diverse areas of human creativity. Computer graphics are right before your eyes as part of the software you use. On the professional level, the computer musician who works with MIDI will at some point undoubtedly work with video or film, or possibly with a slide show, or may edit digital audio files…

…or will most likely work with a project using all of the above: a multimedia project.

Multimedia and Interactive Multimedia Defined

Media refers to a means of communicating. *Multi* refers to more than one. *Multimedia* is a communications arena where presentations are designed

that use many different communications media, such as digitized still photos, digitized video, digitized sound, text, computer animation and graphics, CD (Red Book) audio, and/or MIDI. Computer games are a popular and fun form of multimedia. Those kiosks you work with at the local museum often present their information in an entertaining, yet educational, multimedia form.

Some multimedia presentations are *noninteractive.* You click a mouse or a start button and watch as the presentation is played back for you. Noninteractive presentations are often used in business meetings, where multimedia in effect

replaces the traditional slide show presentation. But other multimedia presentations are *interactive.* This means that the viewer can control the way in which the media are played back. This is the really fun stuff.

Assembling these various media into a completed work is usually called "authoring." Figure 15.1 shows a screen from one multimedia authoring program, Producer, by Passport. I used this software, which currently comes bundled with the NuMedia audio card for the Mac, to author a multimedia presentation that I've used to tell people about this book. Icons in the Cue Palette

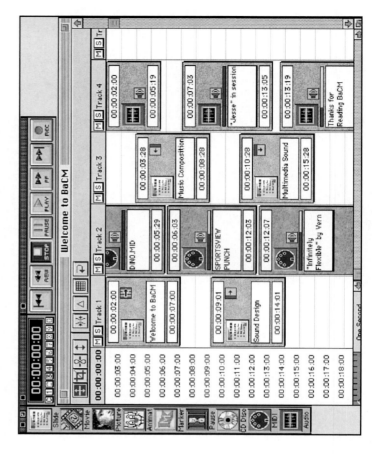

Figure 15.1. A screen from a multimedia presentation authored with Passport's *Producer.*

strip on the left side of the screen represent various types of digitized "media," such as slides (still photos), animations, audio, MIDI files, and audio. Producer enables you to click and drag these media cues onto the tracks of the cue sheet to create a layered presentation that plays backs these multiple media—multimedia!

Interest in multimedia is very logical for the computer musician who has been exposed to all of these media. In fact, the booming multimedia industry is looking to the music industry as the most likely source of talent for the development of multimedia titles. No kidding! Check out the following interview with Virtual Entertainment entrepreneurs Jeff Pucci and Richard Viard, whose computer music skills helped them author the first commercial MPC software title, Composer Quest. What a great story!

With the relatively recent public acceptance of the new digital media—multimedia and CD-ROM—there are extremely exciting career opportunities…for so many people. It's as if a big door of opportunity has just been opened for creative types—for so many artists and musicians just like us.

The First MPC Title in History

An Interview with Jeff Pucci and Richard Viard of Virtual Entertainment

I can think of no better example how the future of the computer-assisted musician can take an interesting course than the story of Jeff Pucci and Richard Viard of Virtual Entertainment. These two former Berklee College of Music students have been exclusively involved in the conception, development, and marketing of entertainment, educational, and some of the world's best known music-related software since the

mid-80s. They are credited with developing the *first* commercially shipping MPC title in history. The following are segments from a late-night March 1994 conversation with the author.

Jeff: "We'd been working for these music software companies, and we'd met in 1988 while we were both employed at one called Dr. T's Music Software. Richard and I had a bunch of common interests. One was this fascination with how music, the visual arts, and sociology often shared significant parallels through history—how there was often this really discernible thread that tied those topics together. We'd also shared an interest in pop culture, and the broad mass market and mass media in general."

"You know, we loved MIDI and everything that you could do with it, yet we were looking to create some kind of software program that would potentially reach a much greater audience than just folks who even *had* the MIDI-dependent tools at the time. There are a lot of smart people out there who still don't even know what the heck MIDI really is. So, Richard and I drew up a product specification for what was to become a sort of musical 'tour through time,' which ended up being called Composer Quest. Richard had no formal computer training, and me, well, I'm not much of a technical guy at all—we're both musicians, you know."

Richard: "What happened was, we were trying to find a way to create a prototype of this thing that we could present to a real C programmer, then hopefully convince that person to work with us—at the time, we really didn't have any money to pay such a person."

Jeff: "So Richard did the hands-on part of doing a mockup of Composer Quest in an authoring tool called AmigaVision, an Amiga-based programming language from Commodore. We took this mockup to the headquarters of Commodore Business Machines in Westchester, PA, called a meeting with a bunch of their VPs, and they were completely blown away. I remember one of them saying 'this is the best educational title I've ever seen.' Then, I got invited to show this thing at an event at the Getty Museum in Malibu, a Commodore-sponsored event. That resulted in USA Today doing a piece on Composer Quest, which was really cool, I thought. At that point—with a little recognition, you know—we began to take ourselves more seriously."

Richard: "Actually, what happened sometime in there was we'd presented the nearly completed Composer Quest to our employer at that time (Dr. T's). They were impressed and expressed an interest in publishing it. Meanwhile, Dr. T's had recently been contacted by Microsoft, who at the time was creating what was to become a true multimedia environment. It combined MS Windows with CD-ROM and a whole bunch of ways to tie audio, video and graphics together. It would…"

Jeff: " …become the MPC."

Richard: "Exactly."

Jeff: "Then, once again, we were one out of maybe only a dozen development teams that sort of jumped into the fire at that point to address this new potential standard. You know, it was interesting because we got to work with certain people at Microsoft that we never would have had access to otherwise—a couple of executives that really had some vision—but they needed to evangelize this thing, so we got kind of open-door treatment and we committed."

Richard: "We converted over stuff that we had done on the Amiga to the PC using the Asymetrix Toolbook authoring language, which is sort of like a Windows version of HyperCard. Since we had the whole application designed and everything, the only real trick was to find tools that would let us convert the sound files over to the format that Windows needed, and the graphic formats. So, we ended up with, basically, one of the first ever MPC titles."

Jeff: "Well, it's actually the first one that shipped, period. We can say that for sure. Our main contact person at Microsoft took it and showed both Bill Gates and Min Yee, the guy who was the VP of Multimedia at Microsoft at the time. He said that Min jumped up and down, yelling 'Five stars! Five stars!' I thought 'coo-oool!' I asked what Bill Gates thought. Our guy told me that Bill gave it four out of five stars. Anyway, Min was nice enough to give us this great product endorsement quote that we stuck on the box."

"Composer Quest was the first product that Richard and I developed together totally independent of any company, as a team. That was the beginning. And Composer Quest, in relative terms, has sold very, very well—something like 20,000 copies, anyway. So that was our first title. We were really encouraged by its success, and it gave us the confidence to press on. So I guess that's the story of Composer Quest."

"What happened next was we realized that we probably could do a lot more, and have a lot more flexibility in our career if we jumped ship and started our own company. So, two years ago, we left Dr. T's. I bumped into Chris Halaby, the President of Opcode Systems, at some trade show in Frankfurt, Germany. And he just said, 'what are you doing?' I said, 'well, you know I'm doing these multimedia titles.' And he goes, 'well, if you want to do some more music titles, consider doing some with us.' Chris had some interesting ideas already, and we both liked the same jazz musicians and stuff. I liked the idea... came back to the states, and Chris called me at home one night and said, 'How about Opcode finances you guys to do a couple titles to be published by Opcode Systems?'"

And of course, we really didn't have much money back then, and we liked the folks at Opcode anyway, so we figured, well, we'll do this as a contracted job and do these two titles, The Musical World of Professor Piccolo and Allie's Playhouse, which would ultimately be owned by Opcode Systems. Just for the record, I've got nothing but good stuff to say about Chris Halaby, and Opcode does own and publish those two titles. Anyway, The Musical World of Professor Piccolo [is] sort of a complete music theory course and covers the history of a couple of genres of music—symphonic music and jazz and rock…"

Richard: "It covers ages 8 and up."

Jeff: "You know, the heart of the program on that one is a pretty much full-blown music theory course, like a 12-step music theory course—pretty much full-blown involved. Allie's Playhouse is more of a general educational title, targeted at, primarily, pre-readers, age 3-7, specifically ages 3-7."

Richard: "You play in Allie's playhouse; Allie is a little green alien. It's really very fun. And the main room is like a playhouse with a lot of cool stuff in it, a lot of toys and cabinets, and you can click on things and some things launch a full-blown game, or an activity, other things are just like funny little sequences of animation and sound."

Jeff: "It covers just a whole bunch of diverse topics. It's learning about the continents and our solar system. There's a little musical synthesizer in there to play…kids can compose a little music. There's identifying the different animals. There are puzzles, mazes—all kinds of stuff. Everything but the kitchen sink."

Richard: "No, we've got the kitchen sink, too! You can go into the kitchen room, which is a sound recognition game, and there's really a kitchen sink in it too!"

Jeff: "I'll say that one area that is particularly exciting to me is the whole concept of how we are going to interact with the television set. So far, it remains a passionate interest of ours here, and we think that in the next 3-5 years or so, it's going to be a place where people spend huge amounts of time, interacting two-way with the television. We've sure been in the thick of it, trying to adapt applications that would be suitable to interact with on your TV set in the living room, which is a different experience than with the computer in the den. As far as technologies that are coming up, we've got our sights set on the portent of interactive TV, and I think, if I can speak for Virtual Entertainment, I think the real value is in the content. The technology is just a delivery medium. For us, anyway, the

Interactive Multimedia and the Recording Industry

Early in 1994, Geffen Records held a Multimedia Presentation Contest, inviting interested contestants to submit an original multimedia presentation using sound and graphics from the Geffen library, which is available on CompuServe[1] under (Go Geffen) in the Music Vendor forum. This project was the brainchild of Robert von Goeben, and literature from Geffen Records states that the label "hopes to encourage and nurture new talent in the multimedia format while exploring the possibilities that multimedia holds for artist exposure."

Robert von Goeben and the staff at Geffen have a crystal-clear vision. Some of the most interesting applications of multimedia technology are being developed in the recording industry, where established recording artists are exploring the use of this new vehicle to make an even bolder musical statement than ever before. David Bowie, the Residents, Billy Idol, Thomas Dolby, Todd Rundgren, and Peter Gabriel are artists who aren't just talking about interactive multimedia projects—they've done them! I find the XPlora 1

content that we create, like a, you know, like a Walt Disney Company or a Time Warner who own tons of endearing and engaging content, is where the real value lies. And, as far as the technology, whoever figures out whether it's going to be the wires, you know, the fiber optic cables or the satellite feeds, or whatever—a Bell Atlantic, a TCI, or a Microsoft—whoever does that, we'll sit back and let them fight it out. We can in turn just keep creating our characters and content, with [hopefully] great ideas and storyline plots to back them up; and whoever wins the transmission wars—the technology behind transmitting the data stream to your home TV set—we'll just have this bastion of content ready, adaptable to whatever format."

Richard: "I can see now that the major new technologies are already here but we need more powerful machines to really exploit them and make them available to the consumer market. But I think…I'm very personally excited about what is possible with digital video and virtual reality communications in general, the way we can just zoom data across wires and work on projects across the country—stuff like that. And that technology is only going to improve."

Jeff: "I think that we're going to see an incredible convergence of this stuff. The lines will be so blurred in a few years, maybe

3-5 years, and I think that the really great artists, even pop music artists…I think that there is really going to be a place for musicians to do exciting stuff with the continued digital convergence of audio, music and video images—I don't know exactly what shape it is going to take, but I don't guess anyone really does yet; it remains pretty vague now. But I feel certain that all these elements will converge further, and I'm sure that there will be incredible opportunities out there for the musicians working within this interactive CD-ROM environment."

"To the people who are going to be reading this book: We were just a couple musicians, you know, and look what happened—the whole face of our career potential took a dramatic change, because we were early adopters in this whole multimedia game. After a couple of pretty successful products, we're suddenly a publisher with a lot of staff and great resources. It's pretty much like the sky's the limit now. The point is, with the relatively recent public acceptance of the new digital media—multimedia and CD-ROM—there are extremely exciting career opportunities becoming available now, for so many people. It's as if a big door of opportunity has just been opened for creative types—for so many artists and musicians just like us."

[1] An enormous collection of music information is available on online networks such as PAN, CompuServe, the Internet, America Online, and Prodigy. There's even a specialized online service that caters to the specific needs of church and school music directors. This service, called Pepper National Music Network, enables a music director to ask questions of industry representatives in an open public forum, to communicate with music and software publishers, to browse band and choral score listings, and even to place orders electronically. Call Lee Paynter at 1-800-345-6296 for more info.

project by Peter Gabriel and Real World to be especially interesting.

XPlora 1, Peter Gabriel's Secret World

During the week of December 13, 1993, Peter Gabriel and Real World Multimedia released the astonishing (in my opinion) CD-ROM XPlora 1. Figure 15.2 shows one of the still "slides" from this interactive multimedia program. The slide contains a section of the music video for the song "Kiss That Frog." You can click the icons in the upper part of the screen to select music videos for other songs. Click the shovel to cue up "Digging in the Dirt" and on the heart to select "Love to be Loved."

Figure 15.2. A slide from the interactive CD-ROM XPlora 1.

Steve Nelson, of San Francisco-based Brilliant Media, Inc., helped Peter conceive and produce XPlora 1, and a staff of over 40 people used Macintosh computers with Adobe Premier to author it. All sound and music was edited and processed with Digidesign software and hardware. The CD-ROM began shipping in Mac format in late 1993, and PC and other formats are expected to ship later in 1994.

 Peter and the staff at Real World have graciously provided me with two video clips from their promotional XPlora 1 EPK (Electronic Press Kit). These are featured on the

MusicPower CD-ROM enclosed with this book. The selected clips feature Peter as your on-screen guide, telling you about XPlora 1 and showing you how the interactive tour takes place.

XPlora users will be able to do the following:

Mix their own version of "Digging in the Dirt"

Interact with producer Brian Eno to create their own "jam" session with artists from around the world

Discover and play instruments from around the world

Take a tour of the WOMAD festival

Peter also uses this multimedia experience to explain his work with human-rights organizations, such as Amnesty International and the Witness Project. XPlora 1 contains 100 minutes of video, over 30 minutes of audio, 100 full-color photo images, and an entire book's worth of text.

I absolutely love XPlora 1. Congrats to Peter and Steve, and to all involved.

CD-Interactive (CD-I)

CD-Interactive (CD-I) is a medium in which the composer creates music in a nonlinear style—that is, in pieces, such as verses, choruses, bridges, intros, and outros. These musical segments can then be assembled in any order the user desires. In some cases, the user can add different reverbs or eq settings and can change the mix, even to the point of selecting which instruments are playing at any given time. Innovative musician Todd Rundgren is credited with producing the first CD-I music product.

No World Order: Todd Rundgren Interactive, or TR-i

Todd Rundgren (Figure 15.3), whose "Time Heals" video was the second video ever broadcast on MTV, also has the distinction of having created the world's first completely interactive, nonlinear, music-only CD, *No World Order*.

The title is a reference to the fact that the listener can arrange four hours' worth of musical elements, such as verses, choruses, and phrases, into *any*

desired order (thus the title)! Todd includes a linear, 53-minute noninteractive version to show the listener one way this interactive album could turn out. But experimentation is encouraged; Todd believes the listener will then use the musical product for a longer period of time and in a more enjoyable fashion. One of Todd's thoughts that I find especially interesting regards the marketing and promotion of music CDs. In 1993 he stated, "Most people are aware that in the future—and not that distant, perhaps within five to ten years— most media is going to be delivered directly into your home. You will no longer go out and buy records or video tapes...that normally would appear in your home entertainment system. You will get it through fiber optic lines and more or less

interact with a database somewhere.... Music starts looking more like computer software than... traditional records. Just as computer software... updates are made available to the audience, there will appear a *No World Order* 1.1. And at some other point there will be *No World Order* 1.2. It's possible to get musical updates if you send in your registration card...at a mere fraction of the cost of the original program. [Interactive music] has the potential to extend the shelf life of music, but also to have some kind of assurance or idea of the size of your potential audience before you release a new version."

Virtual Reality Is a Reality

The 3-D movie was a first step in the direction of virtual reality, an attempt to immerse the viewer in an environment that might not actually exist. Really good examples of this can be found in films shown in the Kodak Imagination exhibit at Epcot Center. In one film, the viewer actually flies through an orchard filled with apple blossoms, dodging them as they fall to the ground. You actually think you'll hit the petals, it's so real. Silicon Valley is turning into a hotbed for the development of the new 3-D experience called Virtual Reality (VR), which provides an interesting environment for the creation and production of 3-D surround sound. Recording artist Thomas Dolby uses his vast knowledge of electronic music to create sound environments for VR programs called VR "experiences."

Figure 15.3. *Todd Rundgren, Forward Records, and Philips Interactive Media released the interactive CD* No World Order *in the summer of 1993. Photo by Jean Lannin and Danny O'Connor.*

Thomas Dolby Makes Virtual Reality "Real"

Dolby teamed up with virtual-reality pioneer Eric Gullichsen to create a program called The Virtual String Quartet, which was installed in the Guggenheim Museum in Soho, New York, in October of 1993. This project was sponsored by the Intel Digital Education and Arts (IDEA) division. It uses goggles and glove-controlled software to immerse users in a user-controlled 3-D sound environment. In this VR experience, you wander through a music rehearsal room where a digitized string quartet is practicing a well-known Mozart composition. You can walk around the musicians and actually lean closer to each instrument to hear it better. You can tickle a musician, and he will veer off into a wild jazz or bluegrass improvisation while the other musicians continue with Mozart.

Dolby (shown in Figure 15.4) states, "My belief is that although realistic and affordable VR graphics may be a few years away, audio is a large part of the experience, and that technology is already here. I would like to develop The Virtual String Quartet into a larger virtual music conservatory where you can wander between several rooms and interact with all sorts of musicians; next door, for example, there could be an Afro-Cuban percussion section.... This is not a game for arcade addicts—there is no goal or points system. It is designed as an experience your granny could enjoy, and a creative application of VR that goes beyond the

Figure 15.4. *Recording artist Thomas Dolby is cutting a path into the new frontiers of virtual reality and interactive multimedia—logical extensions of using computers for musical applications. Photo by Leslie Burke.*

current shoot-em-up mentality of most computer games."

Thomas has also founded Headspace: A Full-Service Audio MultiMedia Company, which has produced music and sound for three amusement ride simulators using IWERKS large-format film, and for the Double Switch interactive CD-ROM computer game by Sega. Headspace is looking for other artists who want to be involved in the VR process. Says Thomas, "As an artist, I think that it's really important that creative minds apply themselves to doing something useful, with virtual reality and these other new platforms becoming available."

Multimedia and Education

When I visited the 1994 Music Educators National Conference, I was amazed at how many interactive CD-ROM titles were already available for music education. Catalogs from McCormick's Enterprises (1-800-333-5201) and Electronic Courseware Systems (1-800-832-4965) each list around two dozen interactive multimedia titles that teach music history, composition, music theory, and music appreciation. It's obvious that using multimedia as a teaching assistant is here to stay.

Becoming Mulimedia-Savvy

You may be using multimedia and don't even know it. For example, when you transfer your family photos to a CD and play them back through the computer, that's multimedia. The computer games and video games you play are multimedia, too. Manufacturers are racing to make multimedia more flexible, more reliable, easier to use, and less expensive. In the time it has taken me to author this book (only a few months), the cost of MPC systems has dropped a couple of hundred dollars. You can now buy a 486DX2 system for the same price you paid for your 386SX a couple of years ago. And ferocious competition is driving the quality of multimedia kits up. Sound cards are appearing with the same sounds and sampling capabilities as many of the "big-guy" synths.

Expect to see multimedia development and production courses added to the curriculae of progressive arts colleges. Many computer stores currently offer multimedia workshops and classes. Watch the newspapers and sales flyers for information pertaining to these.

Read, read, read. A wealth of printed information is available in bookstores, libraries, and magazines. The important thing is that you get started.

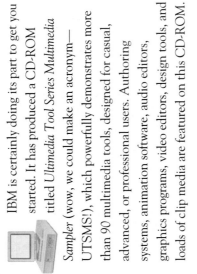

IBM is certainly doing its part to get you started. It has produced a CD-ROM titled *Ultimedia Tool Series Multimedia Sampler* (wow, we could make an acronym—UTSMS!), which powerfully demonstrates more than 90 multimedia tools, designed for casual, advanced, or professional users. Authoring systems, animation software, audio editors, graphics programs, video editors, design tools, and loads of clip media are featured on this CD-ROM.

The price is only $29.95! Call (800) 887-7771 to order your copy. Highly recommended.

And check out what your local university or even high school is doing with multimedia. Don't just look over kids' shoulders to see what the heck they're doing with the computer that you can't get them away from. Turn it on and try it yourself. Ask them to help you...students love to teach.

[2]This comment is especially interesting if you note Dolby's involvement in the 1992 movie Toys, starring Robin Williams and Joan Cusack. Toys explored the debate between using computer games and VR technology for violent applications versus using them for the good of peace. In my opinion, this movie's soundtrack features the most impressive collection of technically astute musicians ever assembled for one project, including Thomas Dolby, Trevor Horn, Enya, Tori Amos, Pat Metheny, Hans Zimmer, Michael Gambon, Grace Jones, Peter Gabriel, Pete Haycock, and Steve Howe, to name a few. The symphonic and techno-pop compositions, arrangements, and production values are absolutely first-class, and I highly recommend repeatedly listening to this CD (Geffen Records GEFD-24505).

The Pep Talk

"Well, uh, just win one for the Gipper." No, no, not that kind of pep talk. But I hope this book has excited you about the possibilities of using computers for musical and multimedia applications. Whether you fool around with computers and music at the hobbyist level, use computers as an aid in the noble profession of teaching music, or are really serious about a computer-assisted music career, once you get up and running I guarantee you'll have a great time. I do.

Thanks for selecting *Becoming a Computer Musician* to serve as your computer music assistant. You can send ideas and comments to me at:

Jeff Bowen
Bowen Music Productions
3590 N. Meridian
Indianapolis, IN 46208
fax: (317) 923-3871

PROGRAMS
THAT TEACH
MUSIC

For addresses, phone numbers, and fax numbers, see Appendix E.

Educational Software for the PC

Software	Company
Band in a Box	PG Music, Incorporated
Composer Quest	Virtual Entertainment, Incorporated
Allie's Playhouse	Virtual Entertainment, Incorporated
The Musical World of Professor Piccolo	Virtual Entertainment, Incorporated
Music Lessons	MiBAC
Super Jam	Blue Ribbon Soundworks
Music Mentor	Midisoft
DO-RE-ME	Midisoft
Miracle Piano Teaching System	Software Toolworks
Piano	Musicware
The Orchestra	Electronic Arts

Educational Software for the Macintosh

Software	Company
Claire	Opcode Systems
Listen	AMAJA
MiBAC Jazz	MiBAC
Music Lessons	MiBAC
Miracle Piano Teaching System	Software Toolworks
Exploring Keyboard Fundamentals	Stipes Publishing, Electronic Courseware

PRINTED SCORE SAMPLES

B

These scores can be used with the tutorials in
Chapters 2, 3, 7, 9, 12, and 13.

"Hail to the Chief"

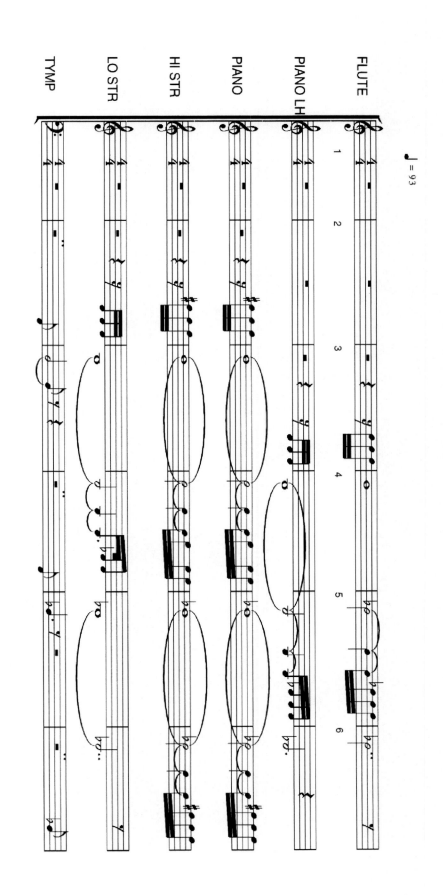

"Beethoven's Fifth"

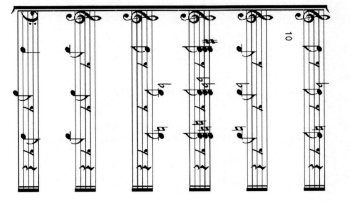

"Away in a Manger"

"Brandenburg"

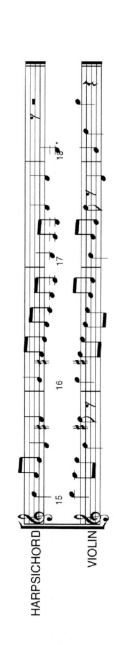

GENERAL MIDI
SOUND TABLES

Standard Patches

General MIDI Level 1 defines a set of 128 recommended instrument patches that all conforming sound devices must support. Following is the complete list of General MIDI patches, which may be selected within MIDI Tune-Up. Sound tables courtesy of Turtle Beach Systems.

> **Note:** Some software and GM synthesizers number these patches 0-127. Also, some synthesizers may call these patches by slightly different names, although the character of the sound matches GM specs.

1-8: Piano

1   Acoustic Grand Piano
2   Bright Acoustic Piano
3   Electric Grand Piano
4   Honky-tonk Piano
5   Electric Piano 1
6   Electric Piano 2
7   Harpsichord
8   Clavinet

9-16: Chromatic Percussion

9   Celesta
10   Glockenspiel
11   Music Box
12   Vibraphone
13   Marimba
14   Xylophone
15   Tubular Bells
16   Dulcimer

17-24: Organ

17   Drawbar Organ
18   Percussive Organ
19   Rock Organ
20   Church Organ
21   Reed Organ
22   Accordian (French)
23   Harmonica
24   Tango Accordian

25-32: Guitar

25   Acoustic Guitar (nylon)
26   Acoustic Guitar (steel)
27   Electric Guitar (jazz)
28   Electric Guitar (clean)
29   Electric Guitar (muted)
30   Overdriven Guitar
31   Distortion Guitar
32   Guitar Harmonics

33-40: Bass

33   Acoustic Bass
34   Electric Bass (finger)
35   Electric Bass (pick)
36   Fretless Bass
37   Slap Bass 1
38   Slap Bass 2
39   Synth Bass 1
40   Synth Bass 2

41-48: Strings

41   Violin
42   Viola
43   Cello
44   Contrabass
45   Tremelo Strings
46   Pizzicato Strings
47   Orchestral Strings
48   Timpani

49-56: Ensemble

49   String Ensemble 1
50   String Ensemble 2
51   SynthStrings 1
52   SynthStrings 2
53   Choir Aahs
54   Voice Oohs
55   Synth Voice
56   Orchestra Hit

57-64: Brass

57   Trumpet
58   Trombone
59   Tuba

60 Muted Trumpet
61 French Horn
62 Brass Section
63 SynthBrass 1
64 SynthBrass 2

65-72: Reed
65 Soprano Sax
66 Alto Sax
67 Tenor Sax
68 Baritone Sax
69 Oboe
70 English Horn
71 Bassoon
72 Clarinet

73-80: Pipe
73 Piccolo
74 Flute
75 Recorder
76 Pan Flute
77 Blown Bottle
78 Shakuhachi
79 Whistle
80 Ocarina

81-88: Synth Lead
81 Lead 1 (square)
82 Lead 2 (sawtooth)
83 Lead 3 (calliope)
84 Lead 4 (chiff)
85 Lead 5 (charang)
86 Lead 6 (voice)
87 Lead 7 (fifths)
88 Lead 8 (bass+lead)

89-96: Synth Pad
89 Pad 1 (new age)
90 Pad 2 (warm)
91 Pad 3 (polysynth)
92 Pad 4 (choir)
93 Pad 5 (bowed)
94 Pad 6 (metallic)
95 Pad 7 (halo)
96 Pad 8 (sweep)

97-104: Synth Effects
97 FX 1 (rain)
98 FX 2 (soundtrack)
99 FX 3 (crystal)
100 FX 4 (atmosphere)
101 FX 5 (brightness)
102 FX 6 (goblins)
103 FX 7 (echoes)
104 FX 8 (sci-fi)

105-112: Ethnic
105 Sitar
106 Banjo
107 Shamisen
108 Koto
109 Kalimba
110 Bagpipe
111 Fiddle
112 Shanai

113-120: Percussive
113 Tinkle Bell
114 Agogo
115 Steel Drums
116 Woodblock
117 Taiko Drum
118 Melodic Tom
119 Synth Drum
120 Reverse Cymbal

121-128: Sound Effects
121 Guitar Fret Noise
122 Breath Noise
123 Seashore
124 Bird Tweet
125 Telephone Ring
126 Helicopter
127 Applause
128 Gunshot

Standard Percussion Map

General MIDI devices respond to key notes 35 through 81 on channel 10, sounding the following instruments:

#	Instrument	#	Instrument
35	Acoustic Bass Drum	59	Ride Cymbal 2
36	Bass Drum 1	60	Hi Bongo
37	Side Stick	61	Low Bongo
38	Acoustic Snare	62	Mute Hi Conga
39	Hand Clap	63	Open Hi Conga
40	Electric Snare	64	Low Conga
41	Low Floor Tom	65	High Timbale
42	Closed Hi-Hat	66	Low Timbale
43	High Floor Tom	67	High Agogo
44	Pedal Hi-Hat	68	Low Agogo
45	Low Tom	69	Cabasa
46	Open Hi-Hat	70	Maracas
47	Low-Mid Tom	71	Short Whistle
48	Hi-Mid Tom	72	Long Whistle
49	Crash Cymbal 1	73	Short Guiro
50	High Tom	74	Long Guiro
51	Ride Cymbal 1	75	Claves
52	Chinese Cymbal	76	Hi Wood Block
53	Ride Bell	77	Low Wood Block
54	Tambourine	78	Mute Cuica
55	Splash Cymbal	79	Open Cuica
56	Cowbell	80	Mute Triangle
57	Crash Cymbal 2	81	Open Triangle
58	Vibraslap		

TABLE OF MIDI EVENTS

D

This is a list of the standard MIDI controller numbers. Chapter 11 discusses the various types of MIDI events and their effects.

Controller Number	Event
MIDI 01	Modulation Wheel
MIDI 02	Breath
MIDI 04	Foot
MIDI 05	Portamento Time
MIDI 06	Data Entry
MIDI 07	Volume
MIDI 08	Balance
MIDI 10	Pan
MIDI 11	Express
MIDI 64	Sustain
MIDI 65	Portamento Switch
MIDI 66	Sostenuto Switch
MIDI 67	Soft Switch
MIDI 91	External Effects Depth
MIDI 96	Data Increment
MIDI 97	Data Decrement
MIDI 123	Panic (All Notes Off)

Here's the main control source list:

Note ON (ON)

Note OFF (-ON)

Mono Pressure
(also called Channel Aftertouch)

Polyphonic Pressure
(also called Polyphonic Aftertouch)

Pitch Bend Wheel

Attack Velocity

Release Velocity

Patch/Song Changes

System Exclusive

Tune Request

Mode Changes

Markers

Tempo Changes

Meter Changes

Key Changes

Loops

THE RESOURCE GUIDE

E

Amazing! This list actually goes from A to Z.

Address:	Phone:	Fax:
Akai Professional MIDI Controllers, P.O. Box 2344, Fort Worth, TX 76102	(817) 336-5114	(817) 870-1271
Alaska Software, 1197 Pomelo Court, Sunnyvale, CA 94087	(408) 738-3320	(408) 524-9699
Alesis, 3630 Hordrege Avenue, Los Angeles, CA 90016	(310) 558-4530	(310) 836-9192
Apple Computer, 20525 Mariani Avenue, Cupertino, CA 95014	(408) 996-1010	
Audio Technica, US, 1221 Commercial Drive, Stowe, OH 44224-1760	(216) 686-2600	(216) 686-0719
Berklee College of Music, 1140 Boylston St., Boston, MA 02215-3693	(617) 266-1400	(617) 247-6878
Blue Ribbon Soundworks, 1605 Chantilly Drive, #200, Atlanta, GA 30324	(800) 226-0212	
J.L. Cooper Electronics, 12500 Beatrice St., Los Angeles, CA 90066	(310) 306-4131	(310) 822-2252
Creative Labs, Inc., 1901 McCarthy Blvd., Milpitas, CA 95035	(408) 428-2394	
Digidesign, 1360 Willow Rd., Menlo Park, CA 94025	(415) 688-0600	(4150 327-0777

Address:	Phone:	Fax:
Electronic Arts, 1450 Fashion Island Blvd., San Mateo, CA 94404	(415) 513-7609 or (800) 245-4525	
Electronic Courseware Systems, 1210 Lancaster Drive, Champaign, IL 61821	(217) 359-7099	(217) 359-6578
E-mu Systems, Box 660015, Scotts Valley, CA 95067-0015	(408) 438-1921	(408) 438-8612
Ensonic Corporation, 155 Great Valley Parkway, Malvern, PA 19355-0735	(215) 647-3930	(215) 647-8908
Fostex, USA, 15431 Blackburn Avenue, Norwalk, CA 90650	(310) 921-1112	(310) 802-1964
Gibson Guitar Corporation, 641 Massman Drive, Nashville, TN 37210-3781	(615) 871-4500	(615) 889-0564
IBM Ultimedia Tools, 1055 Joaquin Rd., Mountain View, CA 94043	(800) 887-7771	
IMAJA, P.O. Box 6386, Albany, CA 94706	(510) 526-4621	(510) 526-4621
Kurzweil Music Systems, 13336 Alondra Blvd., Cerritos, CA 90701	(310) 926-3200	(310) 404-0748
Mackie Designs, 20205 144th Avenue N.E., Woodinville, WA 98072	(800) 258-6883 (800) 363-8855 Canada (206) 487-4333 outside U.S.	(206) 487-4337

Address:	Phone:	Fax:
Mark of the Unicorn 1280 Massachusetts Avenue Cambridge, MA 02138	(617) 576-2760	(617) 576-3609
Media Vision 47300 Bayside Parkway Fremont, CA 94538	(800) 348-7116	
MiBAC Music Software P.O. Box 468 Northfield, MN 55057	(507) 645-5851	(507) 645-2377
Midisoft Corporation P.O. Box 1000 Bellvue, WA 98009	(206) 881-7176 or (800) 776-6434	(206) 883-1368
Morning Star Solutions 7 Kings Pine Rd. Westford, MA 01886	(508) 692-0373	(508) 692-6535
Multimedia Products Corp. 300 Airport Executive Park Spring Valley, NY 10977-9868	(914) 426-0400	
Music Quest, Inc. P.O. Box 260963 Plano, TX 75026-0963	(800) 876-1376	(214) 422-7094
Musicware 8654 154th Avenue N.E. Redmond, WA 98052	(800) 99-PIANO	(206) 881-9664
Opcode Systems, Inc. 3950 Fabian Way Suite 100 Palo Alto, CA 94303	(415) 856-3333	(415) 252-0560
Orchid Technology 45365 Northport Loop West Fremont, CA 94538	(800) 7-ORCHID	(510) 490-9312

Address:	Phone:	Fax:
OSC 480 Potrero Avenue San Francisco, CA 94110	(415) 252-0460	(415) 252-0560
PG Music, Inc. 111-266 Elmwood Avenue Buffalo, NY 14222	(800) 268-6272	
Passport Designs, Inc. 100 Stone Pine Rd. Half Moon Bay, CA 94019	(415) 726-0280	(415) 726-2254
Roland, USA 7200 Dominion Circle Los Angeles, CA 90040-3696	(213) 685-5141	(213) 722-0911
Samson Technologies P.O. Box 9068 Hicksville, NY 11802-9068	(516) 932-3810	(516) 932-3815
Softronics Sales 5058 List Drive Colorado Springs, CO 80919	(800) 225-8590	
Software Toolworks 60 Leveroni Court Novato, CA 94949	(800) 234-3088	
Spectral Innovations 1885 Lundy Avenue, Suite 208 San Jose, CA 95131	(408) 321-7680	(408) 955-0370
Steinberg-Jones 17700 Raymer St., #1001 Northridge, CA 91325	(818) 993-4091	(818) 701-7452
Sweetwater Sound 5335 Bass Rd. Fort Wayne, IN 46808	(219) 432-8176	

Address:	Phone:	Fax:
Tascam, USA 7733 Telegraph Rd. Montebvello, CA 90640	(213) 726-0303	(213) 727-7656
Turtle Beach Systems 52 Grumbacher Rd. York, PA 17402	(717) 767-0200	(717) 767-6033
Twelve Tone Systems P.O. Box 760 Watertown, MA 02272	(800) 234-1171	(617) 924-6657
Virtual Entertainment, Inc. 200 Highland Avenue Needham, MA 02194	(508) 660-1223	(508) 660-8865
Yamaha Corporation of America P.O. Box 6600 Buena Park, CA 90620	(714) 522-9011	(714) 522-9832
ZETA Music 2230 Livingston St. Oakland, CA 94606	(510) 261-1702	(510) 261-1708

Periodicals

My favorite magazines:

Address:	Phone:	Fax:
Electronic Musician P.O. Box 41525 Nashville, TN 37204	(800) 888-5139	
EQ 2 Park Avenue #1820 New York, NY 10016	(212) 213-3444	(212) 213-3484
Keyboard Box 58528 Boulder, CO 80322-8528	(800) 289-9919	
MIX P.O. Box 41525 Nashville, TN 37204	(800) 888-5139	
Morph's Outpost on the Digital Frontier Box 578 Orinda, CA 94563	(510) 238-4545	(510) 238-9459
Multimedia World 501 Second St. San Francisco, CA 94107	(415) 281-8650	(415) 281-3915
National Geographic Traveler 1251 Avenue of the Americas New York, NY 10020	(212) 974-1700	
The World of Macintosh Multimedia Redgate Communications Corporation 660 Beachland Blvd. Vero Beach, FL 32963	(407) 231-6904	

CONTENTS OF
THE *MusicPower*
CD-ROM

F

This CD-ROM contains a wealth of PC and Macintosh software that will enhance your enjoyment of the book. You'll find many different kinds of software, including the following:

♪ Special working versions of the programs used in the chapter lessons

♪ Working demo versions of popular music programs

♪ MIDI, .WAV (PC) and .SND (Mac) music files used in the chapter lessons

♪ Professionally recorded CD audio tracks of music projects from the book

♪ Video clips from Peter Gabriel's *XPlora* CD-ROM, Kenny Aronoff's *Power Workout* tapes, and work by the author

The *MusicPower* CD-ROM will work on both PC and Macintosh computer systems. Your computer will "see" only the portion of the CD-ROM that is meant for it. Before you get started using any software from the CD-ROM, read either "Getting Started: Windows Systems" or "Getting Started: Mac Systems" later in this appendix.

The next two sections cover Windows software, followed by two sections on Mac software. After that, you'll find information on DOS software, music files, and video clips on the disc.

Note: You can work with the software featured in Chapters 2 and 3 using nothing more than your PC or Mac. No additional hardware is required.

PC users need to have one of these items to use most of the software on *MusicPower*:

A MIDI capable sound card and speakers

or

A MIDI interface, a MIDI synthesizer and speakers

Mac Users will need the following to use most of the *MusicPower* software:

A MIDI interface and a MIDI synthesizer

Any of these synthesizers can be a MIDI sound module or a keyboard version.

The working demos on the disc will give you hands-on experience with the full program's capabilities. They are usually the same as the complete product, with the limitation of not being able to save or print your work.

Obviously, the companies who created these demonstrations hope you will be impressed enough with what you experience to purchase their product. You'll find the addresses and phone numbers for these companies in Appendix E, "The Resource Guide."

Getting Started: Windows Systems

Most of the software demos on the *MusicPower* disc run within Microsoft Windows. See the section "DOS Software Demos," later in this appendix, for information on DOS music software.

Insert the *MusicPower* CD-ROM in your drive and follow these steps from within Windows to set up the software:

1. Switch to Program Manager or File Manager.

2. Select **File**, then **Run**, from the menu bar.

3. Type D:\SETUP and select OK. This assumes that your CD-ROM drive is D. If it is another letter, substitute that letter for D. For example, if your CD-ROM drive is F, type F:\SETUP.

4. The setup program creates icons in several Program Manager groups. Select OK to continue and follow the instructions in the setup program. A Program Manager group named MusicPower Book Software is created.

5. The setup program informs you that it will create a second Program Manager group. Follow the instructions, and a group named MusicPower Software Demos will be created.

6. When the setup program is complete, it will automatically run another setup program that installs Microsoft's *Video for*

Windows™ viewing software. You'll need this for viewing the video clips.

7. When the Video for Windows setup is complete, you'll need to exit and restart Windows.

The MusicPower Book Software group contains icons for

♪ Installing the software used in the book's tutorial lessons

♪ Listening to the sound clips used in the book's lessons

♪ Viewing the video clips on the CD-ROM

The MusicPower Software Demos group contains icons for installing the working demos of popular Windows music software. You'll find a complete list of this software in the next section.

Make sure you double-click the Important MusicPower Info icon. This file contains important information about installing the demos.

Windows Software Demos

The first three product demos listed are used in the chapter tutorials. You can install them by double-clicking their icons in the MusicPower Book Programs group. The other demos are installed by double-clicking their icons in the MusicPower Software Demos group.

Cakewalk Professional

Twelve Tone Systems

Location on CD-ROM: \WINDEMOS\CAKEWALK

Cakewalk Professional is a Pro-level MIDI sequencer.

Studio for Windows

Midisoft Corporation

Location on CD-ROM: \WINDEMOS\STUDIO

Studio is a MIDI sequencer and notation program.

WinSong

Softronics

Location on CD-ROM: \WINDEMOS\WINSONG

WinSong combines a MIDI sequencer with notation and multimedia tools.

MiBAC Music Lessons

MiBAC Music Software

Location on CD-ROM: \WINDEMOS\MIBAC

Music Lessons is a complete, fundamental music education program.

Master Tracks Pro

Passport Designs

Location on CD-ROM: \WINDEMOS\MTRAXPRO

Master Tracks Pro is a high-quality MIDI sequencer program.

Encore

Passport Designs

Location on CD-ROM: \WINDEMOS\ENCORE

Encore is a popular music scoring and MIDI sequencing program.

MusicTime

Passport Designs

Location on CD-ROM: \WINDEMOS\MUSTIME

MusicTime is an inexpensive music notation program, based on Encore.

Cakewalk Home Studio

Twelve Tone Systems

Location on CD-ROM: \WINDEMOS\HSTUDIO

Cakewalk Home Studio is an entry-level MIDI sequencer program.

Cubase

Steinberg Jones

Location on CD-ROM: \WINDEMOS\CUBASE

Cubase is a MIDI recording and sequencing program.

Cubase Lite

Steinberg Jones

Location on CD-ROM: \WINDEMOS\CUBASEL

Cubase Lite is a simpler version of the Cubase MIDI recording and sequencing program.

Sound Forge

Sonic Foundry

Location on CD-ROM: \WINDEMOS\SFORGE

Sound Forge is a digital sound-editing program.

WinJammer Pro

WinJammer Software

Location on CD-ROM: \WINDEMOS\WJPRO

WinJammer Pro is an inexpensive MIDI sequencing program.

SuperJAM!

Blue Ribbon Soundworks

Location on CD-ROM: \WINDEMOS\SUPERJAM

SuperJam allows you to write music without knowing musical notation.

Power Chords

Howling Dog Systems

Location on CD-ROM: \WINDEMOS\PCHORDS

Power Chords is an easy-to-use song creation program.

MIDI Quest

Sound Quest

Location on CD-ROM: \WINDEMOS\MIDIQ

MIDI Quest is a MIDI editor and librarian.

Getting Started: Macintosh systems

The folders on the Mac portion of the *MusicPower* CD-ROM are color-coded according to the type of software. For instance, folders for the software used in the chapter lessons are a different color from the folders for the other music software demos.

To view the video clips, you'll need to have Apple's QuickTime™ installed on your computer. Double-click the QuickTime Readme file in the QuickTime 1.6.1 folder before proceeding. Follow these steps to install QuickTime:

1. Open the folder labeled QuickTime 1.6.1.

2. Select the QuickTime™, Scrapbook and MoviePlayer icons and drag them to your System folder.

3. Select OK when your system asks you if it's okay to place these items in the correct locations within the System folder.

4. Restart your Mac for these changes to take place on your system.

Note: If you have anything less than System 7.0.1 on your Mac, read the QuickTime Readme file for important information.

tion about system requirements or things you need to do before running the demo.

Macintosh Software Demos

Most of the software demos can be run directly from the CD-ROM—double-click the folder to open it, then double-click the demo program.

Always read the Readme file for the software before running it. These clearly labeled files contain instructions for running the demo, system requirements, and other important information.

Some of the software must be installed to your hard drive before using it, though. In these cases, you'll find a program that says something like "Install Vision" or "Installer." Running this program will install the software on your hard drive.

The Musicshop, Vision, and DeluxeMusic demos are used in the book during the chapter tutorials, and they are listed first in this section.

Make sure you double-click the Readme First file. It contains important information about the demos.

Vision

Opcode Systems

Vision is one of the hottest Mac-based MIDI sequencers in the world. You must install this demo to your hard drive before you can use it.

Be sure to read the Readme file for a particular demo, along with the information about the demo in this section. It may contain important informa-

The OMS (opcode MIDI system) software must be installed before you can run the Vision demo. Open the OMS folder on the CD-ROM and double-click the OMS Installer icon.

Musicshop
Opcode Systems

Musicshop is a very good MIDI sequencer program and is great in color. You must install this demo on your hard drive before you can use it.

DeluxeMusic 3.0
Electronic Arts

DeluxeMusic is a powerful MIDI sequencer with very good notation and printing capabilities.

Master Tracks Pro
Passport Designs

Master Tracks Pro is a high-quality MIDI sequencer program.

MusicTime
Passport Designs

MusicTime is a professional-quality music notation program.

Claire
Opcode Systems

Claire is a music education program that includes ear training, sight-reading, and music theory. You must install this demo to your hard drive before you can use it.

Metro
OSC Software

Metro is a professional-level MIDI sequencing. It can use internal Mac sound.

Cubase
Steinberg Jones

Cubase is a popular, high-quality MIDI sequencer.

MiBAC Music Lessons
MiBAC Music Software

Music Lessons is a complete, fundamental music education program.

MiBAC Jazz
MiBAC Music Software

MiBAC Jazz provides serious, user-definable automatic musical accompaniment. It really is fun, but it's not a toy.

DigiTrax
Alaska Software

DigiTrax is a professional-level, direct-to-disk recording system.

This demo will work only on Quadra/Centris 660AV or 840AV computers, or Macs with a NuMedia Sound card installed.

SoundEdit Pro
Macromedia Corporation

SoundEdit Pro enables you to edit digital sound files, such as .SND and AIFF files.

Band-In-A-Box
PG Music, Incorporated

Band-In-A-Box provides automatic musical accompaniment.

MIDI Quest
Sound Quest

MIDI Quest is a MIDI editor and librarian.

DOS Software Demos

Most PC music software is written for Windows systems, but there is still good DOS music software available, as you'll see from these demos.

To install any of these DOS demos to your hard drive, insert the *MusicPower* disc in your drive and follow these steps at the DOS prompt:

1. Switch to the drive that holds the CD-ROM. For example, if the disc is in drive D, type D: and press Enter.

2. Type \MENU and press Enter. This will start the DOS menu program that enables you to choose which program to install.

3. When you choose a program, the install routine for that software will run. You'll see how many megabytes the program will take up on your hard drive before the installation proceeds.

When one of the DOS installation programs finishes, you'll be informed where the software was installed on your hard drive and what command starts the software.

If you're running DOS and you do not have Windows on your system, you will be able to run only these DOS demos. The .WAV music files and video clips will run only under Windows.

Noteplay

Ibis Software

Location on CD-ROM: \DOSDEMOS\NOTEPLAY

Documentation: (see the online help)

Noteplay is an interactive sight-reading program.

Soloist

Ibis Software

Location on CD-ROM: \DOSDEMOS\SOLOIST

Documentation: SOLOIST.DOC and READ.ME

Soloist is designed to teach you fundamental sight-reading using almost any musical instrument, acoustic or electronic.

Band-In-A-Box

PG Music, Incorporated

Location on CD-ROM: \DOSDEMOS\BANDBOX

Documentation: DEMOHELP.BB (can be read within program)

Band-In-A-Box is a program that provides automatic musical accompaniment. It is also available in a Windows version.

Laser Music Processor

Teach Services

Location on CD-ROM: \DOSDEMOS\LMP

Documentation: LMPDEMO.DOC

LMP provides high-quality music notation and score printing.

MIDI Quest

Sound Quest

Location on CD-ROM: \DOSDEMOS\MIDIQ

Documentation: TUTORIAL.TXT

MIDI Quest is a MIDI editor and librarian.

Music Files

The music and sounds discussed in the book are available on the CD-ROM in various formats. Most of the music is available in MIDI files, .WAV or .SND files, and CD audio tracks. The sounds are in .WAV or .SND format.

Windows Sounds

To play any of these sounds, open the MusicPower Book Software group and double-click any of the sound file icons.

To play these files, you must have a sound card with Windows drivers installed.

Bonus PC MIDI Files

These MIDI files are all arranged and/or composed by the author. I've taken time to arrange many of these with full symphonic orchestration. Be sure to take time to experiment with them. You'll find them in the \JEFFMIDI directory.

They're all in General MIDI configuration, complete with Program Change commands. Chapter 12 shows you how to remove program changes, using a MIDI event list. Do this if your MIDI synthesizer is not General MIDI-compatible.

Mac Sounds

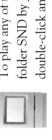

To play any of these sounds, open the folder SND by Jeff on the disc and double-click any of the sound file icons.

These files were recorded as 8-bit sounds, so they should play on nearly any Mac system.

Bonus Mac MIDI Files

These MIDI files are all arranged and/or composed by the author. I've taken time to arrange many of these with full symphonic orchestration. Be sure to take time to experiment with them. You'll find these files in the MIDI by Jeff folder. They're all in General MIDI configuration, complete with Program Change commands. Chapter 13 shows you how to remove program changes, using a MIDI event list. Do this if your MIDI synthesizer is not General MIDI-compatible.

CD Audio Tracks

The CD audio tracks on the disc enable you hear completely orchestrated versions of the music discussed in the book—the way these compositions were meant to sound. I used MIDI plus other modern recording hardware to produce these CD tracks.

Some of these tracks have corresponding .WAV and .SND versions on the CD-ROM. Of course, these audio tracks (listed in Table F.1) will sound much better than the .WAV or .SND files.

> **Warning:** You can play these audio tracks through your computer or you can play them on your audio CD player. If you play them on your audio CD player, *do not play track one!* This track contains computer data; most CD players will automatically mute the audio on this track, but some professional players or older home CD players may not. If you try to play track one and your volume is turned up high, you could damage your speakers.

Table F.1. *MusicPower* CD audio tracks.

Track Number	Contents
1	PC and Mac data—**do not play!**
2	Infinitely Flexible— Internal Mac sounds
3	Infinitely Flexible—MIDI synthesizer sounds
4	Dino Disaster
5	SportsView—Chimey version
6	SportsView— version
7	SportsView—Trumpet version
8	SportsView—Final version
	SportsView—Alternate mix
9	To the Stars
10	Reach for the Stars
11	Key Club '94
12	You'll Love MIDI (short clip)
13	Piano Riff (short clip)
14	Bach (short clip)
15	Mozart (short clip)

Video Clips

You'll have fun playing back these special video clips from Peter Gabriel, Kenny Aronoff, and work done by the author.

Windows users: Open the MusicPower Book Software Program Manager group, and double-click any of the video clip icons. You must have Video for Windows installed on your system; this software is automatically installed when you run the Windows setup program on the CD-ROM.

Mac users: Open the Video Clips folder and double-click any of the video clip icons. You must have QuickTime installed on your system; if you haven't already installed this software from the CD-ROM, see section "Getting Started: Mac Systems," earlier in this appendix.

Peter Gabriel

These two short clips show Peter talking about his *XPlora* CD-ROM project. You'll find an interview with Peter in Chapter 15. These video clips are provided courtesy of Real World, Ltd.

Kenny Aronoff

This video clip was provided courtesy of Kenny Aronoff. It shows Kenny talking about drumming and about his *Power Workout* tapes. You'll find an interview with Kenny in Chapter 5.

SportsView

The music discussed in chapters 12 and 13 was composed by the author for this video clip, which is provided courtesy of Fox TV-affiliate WXIN-59.

Also see the video that was used to compose the music found in the Chapter 12 and 13 tutorials.

Macintosh QuickTime

The section "Getting Started: Macintosh Systems" details how to install the Mac QuickTime system files.

GLOSSARY

ADAT Alesis Digital Audio Tape. A popular digital 8-track tape recording format that has become a standard for interstudio exchange of digital multitrack recordings.

Aftertouch Sometimes called *pressure*. Aftertouch enables the computer musician to control a number of user-defined MIDI synthesizer parameters relative to how hard the fingers press on the keyboard after keys are struck.

Archive To back up or make a storable copy when a project is completed.

ATR Audio Tape Recorder.

BPM Beats Per Minute; also known as *tempo*.

Byte A unit of computer data consisting of 8 bits.

CD-I Compact Disc-Interactive. A read-only media format that uses compact disk as a source of digital material. CD-I enables the user to interact with and custom-design the playback of the CD-I material.

CD-ROM Compact Disc Read-Only Memory. A read-only media format that uses a high-capacity compact disc as a source of digital material.

Channel In MIDI, an electronic pipeline for the transfer of MIDI data between MIDI devices. A very basic MIDI setup allows 16 MIDI channels, although advanced technology allows for dozens of MIDI channels.

Click Recording-studio term for a metronome.

Controller Usually a keyboard instrument. A MIDI-equipped device that generates MIDI event data that can be received, recorded, and processed by other MIDI-equipped software and hardware.

Count-off Used in MIDI recording. A sequencer plays a user-defined number of countoff measures, which provide a click. This countoff enables the musician to feel the tempo before starting a recording. Similar to a live drummer counting off "1-2-3-4."

DAT Digital Audio Tape. A tape-based recording medium that uses 4mm digital certified tape for storage of digital audio data.

DMA Direct Memory Address. A DMA channel allows the transfer of data between computer memory and any peripherals, which frees the CPU for other work assignments. DMA conflicts are a common source of problems when configuring sound cards and other PC peripherals.

Digital For the purposes of this book, the representation and manipulation of sound and visual information in a computer-based binary format as opposed to analog formats.

Digital audio workstation A computer-based, direct-to-disk or random-access recording system that uses analog-to-digital converters to digitize sound. These digitized sound files are then stored on various disk formats and may be uploaded and processed by the workstation software at any time. A digital-to-analog converter then converts the

digitized sound files into a standard analog format that can be listened to through a standard audio system.

Digitized To be converted into a digital format, which can be processed by computers and microprocessors.

Direct-to-disk A digital recording process using the hard disk and other disk hardware for the storage of digitized sound.

Fader A slider control on a mixer that is usually used for volume control.

FM Frequency Modulation. A form of synthesis developed by Dr. John Chowning and popularized by Yamaha Musical Instruments. FM synthesis is a popular form of inexpensive synthesis and is used on many sound cards. See Chapters 4 and 11 for more about FM synthesis.

Frame rate Also see *SMPTE time code*. The frame rate of SMPTE time code refers to how many SMPTE-defined frames pass per second. Thus, frame rate is measured in frames per second (FPS).

FSK sync Frequency Shift Key synchronization. One of the earliest tools for synchronizing MIDI devices with audio and video tape machines. See Chapter 14 for details.

GM General MIDI. A MIDI system configuration supported by manufacturers who really care about MIDI music production by the masses. The

GM configuration determines 127 standard instrument sounds and 46 drum and percussion sounds that appear in the same patch configuration on any GM compatible synthesizer, sound module, or sound card. This makes the playback of MIDI files much, much easier. More about GM in Chapter 5 and Appendix C.

Interactive Refers to the ability of the user to participate in and alter the performance of a sound or visual presentation so as to personalize the program. Chapter 15 discusses interactive multimedia and music applications.

IRQ Interrupt Request. An interrupt request allows peripheral devices to share the resources of an IBM-compatible computer. Each peripheral device is assigned an IRQ address or number. If two devices share the same IRQ, the two devices will either not operate or will operate unreliably. This comes into play when configuring PC sound cards and MIDI interfaces.

Jam sync Also called *regeneration*. Source SMPTE time code from a video or audio tape machine is input to a time code generator, which then regenerates fresh time code with exactly the same frame rate and time code numbers as the source code. Jam sync actually refers to the situation when the generator continues to generate frame-accurate time code even if the source code is damaged or drops out completely. See Chapter 14 for more information. Also see *SMPTE time code*.

KB Kilobyte. 1,024 bytes of data. Also see *byte*.

MB Megabyte. 1,024 kilobytes of data. Also see *kilobyte*.

.MID A Windows file extension for standard MIDI files.

Mixdown The process of combining multiple channels of sound, usually into a two-channel stereo "mix."

MIDI Musical Instrument Digital Interface. An internationally standardized data protocol that allows communications between MIDI-equipped instruments, software, and computers.

MIDI clock Also known as *MIDI beat clock*. A tempo-based timing reference used for synchronizing MIDI devices. Chapter 11 discusses MIDI clock in detail.

MIDI event A MIDI message or command, or a packet of MIDI information. More about MIDI events in Chapters 5, 11, 14, and Appendix D.

MIDI IN A connector on a MIDI-equipped device that receives MIDI event data.

MIDI interface An electronic device that converts and transfers computer and MIDI data.

MIDI Manager An extension to the Macintosh operating system developed and distributed by Apple. MIDI Manager allows the simultaneous operation of multiple MIDI applications and provides manufacturers with a common driver around which to base their software and hardware designs. MIDI Manager places great demands on your operating speed and is not recommended on Mac Plus, SE, Classic, and other, less powerful computers.

MIDI Mapper A Windows 3.1 application that routes MIDI to and from MIDI devices used with your PC. The MIDI Mapper enables you to reconfigure your PC-based MIDI system.

MIDI OUT A connector on a MIDI-equipped device that transmits MIDI event data.

MIDI THRU A connector on a MIDI-equipped device that retransmits MIDI event data that is received by the device's MIDI IN port. A MIDI THRU is useful for daisy-chaining MIDI devices.

MO Magneto-Optical. A rewritable, disk-based data storage medium sometimes used for the storage of sound files for digital workstations. Also used for archiving projects completed on a digital workstation.

MPU-401 The first commercially successful IBM PC MIDI interface protocol, and still the PC standard to this day. Most PC MIDI interfaces are MPU-401 compatible.

MTC MIDI Time Code. A timing clock used to synchronize MIDI equipment. MTC allows the transmission of SMPTE time code information over MIDI channels, which allows effective synchronization of multiple MIDI devices with audio and video tape machines. MTC is discussed in detail in Chapter 14.

Multimedia   Computer-based presentations consisting of text, animation, graphics, video, CD audio, MIDI, and digitized sound, usually centered around the use of a CD-ROM player.

MPC   Multimedia Personal Computer. A PC standardization defined as using Windows 3.1 or later with a sound card, a CD-ROM drive, and VGA or better video and graphics capabilities.

Multiport interface   A MIDI interface that enables the use of more than one port, with each port supplying up to 16 channels of MIDI.

Multitimbral   A synthesizer that will play more than one instrument sound (timbre) or patch at a time. Good multitimbral synths enable the use of up to 16 timbres at once.

Multitrack   A recording term referring to the ability to record multiple sounds, each on an isolated track. *Multitrack* can refer to sound recording and/or MIDI recording.

Nonlinear recording   See *direct-to-disk*.

OMS   Opcode MIDI System (now renamed *Open MIDI System* and distributed license-free by Opcode). Opcode's answer to MIDI Manager. OMS acts as a central MIDI driver between OMS-compatible hardware and software. OMS has gained widespread popularity due to its superior operating efficiency as compared to the MIDI Manager.

Online services   Electronic communications systems for business, education, and consumers who use computers and modems for exchanging information. These systems criss-cross the world and enable nearly instantaneous transfer of software, computer files, and databases, as well as troubleshooting and the sharing of new information in a fast, paperless medium.

Overdub   A recording term that refers to the addition of newly recorded information without erasing already existing recorded information. Overdub recording can refer to MIDI and/or sound recording.

Pad   A synthesizer sound term. A pad is usually a wash of sound that provides a textural background onto which melodic and rhythmic instrument parts are layered. Also an electric drum surface played by hand or with regular drumsticks.

Piano roll   A type of MIDI-event–viewing and –editing. Piano-roll viewing uses rectangular lines and spaces to represent the pitch and duration of MIDI key on/key off events and derives its name from the fact that this representation visually emulates the paper rolls used to "play" player pianos. Piano Roll viewing and editing are featured in Chapters 12 and 13.

Polyphony   Refers to the total number of pitches or notes that can be played by a synthesizer or digital workstation at any one instant. Polyphony is discussed in Chapter 4. Also see *multitimbral*.

Post score   Creating a musical arrangement that is designed to match a completed film or video presentation. A post score is produced after "rough-cut" or "on-line" video editing is completed.

Program change   A MIDI event command that automatically changes a patch or program when received by a MIDI synthesizer.

Punch record   According to tech editor Larry Fast, also known as *drop-in* outside North America. Recording between two user-specified points, called the record In-point and the record Out-point. Punch recording enables you to record segments of a track without erasing the entire track. See Chapters 12 and 13 for more details.

Quantize   A type of MIDI error correction. Quantizing moves the attacks and/or releases of MIDI notes to the nearest beat or fraction of a beat, as determined by the user. More about quantizing in Chapters 7 and 9.

Random-access recording   See *direct-to-disk* and *digital audio workstation*. Chapter 14 introduces you to random-access recording.

Red Book audio   CD-quality audio with 16-bit, 44.1 kHz sampling.

Regenerate   See *jam sync*.

Sampler   A digital audio recorder. Usually the term refers to an electronic musical instrument that enables the user to digitally record his or her own sound selections, storing the samples and configuring user-defined wavetables that are then used for music instrument sound synthesis.

Sequencer   A software-based MIDI multitrack recorder.

Shareware   Software available through mail or online services that may be auditioned then purchased if it fits the needs of the user.

Smart mode   Compare to *UART mode*. This MIDI interface mode enables the conversion and transfer of computer and MIDI data, but it also enables more advanced features such as MIDI event-filtering and -remapping, and sync timing. See more about interface modes in Chapters 6 and 8.

SMPTE time code   In the '70s, the Society of Motion Picture and Television Engineers (SMPTE) adopted this digital timing code as a real-time reference for film and videotape production. In the early '80s, SMPTE time code was adopted by the audio industry as the primary tool for synchronizing audio and video tape machines and MIDI equipment as well. Also see *frame rate*. Chapter 14 explains the use of SMPTE time code for synchronization.

.SND   A Macintosh digital sound file format.

Song position pointer   A feature of MIDI Clock that updates the measure and beat location of MIDI devices synchronized to a master MIDI device.

Sound card   A printed circuit board featuring a variety of microprocessors that add expanded sound capabilities to your computer. A sound card fits into an expansion slot inside the host computer.

Sound module   A sound synthesizer with no keyboard controller attached. Usually MIDI-equipped.

Standard MIDI file   The Standard MIDI file format is a format (agreed to by members of the MIDI Manufacturers' Association) that enables the import and export of MIDI sequences between sequencer application programs designed by different manufacturers.

Stripe   Also see *SMPTE time code*. To record SMPTE time code on audio or video tape. Chapter 14 teaches you how to stripe tape.

Syncing   Short for *synchronizing*. To force two or more video, audio, or MIDI devices to run at consistent, predictable, compatible speeds, so that the devices are all in step with each other. Chapter 14 shows how to sync these devices.

Synthesis   The creation of sound from an electronic microprocessor or other electronic circuit.

Sys Ex   System Exclusive. A special type of MIDI data that is reserved for any use a manufacturer sees fit. A Sys Ex message starts with a manufacturer's ID code. Equipment made by another manufacturer will not respond to the Sys Ex MIDI data that then follows this ID. Sys Ex data can be recorded into sequencer tracks and is useful for storing patch configurations, setups, and sound libraries.

Track   A MIDI track in a sequencer stores a recording of MIDI data, not a recording of a sound. An audio track on a tape recorder stores an analog recording of a sound.

Template   A general setup useful as a starting point for MIDI recording. Using a template saves the time of starting from scratch every time you want to have a MIDI recording session.

Transpose   To raise or lower the pitch of a musical instrument's sound.

UART mode   Also called *dumb mode*. This MIDI interface mode enables the simple conversion and transfer of computer and MIDI data. See more about interface modes in Chapters 6 and 8.

Velocity   The strength with which a note is played or released on a MIDI controller.

Virtual tracks   A term invented by computer musicians that refers to tracks of sound not recorded on tape, but rather generated by computers and MIDI devices.

VTR   Video Tape Recorder.

.VOC   A Sound Blaster-oriented digital sound file format. Sound Blaster-compatible sound cards can support this type of sound file as well as .WAV files.

.WAV   A Windows digital sound file format. The most commonly used sound file for multimedia and sound-card applications.

Waveform   A representation of a sound wave. A digital waveform shows a visual representation of a digitized version of a sound. These visual representations may then be used as models for editing digitized sound waves.

Wavetable   A collection of digitally recorded (sampled) and edited sounds that provides building blocks for the creation of synthesized sounds.

Workstation   See *digital audio workstation*.

WORM drive   Write Once, Read Many. A recordable optical drive format used for archiving large amounts of digital data. Sometimes used for direct-to-disk recording. A WORM drive is not erasable.

INDEX
I

ELECTRONIC ARTS®

ORDER NOW THROUGH ELECTRONIC ARTS DIRECT

AND GET DELUXEMUSIC MACINTOSH VERSION 3.0 FOR $89.95

(MANUFACTURER'S SUGGESTED PRICE $149.95).

- Available Fall 1994.
- Offer good until December 31, 1994.

To order, please call 1-800-245-4525, and use Visa, MasterCard, or Discover card.

Authorized Gateway 2000 Licensee

KENNY ARONOFF
EDUCATIONAL MEDIA MATERIAL

**Basics of Rock Drumming
(Laying It Down)**
(VH027) VHS Video $39.95

Power Workout 1
(VH0154) VHS Video $24.95
(MMBK0041AT) Book and
    Cassette $21.95
(MMBK0041CD) Book and
    CD $24.95

Power Workout 2
(VH0155) VHS Video $24.95
(MMBK0042AT) Book and
    Cassette $21.95
(MMBK0042CD) Book and
    CD $24.95

Powerpack
(VH0172) $39.95
*Both Power Workout videos packaged
together as a set.*

Available from:

CPP/Media Group
15800 N.W. 48th Avenue
Miami, Florida 33014

Call toll free:
1-800-628-1528
Monday - Friday

INSTALLING THE CD-ROM

The *MusicPower* CD-ROM

This CD-ROM works with both PC and Macintosh systems. Your computer will "see" the portion of the CD-ROM that is meant for it. You'll find a wealth of cool PC and Macintosh music software, including the following:

♪ Special working versions of the programs used in the chapter lessons. These programs let you follow along with the author and *do* what he does in the book.

♪ Working demo versions of popular music programs. Experience everything from pro-level and beginning music programs to software that teaches you about music.

♪ Complete MIDI files for all chapter lessons.

♪ Digitally recorded .WAV (PC) and .SND (Mac) music files used in the chapter lessons.

♪ Professionally recorded CD audio tracks of music projects from the book.

♪ Video clips from Peter Gabriel's *XPlora* CD-ROM, Kenny Aronoff's *Power Workout* tapes, and work by the author.

Getting Started

If you're itching to get started with the software, here's the very least you need to know:

Run the \SETUP.EXE program on the CD-ROM from within Windows. This sets up Program Manager groups and installs Video for Windows™ software on your hard drive.

Double-click the Read Me First file on the CD-ROM and follow the directions for installing

QuickTime™. Some of the software demos need to be installed to your hard drive.

These are bare-bones instructions, of course. For more information on *MusicPower* and how to use it, read Appendix F. Even if you *think* you don't need more information, he sure to read this appendix!